Las Vegas

Scott Doggett

LONELY PLANET PUBLICATIONS
Melbourne • Oakland • London • Paris

Las Vegas
2nd edition – January 2003
First published – January 2000

Published by
Lonely Planet Publications Pty Ltd ABN 36 005 607 983
90 Maribyrnong St, Footscray, Victoria 3011, Australia

Lonely Planet offices
Australia Locked Bag 1, Footscray, Victoria 3011
USA 150 Linden St, Oakland, CA 94607
UK 10a Spring Place, London NW5 3BH
France 1 rue du Dahomey, 75011 Paris

Photographs
Many of the images in this guide are available for licensing from
Lonely Planet Images.
W www.lonelyplanetimages.com

Front cover photograph
The half-sized replica of the Eiffel Tower at Paris-Las Vegas holds its
own amid palm trees and contains a restaurant and high-speed lift.
(Richard Cummins)

Las Vegas Map Section Title Page
An overview of The Strip from the Las Vegas Stratosphere Tower.
(Richard Cummins)

ISBN 1 74059 169 0

Contents – Text

Contents – Maps

The Author

Scott Doggett

Scott's interest in exotic cultures (Las Vegas included) dates from 1979, when the travel bug bit him good during a high school graduation trip to Europe. The itch to travel remained strong in Scott when he graduated from UC Berkeley four years later. Within weeks he'd made his way to San Salvador, where he shot film for The Associated Press for six months. His initial career was followed by postgraduate work at Stanford University; reporting assignments for United Press International in Los Angeles, Pakistan and Afghanistan; and, from 1989 through 1996, seven years as a staff editor for the *Los Angeles Times*. In 1996 Scott coauthored and coedited (with his future wife, journalist Annette Haddad) the award-winning anthology *Travelers' Tales: Brazil*. Scott began writing for Lonely Planet the next year. Today, he is the author of Lonely Planet's *Panama* and *Yucatan* guides, coauthor of Lonely Planet's *Mexico*, *Havana*, and *Dominican Republic & Haiti* guides, and the author of three non-LP guides. Shortly before this book went to press, Scott had returned to the *Los Angeles Times* as travel editor of *latimes.com*. He divides his time between his homes in the United States and Panama.

Dedication Through sheer determination, Wendy Melissa Louise Doggett overcame enormous obstacles and lived her life her way. With profound love and respect, this book is dedicated to her.

FROM THE AUTHOR

Many thanks to the US Lonely Planeteers who demonstrated supernatural talents during the early stages of this standard-setting 2nd edition, particularly intrepid senior editor Robert Reid. Profound graciases also to commissioning editor and MS-assessment maven Elaine Merrill, superlative regional cartographer Graham Neale, and the point person behind the maps, cartographer Bart Wright. Special kudos also to the wild-at-heart Australian production team, who broke new ground by expertly tracking, polishing and assembling all the parts of this multicontinental product.

This Book

The 1st edition of *Las Vegas* was researched and written by Scott Doggett. This 2nd edition was also written by Scott Doggett.

FROM THE PUBLISHER
This 2nd edition of *Las Vegas* was produced in Lonely Planet's Melbourne office. The production Rat Pack was coordinated by Susannah Farfor (editorial), Bart Wright (mapping) and Nicholas Stebbing (design). Carolyn Boicos played a close hand and applied her keen eye while proof reading and taking the book on its journey through layout, with assistance from Kate James. Chris Tsismetzis assisted with design.

This foray into Sin City was commissioned by Robert Reid and required the able assistance of project manager Huw Fowles, commissioning editor Elaine Merrill, managing cartographer Allison Lyall, and managing editors Kerryn Burgess, Jane Thompson, Michelle Glynn and Bruce Evans. The cover was designed by Ruth Askevold, illustrations were organised by Pepi Bluck and Nicholas Stebbing, and Jesse Fankushen collated readers letters.

Thanks

Many thanks to the many travelers who used the last edition of this book and wrote to us with helpful hints, useful advice and interesting anecdotes. The following people wrote, emailed or faxed in information:

Virginia Arrieta, Lewis Brown, Lucy Dallas, Victoria Embs, Kathy Farr, Tami Fichter, Lisa Haun, Chris Hunneyball, Chris & Rose Hunneyball, Christopher Jones, Teresa Kamieniak, Bas Kempen, Karen Kester, Youval Marks, Minouche Martins, Dana Miller, Roberta Murray, Jo Philip, Linda Rafferty, Julie Reefer, Ronald Schlosberg, Claire Snel, Andy Sparrow, Sarah Tilley, Wendy Tucker, Huub van der Linden, Erica Van Zon, Sally Wade, Andrew Young

Foreword

ABOUT LONELY PLANET GUIDEBOOKS

The story begins with a classic travel adventure: Tony and Maureen Wheeler's 1972 journey across Europe and Asia to Australia. There was no useful information about the overland trail then, so Tony and Maureen published the first Lonely Planet guidebook to meet a growing need.

From a kitchen table, Lonely Planet has grown to become the largest independent travel publisher in the world, with offices in Melbourne (Australia), Oakland (USA), London (UK) and Paris (France).

Today Lonely Planet guidebooks cover the globe. There is an ever-growing list of books and information in a variety of media. Some things haven't changed. The main aim is still to make it possible for adventurous travellers to get out there – to explore and better understand the world.

At Lonely Planet we believe travellers can make a positive contribution to the countries they visit – if they respect their host communities and spend their money wisely. Since 1986 a percentage of the income from each book has been donated to aid projects and human rights campaigns, and, more recently, to wildlife conservation.

Although inclusion in a guidebook usually implies a recommendation we cannot list every good place. Exclusion does not necessarily imply criticism. In fact there are a number of reasons why we might exclude a place – sometimes it is simply inappropriate to encourage an influx of travellers.

UPDATES & READER FEEDBACK

Things change – prices go up, schedules change, good places go bad and bad places go bankrupt. Nothing stays the same. So, if you find things better or worse, recently opened or long-since closed, please tell us and help make the next edition even more accurate and useful.

Lonely Planet thoroughly updates each guidebook as often as possible – usually every two years, although for some destinations the gap can be longer. Between editions, up-to-date information is available in our free, quarterly *Planet Talk* newsletter and monthly email bulletin *Comet*. The *Scoop* section of our website covers news and current affairs relevant to travellers. Lastly, the *Thorn Tree* bulletin board and *Postcards* section carry unverified, but fascinating, reports from travellers.

Tell us about it! We genuinely value your feedback. A well-travelled team at Lonely Planet reads and acknowledges every email and letter we receive and ensures that every morsel of information finds its way to the relevant authors, editors and cartographers.

Everyone who writes to us will find their name listed in the next edition of the appropriate guidebook, and will receive the latest issue of *Comet* or *Planet Talk*. The very best contributions will be rewarded with a free guidebook.

We may edit, reproduce and incorporate your comments in Lonely Planet products such as guidebooks, websites and digital products, so let us know if you don't want your comments reproduced or your name acknowledged.

How to contact Lonely Planet:
Online: e talk2us@lonelyplanet.com.au, w www.lonelyplanet.com
Australia: Locked Bag 1, Footscray, Victoria 3011
UK: 10a Spring Place, London NW5 3BH
USA: 150 Linden St, Oakland, CA 94607

Introduction

Go ahead. Get it out of your system. Say it, even if you don't mean it. It's what everybody expects: 'Las Vegas. It's tasteless, cheap, sleazy and cheesy.'

Ah, feel better? But to be honest, Las Vegas no longer lives up to its long-held reputation. It's become a remarkable and unique city that – like every other big city on our glorious planet – has its tasteless, cheap, sleazy and cheesy elements. Consider Paris, San Francisco, Tokyo, Rome. Every great city mixes the tacky with the sublime.

However, only Las Vegas exists chiefly to satisfy the needs and desires of its visitors, and this it does in spectacular fashion. Sin City has taken or re-created the best that other great cities have to offer and then upped the ante – making it bigger, grander, flashier.

What city has so many superb restaurants? What other city has so much world-class entertainment? What other city has a Manhattan skyline *and* a Parisian skyline *and* a Venetian skyline? What city has produced more instant millionaires? The truth is, no other city has.

Given what we've always been told about Las Vegas, it's almost disturbing to realize this is true. Then again, with Las Vegas' hotel-casinos making so much money, resort owners have the freedom to scour the globe and say, 'I want one of *those*.' No, not a Ferrari. Not an estate house on a hill. Not the stuff regular Joes and Janes dream about.

Listen. When businessman Steve Wynn decided to create Bellagio, he set out to awe the most discerning individuals. 'The challenge,' he said, 'became building a place so preemptive, so overwhelmingly attractive and delicious, that it would attract people who do not come to Las Vegas now – people who are not that impressed with gaming.'

Wynn built a resort that's an aesthetic knockout, truly a sight to behold. For entertainment, Wynn turned to Montreal's Cirque du Soleil to create a show 'that people would talk about in Singapore, Rome, Hong Kong, London, New York and Buenos Aires.' Out of Cirque sprang the critically acclaimed *O*.

For food, Wynn's dream was to hire the best chefs on Earth and put them to work for him. Today, there are seven James Beard award-winning chefs at Bellagio, each with his own restaurant. Perhaps never before has such an exceptional group of chefs and restaurants been assembled under one roof.

Steve Wynn is an exceptional man, but his approach to the Bellagio hotel-casino, which opened in late 1998, is not exceptional. To compete with Wynn: David Cacci opened New York-New York, which captures the excitement and beauty of Manhattan without, ironically, any of its sleaze. Glenn Schaeffer opened Mandalay Bay, home to Shark Reef and other awesome attractions, several superb restaurants and one of the nation's premiere blues clubs. Sheldon Adelson opened The Venetian, the $1.5 billion home of two Guggenheim museums. Arthur Goldberg opened Paris-Las Vegas, which reproduces in exquisite detail the City of Lights' most famous landmarks, and contains not less than 11 outstanding *restaurants français* with a French-trained culinary staff of 500.

Wynn, Cacci, Schaeffer, Goldberg and others that you've probably never heard of (there's no reason you should have) have created a Las Vegas that can no longer be easily dismissed by its derogators. Not only does The Venetian house two terrific museums, but high art can be found even in Las Vegas' restaurants. The Bellagio's Picasso restaurant, for example, is filled with original Picassos. (Bellagio contains many such surprises.)

Likewise, in re-creating some of the magic found in the thrill rides at New York's Coney Island amusement park, New York-New York not only built a roller coaster, but it built one with a blazing top speed of 67mph and a twist-and-dive maneuver that produces the weightless sensation a pilot feels during a barrel roll. Nearby, Stratosphere has a roller coaster too – one that's more than 100 floors above The Strip and is the highest thrill ride in the world.

And so it goes with dozens of Las Vegas attractions. It's impossible to talk about Las Vegas without using the word 'world,' because so many of the city's hotels, restaurants and entertainment options are truly world-class.

Even the natural and human-created splendors surrounding Las Vegas are world-class. There's only one Grand Canyon and only one Hoover Dam (it was built more than 60 years ago and is still one of the world's tallest). The 1450-mile-long Colorado River, which carved the Grand Canyon, attracts white-water rafters from across the globe, and not a road leaves Las Vegas that doesn't stumble through the sparse, wind- and water-carved landscapes of the Southwest's famous red rock desert. All these sites are easy excursions from Sin City.

True, Las Vegas hasn't changed completely. It still has its topless revues, but visitors will also find no shortage of shows featuring some of the greatest stage performers of our time. Yes, Las Vegas still has its notoriously huge buffets, but these days the mounds of spaghetti and the piles of cheap cuts of meat have been replaced with grilled salmon, NY steaks, king crab and sushi.

Las Vegas won't disappoint you if you're searching for all things tasteless, cheap, sleazy and cheesy. But if you arrive with an adventurous spirit, you'll discover that it has a sizzling nightlife, extraordinary restaurants, outstanding production shows and incomparable hotel-casinos – and you'll likely leave town feeling like you've just had the best amusement ride of your life.

Facts about Las Vegas

HISTORY

Contrary to legend and Hollywood movies, there was a lot more to Las Vegas than a dumpy gambling house, some tumbleweeds and cacti the day mobster Benjamin Siegel drove into the Mojave Desert and decided to build a glamorous, tropical-themed casino under the searing sun. People had been living in Las Vegas Valley an entire millennium before the celebrated gangster opened the Flamingo in 1946.

The Paiutes Tough It Out

It was a full thousand years ago – or at about the time Byzantine monarch Basil II ordered the blinding of thousands of Bulgarian prisoners and Asian king Machmud of Ghazni retained 400 poets to entertain him – that a small band of weary Indians followed a bend in the Colorado River to Nevada's Black Mountains, where they crossed the jutting beige peaks and settled in the valley below. These hard-bitten Indians were Southern Paiutes, members of the Uto-Aztecan language family that also contains the better-known Shoshones and Utes of Wyoming and Utah, respectively.

The Paiutes pitched tents near an oasis where the city of Las Vegas now stands. The desert Indians spent their days roaming about the Mojave in small groups, harvesting everything they could eat. Nearly 40 varieties of seeds were gathered and stored in tightly woven baskets. Wild celery, sweet sage and the blazing star were eaten, as were the roots and bulbs of the sego lily, camas and wild caraway. Insects such as crickets and locusts, and their larvae, were relished. The rattlesnake was a special treat.

As time passed, the Paiutes came to occupy the mountains and valleys spreading for 50 miles in all directions from Las Vegas, and they became expert hunters. The Sheep Range, the Spring Mountains, the El Dorado Mountains and the Black Mountains ringing Las Vegas Valley contained elk, bear, deer and antelope, which the Indians felled with arrows and clubs. To protect their skin against the blistering desert sun, the Paiutes smeared red paint on their faces and bodies. To protect their soles from the broiling earth, they wore moccasins made of yucca leaves.

Despite the rigors of their surroundings, the Paiutes were a disciplined people who adhered to certain practices without waver. Births took place in circular brush enclosures. Boys were required to surrender first kills to parents. Though marriage was unimportant, funerals were four-day affairs involving cremation or cave burials, the killing of eagles and abandonment of homes. Elected headmen discoursed on morality and had advisory, not authoritative, functions. In the unforgiving desert, the Paiutes not only endured, but they advanced as a culture.

Just how forbidding was their territory? The Spanish, who were the first Caucasians to claim jurisdiction over southern Nevada, skirted this region during their extensive exploration of North America in the 16th and 17th centuries. They were content to leave this section of their 'domain' uncharted, calling the blank space left on their maps the 'Northern Mystery.' Despite its proximity to well-trodden Mexico and California, Las Vegas Valley and the land around it in all directions for at least two weeks' hike was the last part of the US to be penetrated and explored by white settlers.

Trappers & Traders

Except for infrequent raids by Navajo and Ute slave traders during the 18th century, the Southern Paiutes lived a peaceful, if arduous, existence in and around Las Vegas Valley for more than 800 years. Their undoing as the dominant people of the region began with the arrival of white men seeking buck-toothed rodents with flat tails, beady eyes and a penchant for turning rivers into ponds. Beavers were abundant in the Southwest, and beaver fur was prized for its

9

warmth and beauty. During the 1820s anybody who was anybody in Europe wore a beaver-pelt hat. Making matters worse for the busy herbivores, a secretion from their musk glands was thought to be a cure-all and was as sought after as the fur. Europe couldn't get enough of the fur and musk of the little dam-makers, and some American fur traders went to extreme lengths to meet the demand.

One of those traders was Jedediah Smith, who left his trapping areas along the Utah-Idaho border in mid-1826 in search of untouched beaver country. Heading toward the Pacific, Smith blazed a trail southwest along the Virgin River. While following the river out of Utah, Smith crossed the Nevada border in November 1826 at a point near the modern city of Mesquite, NV, 80 miles east of Las Vegas. Smith thus became the first Caucasian American to enter present-day Nevada. Incidentally, the moniker 'first white person to enter Nevada' belongs to British explorer Peter Skene Ogden, who made a brief foray into northern Nevada earlier in 1826.

Jedediah Smith is also credited with having opened up a major segment of the Spanish Trail – a trading route between Santa Fe, NM, and Los Angeles, CA. The Spanish Trail existed from 1830 until the middle of the 20th century, when large segments of the trail were paved and became sections of Interstate 15.

Smith continued on to California (he was anxious to sell his furs in Los Angeles), and it wasn't long before other adventurers traced his steps into the Northern Mystery. Most were traders, some were settlers anxious to get to California, and all were looking for greener pastures of one kind or another.

At least a few green pastures were found: in the diaries of many Spanish Trail travelers arises an image of Las Vegas in the 1830s and 1840s as having a string of lush meadows linked by a picturesque year-round creek that emerged from a series of springs. (This explains the city's name: Las Vegas is Spanish for 'The Meadows.') Shade created by cottonwoods and willows

near the creek allowed grass to grow, and the grass fed the mules, horses and oxen of Spanish Trail caravans.

Among the Trail's most famous travelers was John C Fremont (after whom the main street of downtown Las Vegas is named), an army officer who spent several years exploring and mapping the area around Las Vegas. The beauty of the region awed Fremont, and his favorable reports, parts of which appeared in many US newspapers, encouraged scores of people on the East Coast of the US to seek opportunity in the West. The encouragement took on a sense of urgency in 1849, when gold was discovered in California. By year's end the Spanish Trail had been overtaken by men hungry for gold.

Mormons on the Move

Amid the legions of hard-drinking Rockefeller wannabes responding to the gold strike was a group of men hell-bent on doing God's work in Indian country. These Mormons were sent from Salt Lake City, UT, by leader Brigham Young to colonize the expanding state of Deseret, as they called their homeland. The faithful were dispatched to Las Vegas to help secure a string of Mormon settlements that would stretch from church headquarters in Utah all the way to the Pacific Ocean. In the process, the Mormons began occupying land that had belonged to the Southern Paiutes for 850 years.

To keep the Indians in check, Young instructed the missionaries to convert them to Mormonism. The Mormon gospel has two underlying principles: church officers believe that they are divinely called to be leaders, and that there must be unquestioned obedience to their orders. Devotion to that system was so strong that only two of the 30 men ordered to go to Las Vegas to build a fort and convert Indians refused to make the trip. On May 10, 1855, a party of Las Vegas–bound missionary-colonists left Salt Lake City after each man had sold sufficient possessions to buy a wagon-load of provisions and had said good-bye to his family.

During their first months in Las Vegas, the missionary-colonists built a fort made of adobe, and they planted corn, squash and other crops. Although the Paiutes tolerated the white men because the missionaries gave them grain and squash, they failed to become evangelized. When the Paiutes showed the Mormons a cliff near the summit of Potosi Mountain, 27 miles southwest of Las Vegas, which contained large quantities of silver ore, the Mormons tried to enlist the Indians into mining the ore. The Mormons offered a thousand Indians a total of 10 shirts and a small amount of food to remove the ore from the mountain. The natives hauled only one load of rock on their backs before they quit. Overlooking the fact that the work was demanding and the pay absurdly low, one missionary involved with the silver venture had only this to say about the Indians: 'There seems to be but little Mormon in them, and they showed me on their finger nails how much.'

The missionary's high opinion of Mormons may have slipped a little over the next few months. During that time, intense conflicts arose among the Las Vegas Mormons, who were anxious to get their hands on the wealth that seemed so near, but were unable to get the Indians to agree to be beasts of burden. Fueling passions further was a power struggle that developed between two church officers. One of them, William Bringhurst, was among the original missionary-colonists. The other, Nathaniel Jones, was dispatched from Salt Lake City after Young had been informed about the silver ore.

Bringhurst was in charge of the mission; there was no denying that. But Jones had a letter from Young saying that he could borrow men from the mission to help him extract silver from the Potosi mine, and Young had instructed Jones to bring the silver to Salt Lake City. Bringhurst didn't want to relinquish control of the mine and the riches within it, so he initially denied Jones the men he needed. Because Salt Lake City was a 45-day hike away, whoever controlled the men temporarily controlled the mine.

Dissension arose within the ranks of the missionaries when some announced they wanted to help Jones at the mine and perhaps become rich in the process. Others

William Bringhurst

sided with Bringhurst, who dispatched a messenger to Salt Lake City with a letter asking Young to name a director of the silver mine. But before a reply arrived, frustration got the better of Bringhurst: although he had advised gentle treatment of the Indians, Bringhurst kicked a Paiute from his house and from the mission when he caught the famished man stealing bread. Word of the incident spread like fire through the Paiute community, and the Mormons lost all credibility with the people they were hoping to evangelize.

At about the same time, some of the missionaries announced a desire to build a church. Others thought a fence around the mission was more important and should be erected first. After much bickering, the men agreed to build a church and then build a fence, but the team spirit that had existed at the mission was lost. Then came news that Young had decided to excommunicate Bringhurst, which in turn resulted in some ill will toward the church leader.

In the meantime, Jones and a handful of missionaries had begun mining the silver, but finding the work extremely painstaking and the heat unbearable, Jones abandoned the mine after only five weeks and returned to Salt Lake City with unfavorable reports concerning the mine and the mission.

Citing the inability of the Las Vegas missionaries to solve social problems, their unsuccessful efforts to convert the Indians and the dissension that arose over the mine, Young ordered the mission closed in February 1857, less than two years after it had been established. Although the mission failed in all of its objectives, it paved the way for settlement of southern Nevada the following decade.

A Silver Mine & A Golden Spike

Many gold miners en route to California via the Spanish Trail learned of the silver in Potosi Mountain as they passed through Las Vegas. When word reached them that the Mormons had abandoned the lode, some of the miners returned to Nevada to try their hand at Potosi. In 1860, these miners, unlike Jones and his men, worked Potosi expertly and extracted lots of silver. Some of the Potosi miners, when returning to Los Angeles for provisions, showed off impressive chunks of silver ore, which fueled excitement about the mine. Soon up to 35 miners a day were arriving at Potosi. Some men got rich. Most did poorly. A few took to farming in Las Vegas Valley.

After the Potosi silver boom subsided in late 1861, those who had tried to farm Las Vegas left their generally uncooperative fields for more fertile ground elsewhere. For four years the valley again belonged

solely to the Paiutes. Then, in 1865, with two associates, an on-again, off-again miner from Ohio named Octavius Decatur Gass reconstructed the buildings that had been the Mormon mission, and revived the fields once used by the missionaries. The resulting 2000-acre Las Vegas Ranch flourished for the rest of the century and its success encouraged other settlers to stake claims in the valley.

No railroads crossed southern Nevada in 1900, but plans had been made to link Los Angeles and Salt Lake City by rail, with a stop in Las Vegas. In January 1905, the final spike, a golden one, was driven in just south of Las Vegas, and train service commenced. By this time Las Vegas was more than just a ranch ringed by cacti and barren foothills. A post office had opened, as had a meat market, a general store and a hotel. But with the new railroad, the town was destined for much more – the railroad company cleared off a patch of desert and staked out 40 blocks' worth of lots in the dirt. Then they held an auction. Over two frenzied days local settlers as well as speculators and real estate investors from Los Angeles and the East Coast bid and out-bid each other for the land, and the barren lots sold for twice to 10 times their original price. The railroad

Desert Survival Tips

Octavius Decatur Gass, who founded Las Vegas Ranch in 1865 and at one point in the mid-1870s owned almost all the water rights in Las Vegas Valley, offered the following desert-travel advice to late-19th-century readers of the *San Bernardino Guardian*:

Never travel alone; have a large canteen; rest before crossing the desert; feed your animal on all occasions where you can get supplies. If you have no means to do this, don't start until you have, as your life is at stake; drink, gorge yourself with water before starting to cross a desert, like an Indian; then keep cool; don't get scared and imagine yourself thirsty the first five miles and commence to gorge your water before you really need any. Ever remember that your life is in your canteen; draw it out with a zealous eye....

Never play with the Indians, like some rattle-brained boy and show them your guns, etc, as many have forfeited their lives for this imprudence.... Invariably (before beginning your travels) get full directions about location of water, which side of the road, etc, etc. Never leave a plain wagon road in search of water (as some have done), thinking vainly that they knew more about water than a road. All wagon roads lead to springs and creeks. If you cannot follow these directions, stay at home with the gal you love so much and drink lager beer.

company made a killing. As the dust settled, on May 15, 1905, the City of Las Vegas was officially founded – as was the town's personality.

The young city was quickly transformed as new buildings and businesses sprung up almost overnight. Railroad freight cars provided easy access to provisions that had previously taken weeks to bring in. After a few months, the initial excitement dimmed somewhat as people coped with the difficulties of desert life, but by January 1906, Las Vegas was home to a jail and a school and dozens of businesses, including two banks and a drug store. Tent homes made of canvas and lumber spread everywhere. The *Los Angeles Times* put the city's population at more than 1500. Electricity arrived by year's end.

By the start of WWI, which had little effect on the Las Vegas economy, ranches and small farms flourished throughout the valley, and the downtown area was developing rapidly. A well had to be sunk at each farm to provide for irrigation, as rainfall was insufficient, but beneath the surface of the desert there proved to be no shortage of water. Many types of fruit, as well as grains and vegetables, were grown. Construction financed mostly by outsiders kept employment high. Anderson Field, Las Vegas' first airport, opened in 1920; scheduled passenger services to Salt Lake City and Los Angeles commenced soon after.

Sin also flourished in Las Vegas during this period, in the infamous red-light district known as Block 16 (between 1st and 2nd Sts and Ogden and Stewart Sts downtown). Home to gambling, booze and prostitution, this row of saloons, with their makeshift 'cribs' out back, survived Nevada's 1911 ban on gambling (the city never recognized the ban, which in any case was lifted in 1931) and the 'dry years' of Prohibition.

Prosperity, or at least opportunity, had embraced everyone – everyone except the Paiutes. Unable to speak English and pressured into giving up their land by numerous business interests, including the railroad, the Indians withdrew from the valley they had occupied since AD 1000. Their withdrawal

from desirable land occurred throughout Nevada as years passed. Today, most Paiutes live in reservations scattered across the state. All of the reservations would easily fit within the Nevada Test Site – an area in southern Nevada presently used by the US Air Force for weapons testing.

Dam Offsets Depression

Many small American cities managed to duck the socioeconomic bullets that struck the United States during WWI, but few escaped the country's Great Depression, which began with an unprecedented stock market crash in 1929 and lasted until the advent of US involvement in WWII. One of the few lucky cities was Las Vegas. The reason: Hoover Dam. Finished at a total cost of $165 million, the world's largest dam was built on the 1450-mile-long Colorado River, a mere 25 miles east of Las Vegas. The dam not only provided, as it still does, a reliable source of water to the seven states through which the river runs, but it also put an end to widespread annual flooding caused by melting snow in the Rocky Mountains.

The dam benefited Las Vegas in many ways. For one thing, a virtual army of well-paid construction workers lived in the area for five years until the dam's completion in 1936, two years ahead of schedule. To aid construction, a good supply road was built from Las Vegas to the project site in the Black Mountains. Once the road was completed, the city's saw mills and cement factories could barely keep pace with demand. The railroad increased the number of rail lines in the region to facilitate the work, and installation of those lines meant more jobs for Las Vegas residents and more money going into the city's economy.

In 1931 that economy once again included gambling. That year, Nevada legalized casino gambling and dropped the state's divorce residency requirement to six weeks; both decisions ran counter to the country's prevailing moralistic fervor and set the course of the state's, and especially Las Vegas', sin-filled future. Dam workers flocked to Las Vegas at night to partake in the flowing illegal booze, the rampant prostitution and the numerous, newly legal gambling halls that quickly sprouted downtown.

After 1936, as construction forces left, some businessmen viewed the 726-ft-high dam and newly created Lake Mead as potential big-time tourist attractions, and the federally funded supply road gave Las Vegas easy access to them. Los Angeles hotelman Thomas Hull, more than anyone else, deserves credit for the Las Vegas we see today. In 1941 Hull opened the city's first plush casino-hotel, El Rancho Vegas, south of town along the two-lane highway that eventually became Las Vegas Blvd, otherwise known as The Strip. Hull promoted the dam and Lake Mead like no one else. As a result, people came in droves to see the colossal dam, to relax by the lake and to gamble at his establishment.

In addition, El Rancho Vegas attracted a new element to the desert – Hollywood movie stars, who enjoyed gambling and rubbing elbows with the 'characters' it attracted. One of these characters was mobster Benjamin 'Bugsy' Siegel, who, along with partner Meyer Lansky, had a dream of building an even more luxurious resort in the desert that would, as Lansky said, draw 'high-rollers from all over the world.' Backed by Lansky's East Coast mob money, Siegel built the $6-million Flamingo hotel in 1946. With its incandescent pastel paint job, tuxedoed janitors, Hollywood entertainers, and eight-story flashing neon-covered towers out front, it became the model for the new Las Vegas casino-hotel that was soon to come.

Unfortunately for Siegel, the Flamingo didn't make a profit, at least not immediately, and that was too long to wait as far as Siegel's backers were concerned. On June 23, 1947, he was gunned down by his associates, and the Flamingo had an instant 'change in ownership.' But the resultant national scandal had a curious effect: more people than ever came to Las Vegas to see its stunning gaming palaces and to consort with their notorious patrons and owners. An explosion of new casino-hotels erupted along The Strip, beginning with the

Thunderbird in 1948, and it has continued, with only a few short pauses, to this day.

At about the same time that the first hotel-casinos were going up, in 1941, the Las Vegas economy got a boost from the army. When the United States entered WWII, the US military opened the Las Vegas Aerial Gunnery School, which was expanded the next year into Nellis Air Force Base, 10 miles northeast of downtown Las Vegas. Initially the site contained only a few shacks, but a large complex was soon constructed to train aerial gunners for combat duty in Europe and the Pacific. The airfield's mission quickly grew to include training copilots for B-17 and B-29 bombers.

At the height of the war the base housed several thousand troops. The arrival of the troops also meant, interestingly enough, the end of prostitution on Block 16. The commander of the gunnery school threatened to make the city off-limits to soldiers if the city didn't clean up its act, and so the city did, effectively putting the illicit 'cribs' out of business for good.

That same year, 1941, Las Vegas benefited greatly from the building of a $150-million magnesium plant in Henderson, NV, 15 miles southeast of Las Vegas. Metallic magnesium is the key component of incendiary bombs, which were widely used by the Allies. The quick, intense heat resulting from such bombs made fire control almost impossible and resulted in scores of munitions plants and other strategic targets in Germany and Japan being destroyed.

Spectacular Las Vegas

By the 1950s, Las Vegas felt like a boomtown again, with casino-hotels popping up at an ever more rapid pace, and everyone – gamblers and hotel owners alike – trying to strike it rich before the good times ended. The lavish $4.5-million Desert Inn set the tone in 1950 by throwing Las Vegas' biggest party yet for its grand opening. The hotel was run by Wilbur Clark, a small-time gambler who enjoyed the media limelight, and it was funded and primarily owned by Moe Dalitz, head of a Cleveland-based organized crime syndicate. In fact, a federal investigation at the beginning of the decade made this emerging trend crystal clear: the Las Vegas casino industry enjoyed ties to, and the hidden backing of, organized crime from across the nation. And why not? The mob loved Las Vegas. It gave them a legitimacy and a glamorous cachet they had never experienced before, and by fixing the games, fixing the local politicians and skimming profits both under and over the table, they were getting rich in a hurry. Las Vegans, for their part, loved them back. Everyone, from low-rolling 'grinds' to Tinseltown starlets, flocked to the desert town to soak up the glittering, extravagant spectacle – a gangster's vision of paradise – and the promise of instant wealth.

After the success of the Flamingo and the Desert Inn, practically every new hotel-casino in Las Vegas tried to best the rest in terms of size, services, flash, taste, entertainment extravaganza or the quality and number of shops and restaurants. There was the Horseshoe (1951), the Sahara (1952), the Sands (1952), the Showboat (1954), and the Riviera, Dunes and New Frontier, all in 1955. Revenue from the gaming tables permitted the casinos to feature the biggest names in show business, which in turn allowed the hotel-casinos to appeal to gamblers and nongamblers alike. The Sands attracted Frank Sinatra and Dean Martin, and later the entire Rat Pack; the Riveria nabbed Liberace; other headliners included Jimmy Durante and Sammy Davis Jr.

By the mid-1950s, Vegas had overbuilt, and a number of casinos had gone under or changed hands, but that didn't stop new, ever-larger casino-hotels from opening, each one topping the last. The Fremont and the Hacienda opened in 1956, the Tropicana in 1957 and the Stardust, which was the biggest hotel in the world (1056 rooms) at the time and had the biggest electric sign, opened in 1958. In 1957 the Dunes grabbed the spotlight when it introduced bare-breasted showgirls in its revue, *Minsky Goes to Paris*, then the next year the Stardust grabbed it back when it boasted that it had *real* French showgirls in its bare-breasted revue, *Lido de Paris*.

The 1950s also heralded the testing of nuclear weapons just 65 miles northwest of Las Vegas. Beginning in January 1951 and over the next 41 years, approximately 1000 nuclear explosions were initiated at the Nevada Test Site for national defense and peacetime purposes. For the first 12 years these tests were mostly above ground, at a rate of about one a month, until the 1963 Nuclear Test Ban Treaty forced them below ground, where they continued until 1992. Initially unconcerned about radiation fallout, Las Vegans took the atomic bomb blasts in stride – and even celebrated the publicity and notoriety they brought by selling atomburgers and crowning a Miss Atomic Bomb. One photo taken from Fremont St at the heart of downtown shows people casually going about their business while a mushroom cloud rises ominously in the distance. The decade ended with the opening of the Las Vegas Convention Center, which presaged the city's future as a major convention destination.

By 1960 the population of Las Vegas had risen to 64,406 residents (up from about 17,000 in 1945), which constituted more than half the population of Nevada. That same year the Convention Center hosted a championship boxing match (the first of many to be held in Las Vegas), and El Rancho Vegas – the grand dame of Sin City – caught fire and burned to the ground. Hotel construction slowed considerably through the first half of the turbulent '60s, with no new grand hotels until the Aladdin opened in 1966; a year later Elvis Presley married Priscilla Beaulieu in the hotel. The Aladdin was followed in short order by Caesars Palace (1966), Circus Circus (1968), the Landmark (1969) and the $60-million International (1969; today the Las Vegas Hilton), which featured Barbra Streisand on opening night.

The slowdown in construction during the first part of the '60s allowed federal and state regulators a chance to redouble their efforts to 'clean up' the gambling industry. Scandal after scandal had plagued the casinos, as charges of mob corruption, racketeering, influence peddling and tax evasion were continually raised and investigated by federal agencies. Nevada's elected officials were finding it increasingly difficult to maintain the fiction that their stringent casino licensing standards and vigilant enforcement were keeping the criminal element at bay. There wasn't a handful of casinos without some proven or alleged link to organized crime, and all the bad publicity was beginning to hurt tourism. Then, in 1966, into the picture stepped eccentric billionaire Howard Hughes.

Hughes arrived at the Desert Inn on Thanksgiving night in the back of an ambulance (for security reasons), and he didn't set foot outside the hotel for the next four years. He took over the high-roller suites of the 9th floor, and when he'd worn out his welcome, rather than move, he simply bought the Desert Inn from Moe Dalitz for $13.2 million. He eventually dropped $300 million in a Las Vegas buying spree when he purchased the Sands, the Castaways, the New Frontier, the Silver Slipper and the Landmark, a TV station, the North Las Vegas Airport and other land along The Strip and around the state. It was a public relations boon for Nevada officials, as Hughes immediately lent the casino business a much-needed patina of legitimacy. If

gambling was a dirty business, local papers declared, then an industrialist like Hughes wouldn't be getting into it.

Hughes received special dispensations to do business in the city, and these led to 1967 and 1969 Nevada legislation that allowed for corporate ownership of casinos. This encouraged publicly traded corporations, such as Hilton, Holiday Inn and MGM, to get involved in the gambling industry, which spurred a new round of construction in the late '60s and '70s. Most importantly, Las Vegas could finally begin to distance itself, in the public's mind anyway, from its notorious link to organized crime. In the end, the only loser was Hughes, who in one short span of time became Las Vegas' largest operator of hotel-casinos, but who ultimately got the short end of his many deals and left town several million dollars poorer.

The Age of the Megaresort

With the arrival in 1973 of the magnificent $120-million MGM Grand, Las Vegas experienced the dawn of the megaresort. With 2100 rooms (roughly double the number at the Stardust), the MGM Grand captured the mantle 'world's largest resort.' A slew of smaller hotels also popped up along The Strip during the decade, including the Holiday Hotel, the Continental, the California, the Barbary Coast, the Imperial Palace and Bob Stupak's Vegas World (which became the Stratosphere in 1996). Master illusionists Siegfried and Roy began turning women into tigers at the Tropicana (a practice they continue today at the Mirage); Dean Martin made a surprise appearance on Jerry Lewis' *National Muscular Dystrophy Telethon* at the Sahara, thus ending a 20-year falling-out between the two comedians; and Tina Turner, Bill Cosby, Steve Martin, Johnny Cash, and Sonny and Cher entertained crowds in Las Vegas' many showrooms.

However, the '70s were a difficult decade for the city. A flash flood swept down a section of The Strip, damaging or destroying hundreds of cars; Atlantic City legalized gambling, causing Vegas tourism to dip; and state and federal investigations into illegalities in the gaming industry continued to

When the Lights Went Out

In the history of Las Vegas, the city's casino chieftains have turned off their marquee lights on only five occasions. The first time was in 1963, when the casinos closed for three hours following the assassination of President John F Kennedy. The casinos closed their doors again in 1968, after an assassin's bullet claimed the life of the Rev Martin Luther King Jr. The casinos remained open for business when Sammy Davis Jr died of throat cancer on May 16, 1990, but their marquee lights were shut off in unison for 10 minutes. Lights were then dimmed again for two more Rat Pack brothers – when Dean Martin succumbed to acute respiratory failure on December 25, 1995, and when Frank Sinatra was silenced by a heart attack on May 14, 1998.

unwind before the public. This remaining taint of corruption kept many traditional banking institutions from freely financing corporate gaming – making it sometimes difficult to raise the enormous funds necessary to build the huge resorts.

The 1980s began tragically for Las Vegas when fire swept through the MGM Grand, killing 84 guests and injuring 700 (Bally's took over the property and quickly reopened it). Yet, the decade ended with a celebration, also of fire – in the form of a 50ft volcano that erupts every 15 minutes from sunset till midnight in front of the gleaming Mirage hotel-casino. As the US economy recovered, and Vegas overcame the competition from Atlantic City, the town experienced a new boom. All the *known* mobsters were finally run out of town and Las Vegas was declared sufficiently 'sanitized.' Nothing signaled the re-arrival of good times like Steve Wynn's 3000-room Mirage, which was also home to a white-tiger garden, a dolphin habitat, a 20,000-gallon aquarium and a rainforest. Frequent Las Vegas headliners during the '80s included singers Dolly Parton and Willie Nelson and funnymen Rodney Dangerfield, Eddie Murphy and Don Rickles.

The 1990s saw the boom get bigger. The Excalibur, a giant medieval-castle-themed hotel complete with moat and staffed with valiant knights and fair damsels, ushered in the decade with trumpets blaring. And blare they should have, because the city's most spectacular megaresort casinos were just around the bend. In 1993 the new MGM Grand reappeared from a massive renovation with 5000 rooms, reclaiming its status as the largest hotel in the world. The same year, the Luxor's black pyramid rose from the desert; Treasure Island launched its pirate battle on The Strip; and the Dunes was intentionally blown to bits. Then came the Hard Rock Café & Hotel (the self-proclaimed world's first rock 'n' roll hotel), the French Riviera–themed Monte Carlo resort and New York-New York, replete with Manhattan skyline. Even more impressive were late arrivals Bellagio, one of the most opulent hotels in the world and home to

$300 million in fine art; Stratosphere, which is a hotel, a casino and an elegant, white viewing tower that is the tallest building in the western United States; Mandalay Bay, which takes 'bundling' into uncharted territory with gourmet restaurants, a world-class spa, a terrific blues club and six-time Tony Award–winning musical *Chicago*; and two more awesome, city-themed megaresorts, The Venetian, replete with canals and splendid Italian architecture, and Paris-Las Vegas, home to an Eiffel Tower and a host of fine French restaurants.

Today, Las Vegas boasts 19 of the world's 20 largest hotels, it attracts 33 million visitors a year (more than any other US city), and annual gaming revenue from Sin City's gambling establishments exceeds $5.25 billion (that equates to $10,000 every 60 seconds!). More than 100,000 marriage licenses are issued in Las Vegas yearly, which is an average of one 'I do' every five minutes. There's more than 17 miles of lighted neon tubing in the city. At any time of day or night in Las Vegas you can buy a refrigerator, get divorced, rent a date, sell your car, pick up your cleaning or arrange for a caterer. It is truly a town that never sleeps. There are other cities with terrific entertainment and gaming opportunities, but there is no place in the world like Las Vegas, and no city even pretending to be.

GEOGRAPHY

Las Vegas is in the Great Basin, a vast region that includes most of Nevada and parts of California, Idaho, Utah, Wyoming and Oregon. It's called a 'basin' because its rivers drain into inland lakes and sinks, not to a sea. Within the Nevada portion of the basin are dozens of north–south mountain ranges, such as those that surround Las Vegas for over 200 miles.

The principal life zone of the Great Basin is high desert, with most of the basins at over 4000ft and most of the ranges topping 10,000ft. The geographic area of the Great Basin that contains Las Vegas is the 15,000 sq mile Mojave Desert, which covers parts of southern Nevada, southeastern California, northwestern Arizona and southeastern

Utah. The city sits in the middle of a valley that's 2174ft above sea level and ringed by barren foothills. There are no year-round rivers in the valley.

CLIMATE

Las Vegas receives a mere 4.13 inches of rainfall and enjoys 310 sunny days during a typical year. The dry weather acts as a magnet for sun-starved retirees and others seeking refuge from blizzards at home, but the heat can be oppressive, particularly from May through September. Tourism officials are quick to note it's 'a dry heat,' which is true: relative humidity rarely tops 20%. But be forewarned: daily temperatures approach 100°F half of the year, and highs during July and August routinely hover around 105°F. August is Las Vegas' 'wettest' month, with an average of 0.49 inches of rain. June is the driest month, receiving an average of 0.12 inches of rain.

Las Vegas doesn't cool off much after sunset. Concrete and asphalt retain and radiate heat. Due to the billions of tons of concrete and asphalt in Las Vegas, temperatures within the city often exceed 75°F well after nightfall. That said, chilly days and cold nights occasionally visit Las Vegas during winter. Although it vanished as soon as it landed, snowflakes descended on The Strip in February 2002. If you'll be in Las Vegas during November through February, you'd be wise to bring a jacket.

ECOLOGY & ENVIRONMENT

Las Vegas is an environmentalist's nightmare. Water usage is the chief concern. The city receives 85% of its water from the Colorado River, which supplies Lake Mead, and 15% from the ground. Las Vegas residents use, on average, 178 gallons of water per day per person; this figure includes the tremendous amounts of water used by hotel-casinos.

The Las Vegas Valley is expected to use its entire water supply by the year 2010. It presently shares Colorado River water with California and Arizona, and none of the communities that currently receive water from the Colorado River want to give up any of it. What's going to happen in the years to come when there's not enough water to go around is anyone's guess.

Water pollution is another big problem in Las Vegas. Lake Mead, despite being the largest human-made lake in the Western Hemisphere, is experiencing rising levels of pollution. The lake receives partially treated effluent pumped back by Las Vegas' sewage plants. More partially treated effluent is going into the lake than ever before, and the amount of water leaving the lake exceeds the amount entering it. This situation is particularly alarming when you consider that Las Vegas is one of the fastest-growing cities in the US.

Air pollution is another unpopular subject in Las Vegas. The city is surrounded by mountains that trap hazardous particulates. Prior to 1980, the view of those mountains was crystal clear every sunny day; now most days the sky above Las Vegas contains a dirty brown inversion layer that's occasionally so thick you can't even see the mountains. With average daily traffic in Las Vegas increasing by nearly 6% a year, and the number of takeoffs at McCarran International Airport on the rise, the probability of improvements in Las Vegas' air quality is low.

FLORA & FAUNA

There are 370 recorded species of birds, 129 species of mammals and 64 species of reptiles in Nevada, and the state boasts an equally impressive variety of plantlife. But no-one's got a clue how many species of birds, mammals, reptiles or plants can be found *in the wild* in Las Vegas Valley.

Domesticated critters in Las Vegas include white tigers, black jaguars, bottle-nosed

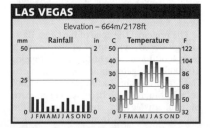

LAS VEGAS
Elevation – 664m/2178ft

Nuclear Waste in the Nevada Desert

The US government stopped exploding nuclear bombs underground at the Nevada Test Site in 1992, but that hasn't meant the end of a possible nuclear future for state residents. In 1998 a US Department of Energy report – which took 15 years and $6 billion to research – recommended Yucca Mountain, near the test site and about 90 miles northeast of Las Vegas, as the best possible location for the nation's only long-term high-level nuclear waste repository.

Did we say long-term? The proposed site – which would eventually hold 77,000 tons of used reactor fuel from nuclear power plants across the country – would remain deadly for 300,000 years. In that time, Earth itself may experience an ice age, and Yucca Mountain, currently one of the driest and most remote places in the United States, may no longer be a desert.

And that's a problem. Scientists agree that water poses the greatest risk to radiation leakage at the site – a far more serious risk than earthquakes (mild ones are common) or volcanic eruptions (which haven't occurred here in 7.5 million years). If ground water seeps down and contacts the waste 1000ft below the surface, it can carry radiation relatively quickly (in less than 50 years, a recent study found) into a water basin below the underground site and into the surrounding countryside.

The Department of Energy acknowledges this risk, but maintains that the corrosion-resistant metal casks will last for at least 10,000 to 100,000 years, even if they get wet, and after that, escaped radiation won't rise above background amounts.

However, no one is arguing that the containers won't deteriorate. And once they do, the only thing keeping the radiation from spreading in substantial amounts is the bone-dry mountain rock – so long as it stays dry.

Would anyone care to predict the weather 200,000 years from now?

Not surprisingly, Nevada officials are fighting the proposed waste site tooth and nail. The problem is that nuclear power plants already have enormous piles of spent fuel rods and radioactive waste that have to be put somewhere – a total of about 40,000 tons of high-level waste in 34 states.

Although the Yucca Mountain nuclear waste repository was approved by Congress, opponents in Nevada have filed federal lawsuits aimed at stopping the project. Should it get the go-ahead, the Yucca Mountain repository would begin taking nuclear waste in 2010. It would continue to receive atomic waste for about one century, and then its 100 miles of tunnels would be capped. The proposed project carries an estimated price tag of $43 billion.

dolphins, Asian elephants – and these represent only the exotic animals found at The Mirage. For years the Flamingo Hilton was home to African penguins, Chilean flamingos, sacred ibises and wood ducks; those beautiful creatures were retired after enough thoughtless individuals offered them chewing gum and cigarette butts.

GOVERNMENT & POLITICS

Las Vegas has operated under a council-manager form of government since January 1, 1944. Under this form of government the citizens elect four council members and a mayor who make up the City Council. The mayor is elected at large by all the voters of the city and each council member is elected from one of four wards in the city. The mayor and the council members serve four-year terms.

A city manager, hired by the City Council, is responsible for the day-to-day operation of the city government. Below the city manager is the city attorney's office and two deputy city managers, responsible for the 14 major departments within the government. Departments are further divided into logistical divisions to perform their respective functions.

On June 8, 1999, in a major blow to official efforts to clean up Sin City's image, Las Vegas voters picked longtime mob lawyer Oscar Goodman to be their mayor. Goodman, who gained fame defending mafia figures such as Meyer Lansky and Tony 'The Ant' Spilotro, caught the voters' fancy with a populist platform that called for developers to pay fees to help solve city traffic and air pollution woes.

The alleged 'barrister-to-butchers,' as an editorial in the *Las Vegas Review-Journal* described him, makes no effort to hide his past. Indeed, the purported 'mouthpiece of the mafia' loves to talk about the old days, when he busted up dozens of government attacks on reputed mobsters and kept Spilotro out of jail despite suspicions that the feared mafia enforcer had committed nearly two-dozen murders.

As Lansky's attorney, Goodman got the mafia's financial genius dropped from a casino cash-skimming trial because of Lansky's failing health. Goodman similarly evoked the disgust of law enforcement officers nationwide when, in 1970, he persuaded a judge to throw out wiretap evidence obtained in 19 cities around the country, crippling a federal campaign against bookmaking.

In his defense, Goodman devoted much of his practice to the poor and the dispossessed, often pro bono. In 1998 he won the release from prison of a cancer-ridden woman who had murdered her abusive husband – a noble thing in the minds of many. And the National Association of Criminal Defense Lawyers once hailed Goodman as 'Liberty's last champion.'

At the time of research, Goodman had been mayor for several years and was enjoying enormous popularity. His popularity was due, in large part, to his frequent use of the mayoral pulpit to comment on many issues (such as medical malpractice, the statewide lottery and the storage of nuclear waste at Yucca Mountain) that fell outside the purview of municipal government but were near to the heart of many Las Vegans. There are some who feel that such subjects are more appropriately addressed by the governor of Nevada.

ECONOMY

Tourism drives the Las Vegas economy. That's no surprise, given that 33-million-plus tourists a year spend an average of four days in town, and most of these people come with money to gamble; the average Vegas visitor in 2001 had a per-trip gambling budget of $535. During the same year, more than 50% of the city's workforce was employed in the service industry.

The stability of Las Vegas' economy fluctuates with the stability of the US economy. The US economy during the late 1990s was record setting: the stock market reached new highs, unemployment was at a 40-year low, and interest rates and inflation were very favorable. Eighty percent of Las Vegas' visitors are American, and with Americans doing so well it wasn't surprising that Las Vegas did well, too.

But, as the saying goes, all good things must come to an end. The Las Vegas economy was already in trouble when terrorists flew a pair of jetliners into the World Trade Center in September 2001. The worldwide travel decline that followed the attacks removed any doubt about the state of the local economy. Air travel plummeted. Hotel occupancies plunged. An estimated 15,000 casino workers lost their jobs, and tens of thousands more had their work schedules reduced.

At the time of writing, a great deal of uncertainty faced Las Vegas. Fear of further attacks on US soil threatened to keep the number of visitors to Sin City down. Although the US economy showed signs of emerging from the economic downturn, the recovery was not certain. Trouble in the Middle East and ongoing US military operations in Afghanistan left Wall Street investors jittery.

POPULATION & PEOPLE

The population of Las Vegas is around 480,000. Of this, around 46% are white, 24% are Hispanic, 10% are black, 5% are Asian, 1% are native American and less than 1% are native Hawaiian or from other Pacific islands. Slightly more than half of the city's residents are male (51% versus 49% female), the median age is 34.5 years and the median household income is $43,170.

If the city's friendliness was measured on a scale of one to 10, with 10 being most friendly, Las Vegas would rate a solid 10. Everywhere you go in town people ask how you are doing, ask if they can be of assistance, stop and say hello. Sure, the city is service oriented. Sure, the city counts on repeat visitors to keep its casinos filled. Sure, its employers place a premium on bright smiles and friendly dispositions.

But spend a few days in Las Vegas and you'll likely leave as so many people do; feeling that Sin City has more than its fair share of genuinely friendly, helpful people. The vast majority of Las Vegans were not born in Nevada, so it's not simply that Las Vegas or Nevada produces warm and fuzzy folks. Rather, its newcomers are friendly people who hail from all parts of our planet.

EDUCATION

State law requires all children between the ages of seven and 17 to attend school. Students attend 180 days of school per year. In 2002 there were 154 elementary schools, 36 middle schools and 31 high schools in the Clark County School District, which includes Las Vegas.

Las Vegas has two institutions of higher learning: the University of Nevada at Las Vegas (UNLV) and the Community College of Southern Nevada (CCSN). The 335-acre UNLV campus has a student body

of 20,000. Its admission requirements are low, and none of its 148 undergraduate, master's and doctoral programs is held in high regard nationally.

Enrollment at CCSN's three campuses hovers around 26,000 students. Sounding somewhat defensive in its literature, the college maintains that its students 'are serious about education and demonstrate a strong work ethic.' In fact, 90% of CCSN's students have part-time jobs.

ARTS

Like clean government in Chicago or sizzling nightlife in Salt Lake City, until recently, cultural arts in Las Vegas would have been just another urban oxymoron. But that's not the case anymore. A glimpse of Vegas' art scene is provided here; see the Things to See & Do chapter for more detail.

Dance

It might surprise and interest you to know that in Nevada there is a professional ballet company, and it presents both classical and contemporary ballet performances. The **Nevada Ballet Theatre** (☎ 702-898-6306; 1651 Inner Circle Dr) offers performances year-round.

Music

Las Vegas is home to the Nevada Symphony Orchestra, the Nevada Opera Theatre, the Las Vegas Civic Symphony and the Nevada Chamber Symphony. Like jazz? You can hear it live every day of the week in Las Vegas. Rhythm and blues? Same deal.

The greatest names in rock 'n' roll appear at MGM Grand, the House of Blues and at

Hollywood Comes to Vegas

More than 130 motion pictures have been filmed in the Las Vegas area since 1932, when John Ford and others visited and made *Airmail*, a routine story of pioneer airmail pilots, starring Pat O'Brien and Ralph Bellamy. Here's a look at some of the famous and infamous movies featuring Sin City.

Love, Las Vegas Style

Viva Las Vegas (1964) – Elvis Presley's a race-car driver and Ann-Margret is the sexy Rusty Martin. Can Elvis win the race and the girl? Of course! But only after a few musical numbers.

Kiss Me, Stupid (1964) – Dean Martin stars as a crooner making the moves on a songwriter's wife in the Nevada desert town of Climax, in this lewd farce by Billy Wilder.

Indecent Proposal (1993) – High roller Robert Redford offers $1 million to a needy couple (Demi Moore and Woody Harrelson) if the wife will have sex with him. It proves to be a poor bargain. It was filmed partly in the Las Vegas Hilton.

Betting the Farm

Lost in America (1985) – This hilarious film starring Albert Brooks finds a middle-class couple looking to escape their yuppie lifestyle, only to lose their 'nest egg' at the Desert Inn.

Rain Man (1988) – Tom Cruise takes his autistic brother (Dustin Hoffman) on a cross-country roadtrip that ends with a triumphant round of cards at Caesars Palace. Many scenes in this Oscar-winning movie were shot in nearby rural Nevada.

Mobsters & Crooks

711 Ocean Drive (1950) – Joseph Newman directs and Edmond O'Brien, Joanne Dru and Otto Kruger star in this racketeer tale with a nail-biting climax at Hoover Dam.

Ocean's Eleven (1960) – This is the movie that gave birth to the Rat Pack: Frank Sinatra, Sammy Davis Jr, Dean Martin, and Peter Lawford attempt to rob five casinos at once. Though overlong and sometimes dull, it's still a quintessential Vegas film.

Ocean's Eleven (2001) – This remake features a host of big-name actors, including George Clooney, Matt Damon, Brad Pitt, Andy Garcia and Julia Roberts, but it's no better than the first. Despite all the talent, it grows monotonous when it ought to be suspenseful.

The Godfather (1972) – There's a brief Vegas interlude in this Oscar-winning tale of an East Coast mafia family.

Bugsy (1991) – Hollywood's take on the Benjamin 'Bugsy' Siegel story. This is a compelling film starring Warren Beatty that takes great pains to recreate the original Flamingo.

The Joint, the 1400-seat state-of-the-art concert venue at the Hard Rock Hotel. Lounge acts playing old favorites? Las Vegas has a million of them. Live country music? Live hip-hop? Big-band sound? Karaoke? Las Vegas has got it all.

Sculpture

Many of the nonprofit and for-profit galleries in Las Vegas have ceramic and wooden sculptures on display. Most of the megaresorts contain statues in their casinos or adjacent shopping wings. The campus of

the University of Nevada at Las Vegas has a rather illuminating piece called *The Flashlight* by Claes Oldenberg; yes, it's a flashlight – a jet-black three-story-tall flashlight located beside the university's Performing Arts Center.

Painting

Caesars Palace still has its kitschy exterior copies of the *Venus de Milo* and other sculptural icons, but Las Vegas now has two Guggenheim museums at The Venetian. At the Guggenheim Hermitage Museum, expect

Hollywood Comes to Vegas

Casino (1995) – This Scorsese film follows casino chief Robert De Niro as Las Vegas changes from a mob-run heaven to a family-fun theme park. Sharon Stone shines amid a heavyweight cast.

Overcoming All Odds

Diamonds Are Forever (1971) – Sean Connery is up to his usual tricks and sexual hijinks as Agent 007 in this James Bond comic-book adventure, which has scenes in Circus Circus and the Las Vegas Hilton.

Rocky IV (1985) – Sly Stallone fights for the USA and Dolph Lundgren the USSR – and James Brown borrows *Jubilee!* props for his musical number – in the third unnecessary sequel to an American classic.

Destroying Vegas

The Amazing Colossal Man (1957) – In this camp thriller, a man turned into a giant by a nuclear explosion terrorizes Vegas. Extremely silly, but there's vintage footage of The Strip.

Honey, I Blew Up the Kid (1992) – See this Disney flick only for its homage to *The Amazing Colossal Man*, in which a giant baby toddles down Fremont St.

Showgirls (1995) – The makers of this film didn't set out to destroy Vegas, but that's what happened. Voted worst movie about Vegas in the *Las Vegas Review-Journal's* 1999 readers' poll.

Mars Attacks! (1996) – Martians attack Earth in this cheeky farce, and Sin City is a prime target. Watch Tom Jones and a bevy of Vegas oddballs fend for their lives!

The Nicolas Cage Series

Honeymoon in Vegas (1992) – Nicolas Cage must love this town. Here, he's a detective on the brink of losing his new wife to sleazy Vegas mobster James Caan. The climax of this engaging farce features the Flying Elvii.

Leaving Las Vegas (1995) – Cage plays an alcoholic bent on drinking himself to death in Vegas in this disturbing yet brilliant movie. He won a Best Actor Oscar for his role.

Con Air (1997) – In this far-fetched action flick, Cage plays a good convict who spoils the escape plans of bad ones. Their plane crashes into the now-demolished Sands hotel-casino, and there's a climactic chase down Fremont St.

Snake Eyes (1998) – This conspiracy thriller, with an often-laughable plot but a visually dazzling style, features Cage as a corrupt cop who unravels an assassination that takes place inside a boxing arena.

to see masterpieces by Claude Monet, Pablo Picasso, Henri Matisse, Vasily Kandinsky, and other artists. The Guggenheim Las Vegas features exhibits that change annually, but regardless of the subject, the treatment is always top notch.

The masterpieces at The Venetian are the pride of Vegas' artistic community these days, but they certainly aren't the only artworks in town. There are no fewer than 22 other private art galleries and 29 nonprofit art galleries in Las Vegas. Among them are the Gallerie Michelangelo, where original works by contemporary artists such as LeRoy Neiman and Erté can be found. See the Things to See & Do chapter for further information.

Architecture

In Las Vegas, structures that predate 1950 cling to life like a trailer park during a tornado. Until recently, buildings with historic value were being blown to pieces with dynamite or slammed apart by wrecking balls, with the machine-gun frequency of Rodney Dangerfield one-liners.

Las Vegas doesn't have any masterpieces of architecture, but the **Huntridge Theater** (☎ 702-477-7703; 1208 E Charleston Blvd) does have a splendid example of Streamline Moderne architecture; a style of clean, austere lines born in the 1930s. The building now housing the Las Vegas Academy of International Studies and Performing Arts is the only full-scale art deco structure in the city.

New monoliths along The Strip celebrate just about every metropolis and epoch except modern-day Nevada. There is a pyramid of ancient Egypt at the Luxor, the famous high-rises at New York-New York, an ersatz Eiffel Tower at Paris-Las Vegas and a *palazzo* at The Venetian. Buildings come in all sizes, shapes and designs in the city of cash and flash.

Hunter S Thompson

Literature

One thing Las Vegas isn't known for is literature. Books by Las Vegas writers or about Las Vegas tend to focus on two topics: beating the casinos at their game *(Henry Tamburin on Casino Gambling* et al) and doing Las Vegas on a dime *(The Cheapskate's Guide to Las Vegas* et al). For these kinds of titles, see Books in the Facts for the Visitor chapter.

In 1971 Hunter S Thompson wrote *Fear and Loathing in Las Vegas*. In many minds, it is the only major literary work linked to Las Vegas. In *Fear and Loathing*, Thompson recounts the humorous story of his trip to Las Vegas to cover the Mint 400 Off-Road Race. The book defined the counterculture of its day.

Literary Las Vegas (1995) is an anthology edited by Mike Tronnos that contains 24 pieces of writing about Las Vegas, penned by Thompson, Tom Wolfe and Noel Coward, to name a few.

Film

Hollywood *loves* Las Vegas. Between 1980 and 2002, no fewer than 92 major motion pictures were shot in whole or in part in Las Vegas or in the desert on the edge of town, and dozens of other movies were made in

the area prior to then (see the 'Hollywood Comes to Vegas' boxed text earlier). In addition to the films mentioned in the boxed text, the following movies were also shot in or near Sin City, some of which now function as time capsules of previous incarnations of this ever-changing place: *Wild Is the Wind* (1957), *The Professionals* (1966), *The Gauntlet* (1977), *Electric Horseman* (1979), *Romancing the Stone* (1984), *Vegas Vacation* (1997) and *3000 Miles to Graceland* (2001).

RELIGION

No one group dominates Las Vegas' religious community. The breakdown: 31% Catholic, 24% Protestant, 20% no affiliation, 16% other, 5% Latter-Day Saints and 4% Jewish.

There are nearly 600 houses of worship in the Las Vegas area. They represent many denominations, including Apostolic, Assembly of God, Baptist, Roman Catholic, Episcopal, Jewish, Lutheran, Latter-Day Saints, Methodist and Pentecostal.

Most tourists seeking religious services while in Las Vegas visit the **Guardian Angel Cathedral** (☎ 702-735-5241; 302 Cathedral Way), which is conveniently located 300ft from Las Vegas Blvd. Mass is held at 8am and 12:10pm weekdays; 2:30pm, 4pm and 5:15pm Saturday; and at 8am, 9:30am, 11am, 12:30pm and 5pm Sunday.

For the locations and phone numbers of hundreds of churches and synagogues in the Las Vegas area, see the listings that appear under 'Churches' and 'Synagogues' in the Las Vegas Yellow Pages (you'll find a phone directory in your hotel room).

LANGUAGE

English is the primary spoken language in Las Vegas. Most of the major casino-hotels have translators on staff to assist guests who are not fluent in English. Also, there are dozens of ethnic/cultural organizations in Las Vegas, including the Cambodian Association, the Deutsche-American Society, the Las Vegas Korean Association and the Polish American Center. Contact **Aird & Associates** (☎ *702-456-3838; 3838 Raymert Dr)* for further information regarding these and other cultural organizations in the Las Vegas area. If you need to communicate with someone who speaks your native language, Aird & Associates can likely assist you.

Facts for the Visitor

WHEN TO GO

You should factor at least two criteria into your travel plans: the weather and conventions. Unless you're cold-blooded or you just really like to perspire, you might want to avoid Las Vegas from May through September. During this time, afternoon temperatures often hit 100°F, and highs during July and August usually hover around 105°F.

You'll also want to avoid Sin City during a big convention (see the boxed text 'Major Convention Dates') – unless you'll be arriving wearing a conventioneer's hat yourself. Not only are colossal crowds annoying – reaching the shrimp pile at the Big Buffet is never more nerve-racking – but they're costly; hotels jack up room rates and buffet prices when the Buggy Whip Manufacturers and other large groups come to town.

Also be aware of certain holidays when you plan your trip. If you don't like crowds, pass on New Year's Eve in Las Vegas; even the mice are bumping shoulders that night. Also, most of the city's revues are 'dark' (shut down) the week before Christmas.

If you'll be in town for only a few days, it might interest you to know that hotel rates are typically 10% to 20% lower from Sunday through Thursday.

ORIENTATION

Two main highways come into Las Vegas: the I-15 and Hwy 95. For downtown, exit Hwy 95 at Las Vegas Blvd (The Strip) or I-15 at Charleston Blvd. I-15 parallels The Strip, so work out which cross street will bring you closest to your destination. If it's your first time in Las Vegas and you're not in a hurry, you might want to exit the I-15 at Blue Diamond Rd and cruise the length of The Strip from south to north, right up to downtown.

Downtown Las Vegas, the original town center, is a compact grid. Its main artery, Fremont St, is a covered pedestrian mall lined with low-brow casinos and hotels for five city blocks. This portion of the street is

---

Major Convention Dates

Listed here are Las Vegas' major annual conventions, their approximate dates and estimated attendance figures. For exact dates, contact the **Las Vegas Convention & Visitors Authority** (☎ *702-892-7575, from anywhere in North America* ☎ *877-847-4858;* Ⓦ *www .vegasfreedom.com).*

January
Consumer Electronics Shows First half of January; 110,000 conventioneers
Sporting Goods Manufacturers Second half of January; 61,000 conventioneers

February
World of Concrete Exposition First half of February; 80,000 conventioneers
Magic Marketplace Second half of February; 110,000 conventioneers
National Association of Home Builders Second half of February; 75,000 conventioneers

March
Associated Surplus Dealers First half of March; 50,000 conventioneers
National Association of Broadcasters First half of March; 120,000 conventioneers
NetWorld-Interop First half of March; 75,000 conventioneers

August
Associated Surplus Dealers First half of August; 50,000 conventioneers
Magic Marketplace Second half of August; 110,000 conventioneers

November
Specialty Equipment Market Association First half of November; 87,000 conventioneers
Comdex Second half of November; 200,000 conventioneers

---

called the Fremont St Experience because of an overhead light show that takes place nightly. Public buildings, like the post office and city hall, are a few blocks north. Shopping is mostly limited to tacky souvenirs.

The blocks around the intersection of Main and Fremont Sts are known as Glitter Gulch, and feature those long-time grinning neon icons, Vegas Vic and Sassy Sally.

Las Vegas Blvd goes through downtown and continues southward for about 10 miles. The Strip, a 4½-mile stretch of this boulevard, has most of the really big hotel-casinos, which are interspersed with parking structures, garish shopping malls, and fast-food outlets. A few small motels are slotted in between the big places, occupying sites awaiting a grander fate.

The colossal, three-legged Stratosphere Tower marks the northern terminus of The Strip. From there to downtown, Las Vegas Blvd is mostly lined with tatty-looking buildings – cheap motels, strip clubs, quickie wedding chapels and so on. Locals refer to the 15-block-long neighborhood as 'Naked City' for its proclivity to prostitution. At the southern end of The Strip, toward the airport, the bright lights peter out a block past the spectacular Mandalay Bay hotel-casino.

Traffic can be heavy on The Strip at times. This is particularly true on Friday and Saturday nights. Unless you want to be part of the street action, use one of the parallel roads (such as Industrial Rd or Paradise Rd), or take the local buses to travel along here.

Aside from the major casinos near The Strip, most of Las Vegas consists of typical residential neighborhoods. North Las Vegas is a pretty tough area, while the city's western fringe has some of the biggest, fanciest houses. Bordering Vegas to the southeast is Henderson, a satellite suburb with some traditional industries, such as chemical manufacturing and metal processing.

MAPS

Lonely Planet publishes a laminated *Las Vegas* map which includes a map of Grand Canyon National Park. Maps are widely sold at hotels, gas stations and newsstands. All of the maps mentioned here can be obtained with little difficulty around town.

For ease of use, Rand McNally's *Las Vegas* is hard to beat. It actually contains several fold-out maps, including Las Vegas Vicinity, Las Vegas Region and Las Vegas Central (which shows the downtown area and The Strip on one long, easy-to-read map). Among the sites shown are the city's major hotel-casinos, 10 shopping centers, and dozens of family attractions and golf courses.

For detail, the *Las Vegas City Map* by Compass Maps is topflight. It shows every single street in the city on one large fold-out map, and has a street and road index on the other side. Beside the index is a thorough but not particularly user-friendly Casino Map and a Glitter Gulch/Downtown Map. The large city map is so detailed it nearly requires a magnifying glass to use. If you think you'll be traveling into the suburbs, this is the map for you.

The Las Vegas Convention & Visitors Authority publishes the fold-out *Las Vegas Maps & Area Information* map that emphasizes The Strip and downtown, and contains only the major boulevards in the vicinity of The Strip. It has an easy-to-use hotel and motel guide, and a small regional map. The reverse side contains the names, addresses and phone numbers of shopping malls, museums, wedding chapels and so on.

The Nevada Commission of Tourism's *Official State Map,* like the Visitors Authority map, is distributed freely. One side has a very detailed map of the state; Lake Tahoe, Las Vegas and Reno-Sparks region maps; a distance chart; and a box showing the location of all of Nevada's campgrounds and recreational areas. The flip side contains lots of good information about the state's history and its attractions.

RESPONSIBLE TOURISM

Las Vegas is the fastest-growing city in the US, with 5000-plus newcomers arriving every month and births outpacing deaths by a margin of two to one. In addition, it seems like every month somebody is opening yet another hotel-casino with several thousand guestrooms. As a result, local officials face enormous challenges with traffic congestion, water conservation, and keeping water and air pollution at acceptable levels.

Tap water is a big concern at City Hall. Nevada receives only 10% of the annual allocation of Colorado River water, and that's barely enough to keep up with demand. Increased water usage has led to a rise in the level of pollutants in Lake Mead. Steps being taken to curb usage include banning lawn watering from May to October in the peak evaporation hours of noon to 7pm.

You can help Las Vegas maintain its water reservoir by taking short showers and by being miserly with your use of towels; don't use three towels when one will suffice. Unnecessary towel-washing not only wastes precious tap water, but it needlessly adds bleach to the area's water supply. Likewise, before leaving your room, be sure to turn off all the lights and the air-con; inefficient use of electricity results in the needless consumption of unrenewable resources.

TOURIST OFFICES
Local Tourist Offices
There are quite a number of tour operators around town with 'Tourist Information' signs posted out front, but the city's only true tourist office is the **Las Vegas Convention & Visitors Authority** (☎ 702-892-7575, 800-332-5333; ⓦ www.vegasfreedom.com). It's across the street from the **Las Vegas Convention Center** (3150 Paradise Rd; open 8am-5pm daily), where Paradise Rd meets Convention Center Dr. The friendly staff is extremely knowledgeable and the office contains so many free brochures, magazines and maps that one copy of each could easily fill a shopping bag.

Tourist Offices Abroad
Las Vegas maintains five visitor information centers overseas.

Australia (☎ 02-9328-5440, fax 02-9328-5443, ⓔ lasvegas@gate7.com.au) Gate 7 Pty. Ltd, Suite 302, Bay House, 2 Guilfoyle Ave, Double Bay, NSW, 2028
Germany (☎ 89-236-6210, fax 89-260-4009, ⓔ think@mangum.de) Mangum Management, Herzogspitalstrasse 5, 80331, Munich
Japan (☎ 3-3358-3265, fax 3-3358-3287, ⓔ oka@kokada.co.jp) Okada Associates, Gyoen Bldg 8F, 1-5-6 Shinjuku, Shinjuku-ku, Tokyo 160-0022

South Korea (☎ 02-777-9282, fax 02-777-9543, ⓔ soniah@itnpr.co.kr) International Tourism Network, Room 506, Shin-A Bldg, 39-1 Seosomun-dong, Chung-ku, Seoul
UK (☎ 1-564-79-4999, fax 1-564-79-5333, ⓔ info@cellet.co.uk) Cellet Travel Services, Brook House, 47 High St, Henley in Arden, Warwickshire B95 5AA

DOCUMENTS
All visitors to the US must have a valid passport and may also be required to have a US visa (see Visas later in this section). Check these regulations carefully with the US embassy in your country before you depart. Immigration and Naturalization Service (INS) officials have the authority to ship you home on the first flight out, without a chance for appeal, if you are caught without proper entry papers.

Your passport should be valid for at least six months longer than your intended stay in the US, and you'll need to submit a recent photo with your visa application. Documents demonstrating financial stability or guarantees from a US resident (in special cases, the INS can demand that someone entering the country be 'sponsored' by a citizen who promises to provide them with financial support) are sometimes required for people from particularly impoverished countries.

Although most visitors to the US have no problem entering the country, you should tread carefully from the time you exit your international flight until you have passed through all the formalities and are in the actual arrivals area of the terminal. In addition to INS staff, who will inspect your passport and collect customs papers, you will encounter customs officials who may search your bags.

Your passport may also prove useful after arrival, as the drinking age of 21 is universally enforced. If you appear younger than 30, bring some form of age identification (such as your passport) with you when you go out.

Visas
A reciprocal visa-waiver program applies to citizens of certain countries, who may

enter the US for stays of 90 days or fewer without having to obtain a visa. Currently, these countries include Andorra, Argentina, Australia, Austria, Belgium, Brunei, Denmark, Finland, France, Germany, Iceland, Ireland, Italy, Japan, Liechtenstein, Luxembourg, Monaco, the Netherlands, New Zealand, Norway, San Marino, Slovenia, Spain, Sweden, Switzerland and the United Kingdom.

Under the visa-waiver program, you must have a round-trip ticket on an airline that participates in the program, and proof of financial solvency, such as credit cards, a bank account with evidence of a balance beyond two figures, or employment in your home country. You will be required to sign a form waiving the right to a hearing over deportation, and an extension to your stay beyond 90 days will not be allowed. Consult with your chosen airline or the closest US consulate or embassy to confirm this information, as regulations are subject to change.

Other travelers will need to obtain a visa from a US consulate or embassy. In most countries the process can be done by mail, but in some countries, notably Turkey, Poland and Russia, you'll need to go to a US consulate or embassy in person. Visa applicants may be required to 'demonstrate binding obligations' that will ensure their return back home. Because of this requirement, those planning to travel through other countries before arriving in the US are generally better off applying for their US visa while still in their home country, rather than while on the road.

The validity period for US visitor visas depends on what country you're from. The length of time you'll be allowed to stay in the US is ultimately determined by the INS officers at the port of entry.

Visa Extensions Tourists using visas are usually granted a six-month stay on first arrival. If you try to extend that time, one of the first assumptions will be that you are working illegally, so come prepared with concrete evidence that you have been behaving like a model tourist, such as receipts to demonstrate you've been spending money brought from home, and ticket stubs that show you've been traveling extensively. Visa extensions in Las Vegas are pondered at the **INS office** (☎ 702-451-3597; 3373 Pepper Lane, Pecos Rd).

If you need to speak with an INS agent and are having trouble getting one on the phone at that location (the line is generally busy), try calling the customs and immigration office at **McCarran International Airport** (☎ 702-388-6480).

HIV & Entering the USA

Anyone entering the US who is not a US citizen is subject to the authority of the Immigration and Naturalization Service (INS), which has the final say about whether you enter or not, and has full power to send you back to where you came from. Being HIV-positive is not grounds for deportation, but it is grounds for exclusion. What this means is that once in the US, you cannot be deported for being HIV-positive, but you can be prevented from entering the US.

The INS does not test people for HIV when they try to enter the US, but the form for non-immigrant visas asks, 'Have you ever been afflicted with a communicable disease of public health significance?' If you answer yes to this question, the INS may try to exclude you when you reach the US.

If you are HIV-positive but can prove to the consular officials to whom you have applied for a visa that you are the spouse, parent or child of a US citizen or legal resident (green-card holder), you are exempt from the exclusionary rule.

For legal information and referrals to immigrant advocates, potential visitors should contact the National Immigration Project of the **National Lawyers Guild** (☎ 617-227-9727; 14 Beacon St, Suite 506, Boston, MA 02108), and the **Immigrant HIV Assistance Project** (Bar Association of San Francisco; ☎ 415-267-0795; 685 Market St, Suite 700, San Francisco, CA 94105).

Travel Insurance

No matter how you're traveling, take out travel insurance. This should cover you not only for medical expenses and missing luggage, but also for cancellations or delays in your travel arrangements. Be sure to obtain coverage for any accident that requires hospital treatment and a flight home. STA Travel offers various travel insurance plans at reasonable prices.

For insurance purposes, it's advisable to keep photocopies of your airline tickets and insurance policy separate from the originals (also, consider leaving photocopies with someone who could fax them to you in a clutch).

Buy travel insurance as early as possible. If you buy it the week before you fly, you may find, for instance, that you're not covered for delays to your flight caused by strikes or other industrial action that may have been in force before you took out the insurance.

Driver's License

Planning to drive? You will need to bring your driver's license, and check with your country's national auto club to see if they recommend obtaining an International Driver's License. Note that this document alone won't allow you to drive; you will need a valid license from your home country as well.

Hostel Cards

There are two youth hostels in Las Vegas, but neither one gives you a discount or otherwise honors a hostel card issued by Hostelling International/American Youth Hostel or any similar organization.

Student Cards

If you are a student, by all means obtain and carry an International Student Identification Card (ISIC), which can get you substantial discounts at museums, tourist attractions and on some plane fares.

Seniors Cards

Seniors are Las Vegas' fastest-growing population group. Retirees make up about 20% of Vegas households. About 12% of Vegas' seniors moved here to retire, attracted by the dry climate, mild winters and affordable retirement developments. As such, many businesses in Las Vegas offer senior discounts on request; you don't need a seniors card but you may be asked for proof of age.

Copies

Whatever documents you're required to bring, carry copies of them separately from the originals. This will speed replacement in the case that the originals are lost or stolen. It's also a good idea to leave photocopies of each of your travel documents with someone at home.

EMBASSIES & CONSULATES
US Embassies & Consulates

US diplomatic offices abroad include the following:

Australia (☎ 02-6214-5600, Ⓔapvcanb@pd .state.gov) Moonah Place, Yarralumla, ACT 2600
Consulates: Melbourne, Perth and Sydney

Canada (☎ 613-238-5335, Ⓔ reference@usembas sycanada.gov) 490 Sussex Dr, Ottawa, Ontario K1N 1G8
Consulates: Calgary, Halifax, Montreal, Toronto, Quebec, Winnipeg and Vancouver

France (☎ 01-43-12-22-22-22, Ⓔ citizeninfo@ state.gov) 2 avenue Gabriel, 75008 Paris
Consulates: Marseilles and Strasbourg

Germany (☎ 30-8305-0, Ⓔ feedback@usem bassy.de) Neustädtische Kirchstr. 4-5, 10117 Berlin
Consulates: Düsseldorf, Leipzig, Frankfurt, Hamburg and Munich

New Zealand (☎ 4-462-6000, Ⓔ irc@actrix .gen.nz) 29 Fitzherbert Terrace, Thorndon, Wellington
Consulate: Auckland

UK (☎ 20-7499-9000) 24 Grosvenor Square, London W1A 1AE
Consulates: Belfast (Northern Ireland) and Edinburgh (Scotland)

Consulates in Las Vegas

Las Vegas has got a lot of things, but it hasn't got a single embassy or consulate. All embassies are located in the nation's capital, Washington, DC. Quite a number of countries also maintain consulates in New York, Miami, San Francisco, Los Angeles and Chicago.

If you would like to speak with a government representative of a particular foreign country and don't know the location of the country's nearest diplomatic mission, you can call directory assistance for Washington, DC (☎ 202-555-1212), and request a telephone number for that country's embassy. The fee for directory assistance is $1.

CUSTOMS

International travelers who haven't already cleared US customs must do so at McCarran International Airport. If you have nothing to declare, just follow the green line on the floor of the terminal; you may or may not be singled out for a spot inspection as you head toward the exit. If you have something to declare, follow the red line and be sure to declare the article, because if you fail to do so and are caught, you could find yourself in serious trouble. If you have illegal drugs, discard them immediately.

Non-US citizens 21 years or older can import 1L of liquor and 200 cigarettes duty free. Gifts may amount to no more than $100 in value. You may bring any amount of money less than $10,000 into or out of the US without declaration. Amounts equal to or greater than $10,000 must be declared. There is no legal limit to the amount of US and foreign cash and traveler's checks you can bring in, but undeclared amounts of more than $10,000 can be confiscated.

MONEY

Nothing works like cash, but in Las Vegas you will find that most forms of payment are welcome. How to get cash is another matter. Read on to consider your options.

Currency

Only US currency is accepted in Las Vegas. The dollar ($) is divided into 100 cents (¢). Coins come in the following denominations, with these names and descriptions.

1¢ penny; copper colored
5¢ nickel; fat and silver colored

10¢ dime; the smallest coin, thin and silver colored
25¢ quarter; silver colored with rough edges
50¢ half-dollar; larger than a quarter and silver colored, with a profile of John F Kennedy
$1 dollar; commonly seen in three forms: a large, silver-colored coin with a profile of Dwight D Eisenhower (minted from 1971–78); a smaller gold-colored coin with a profile of Susan B Anthony (minted 1979–99); and a second gold-colored coin featuring Sacagawea in a three-quarters profile on its obverse and a soaring American bald eagle on its reverse (minted from 2000)

In addition to the coins mentioned here, from 1999 to 2008, the US Mint will issue a new state quarter about every 10 weeks. Each quarter's reverse will celebrate one of the 50 states with a design honoring its unique history, traditions and symbols.

Bills – paper currency – are confusing to many foreign visitors. They are all the same size and color, regardless of denomination. Be careful to check the denomination in the corners of the bills so you don't pay the wrong amount or receive the wrong amount in change. Bills come in denominations of $1, $2 (rare), $5, $10, $20, $50 and $100.

In 1996, the US Treasury began redesigning the bills to thwart counterfeiters, starting with the $100 bill and proceeding down through the valuations, one bill every two years. If you find yourself in possession of both new and old bills, don't worry; the old-design currency will remain valid for at least the next several years.

Exchange Rates

Exchange rates fluctuate daily. At press time, exchange rates for some of the major currencies were as follows.

country	unit		dollars
Australia	A$1	=	US$0.54
Canada	C$1	=	US$0.63
euro zone	€1	=	US$0.98
Hong Kong	HK$10	=	US$1.28
Japan	¥100	=	US$0.82
New Zealand	NZ$1	=	US$0.47
United Kingdom	UK£1	=	US$1.56

FACTS FOR THE VISITOR

Exchanging Money

Cash Casinos exist to separate you from your money, and they will facilitate that end any way they can. This includes swapping major foreign currencies for US dollars. The casinos will charge a fee to exchange money, but it's usually not very high. Most banks will change major currencies; their exchange rates tend to be more favorable than those offered by the casinos.

There is no shortage of foreign-exchange brokers in Las Vegas. The **American Express Travel Agency** (☎ 702-739-8474) inside the MGM Grand Hotel changes many foreign currencies at competitive rates. The **Foreign Money Exchange** (☎ 702-791-3301), on The Strip opposite the Stardust Hotel, also changes many foreign currencies at competitive rates.

Traveler's Checks You can cash traveler's checks at all hotel-casinos and they are accepted by most businesses. If you intend to gamble, you must cash the checks at the casino cashier first, as they are not accepted at the tables. A valid photo identification, such as a current passport or driver's license, is usually required.

American Express cardholders can cash personal checks for traveler's checks at American Express offices. You can cash a check for up to $1000 in any seven-day period with a green American Express card, $5000 with a gold card and $10,000 with a platinum card. If you don't have a check, you can use a counter check; all you need to know is the name of your bank. The funds are charged to your checking account, not your card.

Personal Checks Few businesses accept personal out-of-state checks. However, most hotels will cash a check at the casino cashier if you are a guest of the hotel and have a valid driver's license or passport and major credit card. The hotel-casinos are linked to a central credit system; $500 is about the most you can cash for any single trip unless you have completed a check-cashing application in advance and they approve the limit you set for your stay in the city.

ATMs Every hotel-casino, every bank branch and most convenience stores in Las Vegas have at least one automated teller machine (ATM). You will find ready access to ATMs if you are a member of Plus, Cirrus or Instant-Teller networks (check your card for mention of one of these three). When using ATMs at locations other than your bank, a service charge applies.

Credit & Debit Cards Major credit cards and most debit cards are widely accepted by car rental firms, hotels, restaurants, gas stations, shops, movie theaters, grocery stores, ticket vendors and so on. Only the least sophisticated businesses in Las Vegas don't accept plastic money these days.

Cash advances against your MasterCard or Visa are available at all casinos, but the fee is generally steep: about $50 for each $1000. Local banks will give a cash advance on both cards, and the fee isn't as high. American Express cardholders should see Traveler's Checks.

International Transfers Two words: no problem. In keeping with the idea that they don't want to deny you the chance to fritter your money away on their gaming tables and slot machines, most casinos are equipped to receive wired money (but they won't assist you in sending money from the casino).

Security

Pickpockets *love* Las Vegas. With so many people carrying so much cash on them and drinking like fish as they gamble the day away, what's a pickpocket not to like about Las Vegas? If you intend to carry lots of cash on you, carry it in large-denomination bills to minimize the size of the wad. If you must carry it all in your wallet, be sure to keep your wallet in a front pocket of your trousers or a zippered inside pocket of a jacket. Better yet, keep some money in your wallet and the majority of it in an inside pouch. Never leave money unsecured in a hotel room.

Costs

A trip to Las Vegas can be inexpensive or outrageously costly. It depends upon you.

This is Sin City, baby, where everything is fabulous!

Feeling like a fish out of water?

From neon oasis to urban desert, a Las Vegas suburb

Speared straight through the heart and into the chapel

Take a stroll down Fremont St, the neon capital of the world

Pack a few good luck charms and hit the casinos

… just in case you need to be reminded where you are

Yeehah!

If you don't need to be in town during a major convention (when room rates are jacked up), it's possible to find a double room on or near The Strip in a major hotel-casino for as little as $29.95. However, without special deals, basic rooms are usually $69.95 a night or more (see the Places to Stay chapter for more advice on finding cheap lodging), and if you want to stay in a premium room, the sky's the limit on price.

Gone are the days when most hotel-casinos offered spectacular meal buffets for slightly more than you'd pay for a beer at a regular bar. However, it's still possible to find cheap eats in Las Vegas, and if quality rather than cost is your primary concern, you'll be pleased to know that there's a plethora of gourmet restaurants in town.

As for prices in general, items targeted at tourists – film, sunglasses, jewelry and so on – will cost more on The Strip than they will in other areas. If you're looking for snacks or sodas to bring back to your room, expect to pay much more for them at the store inside your hotel-casino than at a neighborhood grocery store.

There's plenty of free entertainment in Las Vegas, and loads of pricey entertainment as well. International travelers will likely be surprised by the relatively low cost of gasoline in Nevada. Phone calls can cost a lot or a little; see the Telephone section later in this chapter.

In short, unless you come during a convention or during a special event or holiday that's big business for Las Vegas, you can spend as little as $45 a day for room, food and entertainment – or you can spend more than you've ever had in your checking account at one time.

Tipping

Many people employed in tourist-intensive service industries are poorly paid, and they rely on tips to bring their incomes up to decent or enviable levels. However, tips should only be given as a reward for good service. If you receive lousy service, leave a poor tip or none at all; to do otherwise defeats the purpose of tipping, which is to provide a financial incentive for superior

service. Here is a guide to customary tipping amounts in Las Vegas.

Bellhops From $2 total to $1 a bag, depending on the distance covered

Change Persons 10% of winnings when a hint on a slot machine pays off for you

Cocktail Servers 10% to 15%; if drinking for free in a casino, $1 per round

Concierges Nothing for information to $20 for securing tickets to a sold-out show

Doormen $1 or $2 for summoning you a cab, depending on the weather

Hotel Maids $1 to $2 a day, left on the pillow each day

Keno Runners 15% if you're winning and a few dollars during play

Limo Drivers 15% of the total fare

Skycaps At least $1 per bag

Taxi Drivers 10% to 15%

Valet Parking Attendants $2, paid when the keys to the car are handed back to you

Waiters 15% to 20% of the total check, when the service warrants it

Who not to tip: cashiers, ticket vendors working in booths and hotel front-desk employees.

Taxes

Some of the taxes you pay in Las Vegas are included in stated prices and fees. For example, a gallon of gasoline in Las Vegas with a posted price of $1 will cost you exactly $1, but from this amount the gasoline station has to pay the US government 18.4¢, the Nevada government 23¢, and the government of Las Vegas 10¢. More than half of the cost of gasoline in Las Vegas goes to pay taxes, but you won't see any sign or receipt saying so.

Not-so-hidden taxes include a sales tax of 7% that is added to the posted price of most goods and services (gasoline is one of the exceptions) and a 9% tax added to posted hotel rates. The restaurant-meal tax is 7%. Car rental agencies add taxes *and* fees: they add a 7% sales tax and a 6% license-tag fee to their advertised rental rates, and they often assess a 10% airport surcharge. Be sure to ask about additional taxes and costs when reserving a rental car.

There is no value-added tax in the US.

POST & COMMUNICATIONS
Postal Rates
US postal rates are among the lowest in the industrialized world. At the time of writing, it costs 34¢ to mail a 1oz, first-class letter – which includes your typical letter or birthday card – within the US. It's another 24¢ for each additional ounce, and postcards cost 21¢.

International rates (except for those to Canada and Mexico, which are slightly cheaper) are 60¢ for a half-ounce letter, $1 for the full ounce and 40¢ for each additional half ounce. Postcards and aerogrammes each cost 50¢.

Several rate options are available for parcels mailed overseas from the US. First class is the most expensive, but delivery anywhere rarely takes more than 10 days. If speedy delivery is not important to you, consider fourth class. Fourth-class rates can be very low, but delivery can take many weeks. If all you are sending is a published work, such as a book or magazine, tell the postmaster. Special low rates apply to 'printed matter,' as postal workers call it.

Sending Mail
The US Postal Service handles 41% of the world's mail volume and is very efficient and reliable. Just west of The Strip is a **US Post Office** (*3100 S Industrial Rd; open 8:30am-5pm Mon-Fri*), near Circus Circus Dr. There's also a downtown post office (*301 Stewart Ave; open 9am-5pm Mon-Fri, 9am-1pm Sat*). For Las Vegas postal information, call ☎ 800-275-8777.

Most hotel-casinos sell stamps and will mail letters and packages for you. Caesars Palace even boasts a full-service US Post Office in its Forum Shops wing; it's open 10am to 11pm Sunday through Thursday, and 10am to midnight Friday and Saturday.

It's extremely rare for mail sent from one part of the USA to another to disappear in the process. However, important parcels shipped overseas should be sent via **Federal Express** (☎ *800-463-3339*) or **UPS** (☎ *800-742-5877*), because the US Postal Service does not control mail once it has left America. Call FedEx or UPS for details.

Receiving Mail
The best way to receive mail in Las Vegas is to have it sent to where you're staying. If that happens to be a hotel, simply add 'c/o guest (your name)' beneath the name of the hotel in the address ('c/o' stands for 'care of'). Be sure to include the zip code, as the US Postal Service returns mail that doesn't have a zip code. Example: Flamingo Hilton, c/o guest Jack Frost, 3555 S Las Vegas Blvd, Las Vegas, NV 89109. Staff will alert you when your mail arrives.

If you won't be in town very long but need to receive a parcel quickly, ask the sender to use one of the major express mail services (or to send the parcel 'priority mail' or 'express mail' from a US post office). Beware that all of the express mail companies require a street address (no post office boxes) and a phone number for the recipient (the hotel's main phone number if you're staying at a hotel).

Telephone
All phone numbers within the US and Canada consist of a three-digit area code followed by a seven-digit local number. There are two area codes in Nevada: ☎ 702 serves southern Nevada (and, therefore, all of Las Vegas), and ☎ 775 serves the rest of the state. If you are calling locally, just dial the seven-digit number. If you are calling to another area code, dial ☎ 1 followed by the three-digit area code and the seven-digit local number.

The country code for the US is ☎ 1. The international access code is ☎ 011 for calls you dial directly and ☎ 01 for calls made collect or on a calling card; dial it before you dial the country code.

Free calls have area codes of ☎ 800 or ☎ 888, and are generally good throughout the USA and Canada. Numbers that begin with ☎ 900 are charged at a premium rate.

Well Hello There
The first telephone in Nevada was installed in 1907, in a cigar store at the Nevada Hotel in Las Vegas. The telephone number was 1.

You'll most often see them advertised late at night on TV, in ads asking, 'Lonely? Want to have some hot talk?'

Local directory assistance can be reached by calling ☎ 411 or ☎ 555-1212. If you are looking for a number out of your local area code and you're sure of the code it's in, dial ☎ 1 followed by the area code and 555-1212. Directory assistance calls cost between 85¢ and $1, depending on the phone company used.

To obtain a toll-free (800 or 888) number, dial ☎ 800-555-1212.

International Calls Americans can contract with long-distance telephone companies for some very cheap international rates. If you are staying with someone, use his or her phone and reimburse the charges. Every other method will cost much more. To get an international line, dial ☎ 011, the country code, the city or area code (you don't need to dial 0), then the number.

From a pay phone, first dial the number, then wait to hear how much it will be. After depositing your first $1.50 to $3 for the first three minutes, be prepared to keep feeding the slot at a rate of $1 to $2 a minute. If the pay phone has a sign saying it accepts credit cards for long-distance or international calls, check the rates carefully before you punch your credit card number in.

Collect & Country Direct You can call collect (reverse charges) from any phone. The two main service providers are **AT&T** (☎ 800-225-5288) and **MCI** (☎ 800-365-5328). These generally have rates less stressful to the lucky recipient of your call than local phone companies or the dreaded third-party firms.

Pay Phones Coin phones have been deregulated and charge what the market will bear. A variety of companies operate them. Those from Ameritech are the most reliable and cost 35¢ for a local call. However, some pay phones are operated by companies run by unethical people, and they charge exorbitant rates, especially for long-distance or international calls. Always check the rates

carefully. If you use one of these phones to call long-distance using your credit card or calling card number, you may later be horrified to find that the operator charged you $5 a minute, or some other outrageous rate.

Phone Cards Lonely Planet's eKno Communication Card is aimed specifically at independent travelers and provides budget international calls, a range of messaging services, free email and travel information. (For local calls, you're usually better off with a local card.) You can join online at W www.ekno.lonelyplanet.com. To use eKno from Las Vegas once you have joined, dial ☎ 800-706-1333.

Check the eKno website for details on joining, and access telephone numbers from other countries, updates on super budget local access numbers and new features.

Hotel Phones The paradox about hotel room phone charges is that the cheaper the hotel, the more likely phone calls from your room will be free. On the dubious theory that if you're paying $100 a night for your room you won't mind being gouged for a call, some of the finest hotels nick you for $1 or more for local and toll-free calls. Worse, they often add an exorbitant surcharge to long-distance calls. Always inquire about such charges from the hotel operator or from the front desk before calling Japan or wherever for 30 minutes.

Similarly, many Las Vegas hotels offer free local calling from guestrooms. Many others charge 75¢ for the first local call made within a 24-hour period and nothing for each additional local call. If you intend to make many local calls while in Las Vegas, be sure to inquire about the local-calling policy of the hotel you're considering before making a reservation.

Fax

Pay fax machines are located at shipping outlets such as Mail Boxes Etc, copy places such as Kinko's, and hotel business centers. Prices can be high, as much as $1 an outgoing page to a US number and $4 a page to Europe. Receiving faxes costs about half that.

Email & Internet Access

If you set up an email account through a free service, such as hotmail (Ⓦ www.hotmail .com) or ekno (Ⓦ www.ekno.com), you can access your email from any computer with an Internet connection. Otherwise, check with the provider of your account to see how, if possible, you can access it from Las Vegas.

Most of the casino-hotels have business centers that offer Internet access to their guests. Both of Las Vegas' youth hostels offer Internet access. Remarkably, there was only one Internet café on The Strip at the time of writing. The **Cyber Stop Internet Café** (☎ 702-736-4782, fax 702-736-7318; Ⓔ info@cyberstopinc.com; Ⓦ www.cyber stopinc.com; 3743 S Las Vegas Blvd, 112B; open 7am-2:30am daily), inside the Polo Towers Plaza, between the MGM Grand and Aladdin Hotel, offers Internet access for $8/12 per 30 minutes/hour. It also offers printing (50¢ per sheet), photocopying (25¢ per sheet), high-resolution color scanning ($1 per scan), cell-phone rental (85¢/$5 per minute/day) and fax services (continental USA/international $2/3 per page).

DIGITAL RESOURCES

Web resources abound for Las Vegas. The following websites are very informative and could prove useful to you in planning a trip to Las Vegas.

Las Vegas Convention & Visitors Authority (Ⓦ www.vegasfreedom.com) This website is tourist-oriented and contains lots of information on Las Vegas and definitely deserves a look. This is the place to find Las Vegas convention, show and event dates. Be forewarned that the hotel reservations service advertised on the website adds a 5% to 10% surcharge to the rack rates charged by the hotels it represents.

Las Vegas Review-Journal (Ⓦ www.lvrj.com/) Nevada's largest and most respected newspaper features scores of articles on local news, sports, business, lifestyles, special events and weather on its website. There's even an 'Implosions Index,' where you can download videos showing landmark Vegas hotel-casinos being blown to bits.

Virtual Las Vegas Strip (Ⓦ www.intermind.net/ strip/strip.html) This fun site shows a map of The Strip, upon which are photographs of the major tourist attractions that flank Las Vegas Blvd. Click on the photographs and you'll be linked to pertinent information about each one. It's a good website to visit if you're unfamiliar with Las Vegas and want to acquaint yourself with the location of The Strip's chief attractions. It's also a good place to find competitive hotel rates and make reservations.

Gay Vegas (Ⓦ www.gayvegas.com/index.html) This website isn't nearly as thorough as it could be, but it is as it claims the most complete site for gay locals and visitors to Las Vegas. Gay clubs and organizations in Las Vegas come and go with such frequency that only the ones with proven staying power are mentioned in this guide. Gayvegas.com does a fairly good job of staying current with these entities.

Yahoo Las Vegas (Ⓦ dir.yahoo.com/Regional/ U_S__States/Nevada/Cities/Las_Vegas/) There are scores of links to sites in more than 20 categories relating to the city on this website, plus its own extensive guides.

BOOKS

Most of the books listed here are available in the US. Internet surfers often have good luck finding the more obscure titles on the Amazon website (Ⓦ www.amazon.com).

See also the Literature section in the Facts about Las Vegas chapter.

Lonely Planet

Lonely Planet's *California & Nevada* is an indispensable guidebook for people looking to combine Las Vegas and its surrounds with extensive travels in California. *Hiking in the USA* covers great hikes for the experienced hiker and novice alike, including detailed trail notes in the Grand Canyon, Bryce Canyon and Zion Canyon.

Lonely Planet's *Travel with Children*, by Cathy Lanigan, will tell you what to do with the little ones while you're on the road.

Guidebooks

Comp City: A Guide to Free Las Vegas Vacations, by Max Rubin, is perfect for anyone interested in garnering casino freebies such as rooms, meals and shows.

Hiking Las Vegas, by Anthony Curtis, contains descriptions of 60 hikes within 60 minutes of The Strip.

Las Vegas Ride Guide, by Lamont J Singley, provides maps and information for more than 30 trails and destinations that you can explore by mountain bike in the Las Vegas area.

Gambling

The Everything Casino Gambling Book, by George Mandos, describes the rules and etiquette for all the casino games played in Las Vegas, and offers 'tips and strategies you need to beat the house.'

Casino Gambling the Smart Way: How to Have More Fun and Win More Money, by Andrew Glazer, provides easy-to-remember tips for recreational gamblers.

Las Vegas: Behind the Tables!, by Barney Vinson, presents a behind-the-scenes look at casino management. It contains lots of stories, as does *Las Vegas: Behind the Tables! Part 2*.

The Las Vegas Advisor Guide to Slot Clubs, by Jeffery Compton, takes readers on an opinionated tour of southern Nevada slot clubs, and presents some valuable casino tips.

Welcome to the Pleasuredome, by David Spanmier, profiles some of Las Vegas' high rollers, its movers and shakers and its excesses.

History & Politics

Casino, by Nicholas Pileggi, is an intriguing book that describes the fall of organized crime in Las Vegas' casinos.

Las Vegas: As It Began, As It Grew, by Stanley W Paner, gives the history of Las Vegas from the Spanish Trail days up through the building of the Hoover Dam.

Bombs in the Backyard: Atomic Testing and American Politics, by Costandina Titus, examines the 30-year history of atomic detonations outside Las Vegas.

General

Viva Las Vegas: After-Hours Architecture, by Alan Hess, examines Las Vegas' history, and reviews the city's architecture from the 1940s to The Mirage.

A Pictorial History of Las Vegas, published by the *Las Vegas Review-Journal*, tells the story of modern Las Vegas through hundreds of captivating photographs.

NEWSPAPERS & MAGAZINES

Nevada's largest and most respected newspaper is the *Las Vegas Review-Journal*, which hits the streets in the morning. The city also has an afternoon paper, the *Las Vegas Sun*. Widely available are the *Los Angeles Times*, the *New York Times* and the *Wall Street Journal*. Abbreviated national and international news can also be found in *USA Today*.

There are numerous local magazines available in Las Vegas, in addition to the wide variety of US-based magazines available at newsstands throughout America. *Casino Player* is a monthly magazine written for Las Vegas and Atlantic City gamblers. It contains lots of casino and gambling news, as well as opinion pieces – typically addressing the pros and cons of 'doubling up,' an optional built-in feature on most video poker machines.

Another information-packed magazine that's distributed freely to guestrooms in most Vegas hotel-casinos is *What's On*, a weekly guide to current and upcoming shows and events in Las Vegas. Other informative guides available for free at most hotel-casinos and at the Las Vegas Convention & Visitors Authority office at the Convention Center include *Las Vegas: Official Visitors Guide*, *Las Vegas Today* and *Nevada Events & Shows*.

RADIO & TV

You'll find the usual assortment of rock, country and classical radio stations in Las Vegas. Due to the city's sports-betting mecca status, there are no fewer than five radio stations that broadcast sporting events on a regular basis.

720 AM (KDWN) Los Angeles Dodgers games
840 AM (KXNT) NFL games
920 AM (KBAD) UCLA football games
1140 AM (KFSN) Notre Dame football and Arizona Diamondbacks, Phoenix Suns and Phoenix Coyotes games
1230 AM (KLAV) Nebraska football games

All of the seven major US television networks – ABC, CBS, NBC, PBS, Fox, UPN and WB – and several independents broadcast in the valley. In addition to the over-the-air channels available via your standard 'bunny-ear' antennae, most Vegas hotels are linked to the city's sole cable provider, Prime Cable, and an increasing number subscribe to DirecTV.

PHOTOGRAPHY & VIDEO
Film & Equipment
Kodak print film is readily available in Las Vegas. You'll be able to find it in every minimarket in town. Professional print and color transparency films, however, are not available on The Strip or downtown. For these, head to **Nevada Photo Merchandising** (☎ 702-735-2211; 3217 Industrial Rd), a half-block south of Desert Inn Rd, or **Sahara Camera Center** (☎ 702-457-3333; 2305 E Sahara Ave at Eastern Ave), in the Albertson's Shopping Center. Both stores also stock a wide selection of cameras and lenses.

Video Systems
If you are from overseas and you wish to purchase a video here, remember that the USA uses the NTSC video format, which is not compatible with the PAL format used elsewhere in the world. Make sure to check what will work in your country before you buy. Blank film and videotapes are readily available; see Malls in the Shopping chapter.

No Photos Please

Taking pictures inside a casino is a big no-no. The folks manipulating the ceiling-mounted cameras over the card tables and slot machines will immediately suspect that you are scheming to steal from the casino, and this *really* annoys them. If you're caught taking pictures in a gaming area, it's unlikely three huge goons will come out of nowhere to haul you off to a back room for a little 'conversation,' but it is likely you'll be in for a little unpleasantness.

Photographing People
Tourists should apply the same rules of polite behavior when taking pictures of people in Las Vegas as they would anywhere in the world. Americans can sometimes be an overly suspicious people. When strangers start snapping photographs, some tend to take the attitude, 'Why the heck is that person photographing me?' However, most Americans delight in being photographed if they are asked and told why. Example: 'Can I ask you to stand next to the grizzly bear so my friends can have some idea how big it is?'

Airport Security
Other than casinos, airports are the only public places in the state of Nevada where photography is off-limits. To thwart any attempt to undermine the security measures at McCarran International Airport, the taking of photographs inside the airport is strictly prohibited.

X-Ray Machines
The X-ray machines at McCarran International Airport were specifically designed not to harm film. Indeed, security personnel at the airport insist you needn't worry about your film, despite the fact that most items passing through the machines are receiving greater scrutiny these days than they ever did prior to the September 11, 2001, terrorist attacks.

TIME
All of Nevada is in the Pacific time zone, which it shares with California, Washington, Oregon and western Montana. The Pacific time zone is one hour behind mountain time, which is respected by Nevada's eastern neighbors Arizona, Utah and Idaho; be sure to change your watch if you're entering Nevada from the east. Nevada is three hours behind the Eastern time zone states (New York and Florida among them).

From the first Sunday in April till the last Sunday in October, Americans set their clocks ahead one hour to give themselves an extra hour of sunlight in the evening, so that they can be more productive. Americans call this period 'daylight savings time.' Near the end of October, Americans set their clocks back an hour and call the six months that follow 'standard time'; during this period, Nevada is eight hours behind Greenwich Mean Time (GMT)/Coordinated Universal Time (UTC).

ELECTRICITY

Electric current in the US is 110–120 volts, 60 Hz AC. Outlets accept North American standard plugs, which have two flat prongs and an occasional third round one. If your appliance is made for another system, you will need a converter or adapter. These are best bought in your home country. They can sometimes be found in the giftshops at McCarran International Airport.

WEIGHTS & MEASURES

The US continues to resist the imposition of the metric system. Distances are measured in inches, feet, yards and miles; weights are measured in ounces, pounds and tons.

Here are some common measurements that you will encounter: gasoline is sold in US gallons, which are 20% smaller than the Imperial version, and the equivalent of 3.79L. Once you have that down, it will become apparent what a bargain gas is in the US. Beer on tap in bars is often sold in US pints, which are three sips short of international ones. Sandwiches and burgers often have a quarter-pound of meat or cheese on them. Temperatures are given in degrees Fahrenheit. See the inside back cover for metric conversions.

LAUNDRY

Every hostel, motel and hotel mentioned in this book offers laundry service or has a laundry room for guests' use. Additionally, many of Las Vegas' hotel-casinos provide an iron and ironing board in each guestroom.

If you must wash your own clothes and you're staying somewhere that doesn't permit it, either ask at the front desk for directions to the nearest laundromat, or look under 'laundries' in the Las Vegas Yellow Pages (a huge, red directory found in most

guestrooms; if you don't have one, ask at the front desk).

TOILETS

Public restrooms abound in Las Vegas. Every restaurant, casino and bar has them. Some, such as the restrooms in the casino at the Bellagio, are elegant. Others are historic; the men's room in the casino at Main Street Station contains a 15ft-long, 5ft-tall slab of graffiti-covered concrete that was formerly part of the Berlin Wall. The restrooms at Pink E's bar contain dozens of neatly framed pin-ups; those in the women's room are from *Playgirl*, those in the men's room are from *Playboy*.

LUGGAGE STORAGE

At McCarran International Airport it's possible to place your baggage in temporary storage at the Passenger Service Center, located under the escalators between the ticket counters. Lockers are also available near the A, B, C and D gates – on the 'safe' side of the X-ray machines. Bag storage and lockers are an option at the Greyhound bus station. Likewise, most hotels will allow guests to store luggage, but usually not for more than 24 hours. Luggage storage rarely exceeds $2 per item per day.

HEALTH

Las Vegas is a typical developed-nation destination when it comes to health. The only foreign visitors who may be required to have immunizations are those coming from areas that are currently experiencing an outbreak of cholera or yellow fever.

Excellent medical care is readily available, but if you are not properly insured, a collision with the US health care system could prove fatal to your budget. The need for travel insurance when traveling abroad cannot be overemphasized.

Precautions

The water is potable and restaurant sanitation is high. The only health risks you face in Las Vegas are related to accident, violence or the weather. The first is somewhat preventable by paying attention to your surroundings. The second can be minimized; see Dangers & Annoyances later in this chapter. Weather can be almost entirely eliminated as a health risk by behaving intelligently: If it's cold out, bundle up. If it's hot out, don't overexert yourself or get too much sun. If you'll be outdoors a lot, wear sunscreen and drink plenty of water.

Medical Kit

Most medications are readily available, and there's no reason to pack extras; they just weigh on you. If you take a prescription medicine, bring an adequate supply along with your prescription, in case you lose your supply. Other than that, you might want to pack the following items.

- Aspirin, acetaminophen or Panadol
- Antihistamine (such as Benadryl), which is useful as a decongestant for colds, to ease the itch from allergies and to help prevent motion sickness
- Bismuth subsalicylate preparation (Pepto-Bismol, Imodium or Lomotil, for stomach upsets
- Rehydration mixture, to treat severe diarrhea, particularly important if you're traveling with children
- Antiseptic, mercurochrome and antibiotic powder or similar 'dry' spray, for cuts and grazes
- Bandages, for minor injuries
- Scissors, tweezers and a thermometer (airlines prohibit mercury thermometers)
- Sunscreen and lip balm

Insurance

Traveling to or within the US without health insurance is foolhardy. One mishap could cost you thousands of dollars. Visitors from abroad should check what their national or private health insurance will cover. In many cases, you will need to purchase additional travel insurance; read the fine print and make certain that it will cover you for any activity you're likely to engage in.

Americans traveling within the US should check carefully to see what conditions are covered in their policy. This is especially true for HMO members, who may have to call a special number to get approval for health care away from home.

No matter where you're from, save all receipts, records and anything else related to your treatment. You'll undoubtedly need

them for reimbursement. When in doubt about your insurance, call your carrier no matter where you are and see what they recommend. It could save you a bundle of money later.

Medical Attention

If you're ill or injured and suspect that the situation is life-threatening, call ☎ 911 immediately. This is a free call from any phone, and you don't have to make a deposit in a pay phone first. It will connect you to an emergency services operator, who will dispatch the appropriate people to assist you.

If you have a less serious malady, such as the flu or a sprained ankle, and just want to see a doctor, ask staff at your hotel for a recommendation.

The following hospitals offer medical services through their emergency rooms. Call first if your condition is not acute, as many hospitals also have clinics that can see you in a more timely and convenient manner.

Desert Springs Hospital (☎ 702-733-8800) 2075 E Flamingo Rd; 24-hour emergency services available

Sunrise Hospital & Medical Center (☎ 702-731-8000) 3186 S Maryland Parkway; 24-hour emergency services, a poison center and a children's hospital

University Medical Center of Southern Nevada (☎ 702-383-2000) 1800 W Charleston Blvd; medical-surgical hospital with 24-hour emergency services available

Valley Hospital Medical Center (☎ 702-388-4000) 620 Shadow Lane; medical-surgical hospital with 24-hour emergency services available

WOMEN TRAVELERS

Women should not be particularly concerned about traveling on their own in Las Vegas. In bars, some men will see a woman alone as a bid for companionship. A polite 'No, thank you' should suffice to send them off. If it doesn't, don't be afraid to protest loudly. It will likely send the offending party away and bring good Samaritans to your side.

Rape is always a threat to women travelers. The best way to deal with this threat is

Helpful Hotlines

These crisis hotlines are open 24 hours.

AIDS Hotline	☎ 800-842-2437
Alcoholics Anonymous	☎ 702-598-1888
Baby Find	☎ 702-383-1411
Gamblers Anonymous	☎ 702-385-7732
Narcotics Anonymous	☎ 702-369-3362
Poison Center	☎ 702-732-4989
Pregnancy Hotline	☎ 800-322-1020
Rape Hotline	☎ 702-385-2153
Runaway Youth Hotline	☎ 702-385-3335
Suicide Prevention	☎ 702-731-2990
Toughlove Hotline	☎ 702-386-5632
Youth Crisis Hotline	☎ 800-448-4663

to avoid the same kinds of situations that might leave you open to other violent crimes. Don't walk down poorly lit streets or corridors. Be alert to being followed. Self-defense experts suggest that if you are attacked in any way, immediately start screaming as loudly as possible.

If you are attacked, call ☎ 911 from any phone. You will be connected with an operator who can dispatch the appropriate assistance to help you.

Organizations

The following organizations may be of particular interest to some women.

American League of Pen Women Founded in 1897, this club is composed of artists, writers and musicians. Contact Joan LeMere (☎ 702-456-9242) for information.

Jewish Women's International Club This club meets for breakfast on the third Wednesday of each month at the Santa Fe Coffee Co, 4949 N Rancho Drive. Contact Lillian Goodman (☎ 702-242-0842).

Southern Nevada NOW This is the local branch of the National Organization for Women, a political action group for women's rights. Contact Patricia Ireland (☎ 702-387-7552).

GAY & LESBIAN TRAVELERS

Las Vegas attracts all kinds of people, from the outlandishly liberal to the narrowly conservative, including a large number of Mormons, Midwestern cowboys and others with a skin-deep tolerance for people who aren't one of them. Public displays of affection aren't much appreciated in this generally conservative town, and such displays are *strongly* frowned upon when the people doing the hugging and kissing are of the same sex.

That's not to say that the gay scene in Las Vegas isn't active. It is, although not nearly as much as in many other cities in the US. There are numerous gay and lesbian dance clubs (visit the Gay Vegas website W www.gayvegas.com for up-to-date information), and the city has a weekly gay newspaper the *Las Vegas Bugle* (☎ 702-369-6960; W www.lvbugle .com) – which is free and appears in news racks around town.

There are also several long-running female-impersonator shows in town, and numerous annual events such as the Gay New Year's Eve party and the Fig Leaf Christmas Fashion Show (see the *Bugle* for events information).

Organizations

The **Lambda Business Association** (☎ 702-593-287; W www.lambdalv.com; 953 E Sahara Ave, Suite B-25) is a networking, support and development organization that provides lesbian, gay, bisexual, transgender and gay-friendly business and professional resources.

At the time of writing, the city's Gay & Lesbian Community Center had closed and there were no plans to reopen it.

DISABLED TRAVELERS

Las Vegas is a fairly accommodating place for people with reduced mobility. For one thing, nearly every casino in town is on the ground floor. For another, because so many gamblers are senior citizens, the hotel-casinos and area restaurants have in most instances taken the steps to make their establishments wheelchair accessible. The same goes for public restrooms. Where stairs exist, so does an elevator or a ramp. Automatic doors and shaved curbs are standard.

Organizations

There are a number of organizations and tour providers around the world that specialize in the needs of disabled travelers.

In the US, try **Mobility International USA** (☎ 541-343-1284; PO Box 10767, Eugene, OR 97440), an organization that advises disabled travelers on mobility issues and runs an educational exchange program.

Also worth a try is the **Society for the Advancement of Travel for the Handicapped** (SATH; ☎ 212-447-7284; W www.sath.org; 347 5th Ave No 610, New York, NY 10016).

Twin Peaks Press (☎ 360-694-2462; W home.pacifier.com/~twinpeak/; PO Box 129, Vancouver, WA 98666) publishes several handbooks for disabled travelers, including *Travel for the Disabled* and *Directory of Travel Agencies for the Disabled*.

Organizations worth contacting before you leave home include **Nican** (☎ 02-6285-3713, fax 02-6285-3714; W www.nican.com.au; PO Box 407, Curtin, ACT 2605) in Australia, and **Radar** (☎ 0171-250-3222; W www.radar.org.uk; 250 City Rd, London) in the UK.

SENIOR TRAVELERS

Though the age at which senior benefits begin varies, travelers aged 62 and older (though sometimes 50 and older) can expect to receive discounts from hotels, museums, tours, restaurants and various other places. Here are some national advocacy groups that help seniors in planning their travels.

American Association of Retired Persons (☎ 702-386-8661, 800-424-3410, W www.aarp.org) 601 E St NW, Washington, DC 20049

Elderhostel (☎ 617-426-8056, W www.elderhostel.org) 75 Federal St, Boston, MA 02110

Grand Circle Travel (☎ 800-955-1034, W www.gct.com) This organization has a brochure called *101 Tips for Mature Travelers*. Call and leave your name and address if you would like to receive it.

LAS VEGAS FOR CHILDREN

The Las Vegas of downtown and The Strip exists for gamblers, and since the gambling age is 21, most casinos would rather you left the little ones at home. State law prohibits people under age 21 from being in gaming areas. With increasing frequency, hotel-casinos are prohibiting strollers on their grounds.

That said, not every hotel-casino looks upon children like so many sewer rats. Circus Circus has gone to great lengths to appeal to families, providing free children's entertainment within earshot of the casino. The setup allows one parent to gamble while the other baby-sits Janet and Joey in a circus environment that's fun for adults, too. Out back is a theme park for kids; the MGM Grand has one as well. There's a waterpark on The Strip that's open half the year, and two museums designed for kids. There are several spectacular roller coasters in town, and no shortage of arcades, movie theaters and animal attractions. There are even a couple of child-friendly production shows. See the Things to See & Do chapter for more details.

Child Care

Only three hotels in town have child-care centers: the Gold Coast, the MGM Grand and The Orleans. All other hotels encourage parents to contact child-care agencies such as **Around the Clock Childcare** (☎ 702-365-1040), which has a four-hour minimum of $48 per child and $10 for each additional hour. All staff working for Around the Clock Childcare have been fingerprinted by the local police department and background-checked by the FBI.

For the **Gold Coast child-care center** (☎ 800-331-5334; open 9am-12:30am daily), kids must be potty trained, healthy and between the ages of two and eight. Parents must remain on the premises, and they must leave photo identification while their kids are being attended to. Only the parent who leaves the child can pick him or her up. The service is available only to children of hotel guests. There is no fee. A 3½-hour daily limit applies. The center features a story-telling center, a movie theater and a toy room.

The **MGM Grand child-care center** (☎ 800-929-1111; open 11am-11pm Sun-Thur, 11am-midnight Fri & Sat) accepts only potty-trained kids between three and 12 years of age. Its kids activity center features tumbling mats, a playhouse, puppets and so on for the youngest of the bunch, and small pool tables, Foosball and Ping Pong for the older kids. All kids can play in the arts and crafts room. It charges $8.50 per hour per child, with a maximum stay of five hours per day. Parents must remain on the premises.

The **Orleans child-care center** (☎ 800-675-3267; open 9am-midnight Sun-Thur, 9am-1am Fri & Sat) isn't nearly as impressive as the MGM Grand's, but the attendants are as enthusiastic, and the kids seem to really enjoy themselves there. Parents must stay on the premises while the kids are being looked after, and the maximum daily length of each visit is 3½ hours. The cost is $5.40 per hour per child, three hours maximum per calendar day. The center accepts children aged 2½ through 12 years.

LIBRARIES

The **Clark County Library** (☎ 702-507-3400; 1401 E Flamingo Rd; open 9am-9pm Mon-Thur, 9am-5pm Fri & Sat, 1pm-5pm Sun) is the largest library in Las Vegas. Available for check-out are books, videos, CDs and tapes. A library card is issued free of charge to US citizens. Photo identification with current address is requested.

The **James R Dickinson Library** (☎ 702-895-3286), on the campus of the University of Nevada at Las Vegas, has a collection of nearly two million books and photographs. You must live in Clark County to be able to check out materials. Hours vary with the university's schedule.

Military buffs might like to visit the **Nellis Air Force Base Library** (☎ 702-652-4484; 4311 N Washington Blvd; open 10am-8pm Mon-Thur, 10am-6pm Fri & Sat), on the base. The highlight of the library is the collection of photos documenting weapons testing at the base and at the nearby proving ground. Note that except for the library, the base is generally off-limits to the public.

CULTURAL CENTERS

The **Reed Whipple Cultural Center** (☎ 702-229-6211; 821 N Las Vegas Blvd; open 1pm-9pm Mon & Thur, 10am-9pm Tues & Wed, 10am-6pm Fri, 9am-5pm Sat, closed Sun) offers classes for children, teens and adults in dance, theater, music, painting, photography, pottery and weaving. Call for a free

brochure detailing all classes. The classes are open to anyone.

The **Las Vegas Art Centre** (☎ 702-227-0220; 3979 Spring Mountain Rd; open 10am-6pm Tues-Thur, noon-5pm Sat & Mon, closed Sun) conducts classes in drawing, oil painting, calligraphy, watercolor, acrylics and pencil. Call for details. The classes are open to anyone.

DANGERS & ANNOYANCES

Las Vegas survives on tourism. The last thing the city wants is a reputation for crime. To prevent that, more police and private security officers are out and about than you've probably seen anywhere else. They are in cars, on bicycles, on horseback and on foot. Surveillance cameras are everywhere.

If you stick to tourist areas, which are well lit and hopping with visitors, you have little to fear in the way of violent crime. Still, pickpockets thrive in heavily touristed places, and Las Vegas has its share of them. Keep your money in places that are difficult for pickpockets to access, and never leave money or valuables in your hotel room unattended.

A common complaint registered by tourists is cigarette smoke. 'Smoke-free' and 'Las Vegas' are rarely in the same sentence: there are ashtrays at every telephone, elevator, pool and shower, in toilets and taxis, and at the movies. However, nonsmoking sections exist in most restaurants.

Other complaints include traffic and lines, which often accompany big conventions, and the No 1 annoyance: losing money in casinos. Usually it's an annoyance you can live with, but betting the farm and losing it won't be. Don't bet more than you can afford to lose.

If you stroll The Strip, you will likely find yourself being handed fliers advertising room-service strippers. Having strangers thrust ads for strippers at you five times in a day can be annoying, but a simple 'No, thanks' will suffice.

EMERGENCIES

For urgent police, fire and ambulance calls, dial ☎ 911; no coins are required if dialing this number at a pay phone. To report a picked pocket or other minor crime for which you don't need immediate police response, dial ☎ 702-795-3111. You will need a police report in most cases to file for an insurance claim.

If your traveler's checks are lost or stolen, call the check issuer.

American Express	☎ 800-221-7282
MasterCard	☎ 800-223-9920
Thomas Cook	☎ 800-223-7373
Visa	☎ 800-227-6811

Likewise, if your credit card is lost or stolen, call the card issuer.

American Express	☎ 800-992-3404
Diners Club	☎ 800-234-6377
Discover	☎ 800-347-2683
MasterCard	☎ 800-307-7309
Visa	☎ 800-336-8472

LEGAL MATTERS

In tourist-dependent Las Vegas, the cops are on their best behavior. However, if at any time a police officer gives you an order of any kind, do not seize upon that moment for a debate. He or she may have mistaken you for someone else.

If you are arrested, you have the right to remain silent. There is no legal requirement to speak to a police officer if you don't want to, but never walk away from one until given permission. Anyone who is arrested is legally allowed (and given) the right to make one phone call. If you're from overseas and don't have a lawyer, friend or family member to help you, call your consulate. The police will give you the number upon request.

It's against the law to have an open container of an alcoholic beverage while walking down the street, but in Las Vegas this rule is generally waived in the spirit of good public relations. However, if you're *staggering* down a street with a drink in your hand, you may find yourself being led away to jail to sober up. Be advised: drunk-driving laws are strictly enforced. Even having an open container of an alcoholic beverage in a

car is a big no-no, whether or not it's the driver who's drinking.

The drinking age of 21 is strictly enforced. If you're younger than 35 (or just look like it), carry an ID to fend off overzealous barkeeps and the like. In Las Vegas, it is legal to purchase alcohol at any time of day or night.

There is zero tolerance at all times for any kind of illegal drug use. If police find marijuana, cocaine or any other illegal substance on you, you will soon become acquainted with the local jail.

BUSINESS HOURS

Office hours in Las Vegas are typically 8am to 5pm. Shops are usually open at least until 7pm, and most keep Sunday hours. You'll find plenty of convenience stores and supermarkets open 24 hours a day. Banks increasingly keep hours like stores. Fortunately, ATMs never sleep.

Movie theaters and many bars and restaurants are open every day of the year. Smaller restaurants are often closed one or two days a week, frequently early in the week. Most production shows are closed one day a week; the 'dark' day, as show-business folks call it in Las Vegas, varies from show to show.

PUBLIC HOLIDAYS

Christmas is one of the few holidays for which most stores close. The holidays in the following list marked with an asterisk (*) are widely observed, with most businesses closed. When some of these holidays fall on the weekend, they are celebrated on the following Monday.

New Year's Day* January 1
Martin Luther King Jr's Birthday Third Monday in January
Presidents' Day Third Monday in February
Memorial Day* Last Monday in May
Independence Day* July 4
Labor Day* First Monday in September
Columbus Day Second Monday in October
Veterans Day November 11
Thanksgiving Day* Fourth Thursday in November
Christmas Day* December 25

Trivial Las Vegas

Average number of persons per household	2.6
Median home price	$139,000
Average monthly apartment rent	$648
Percentage of homeowners	63
Number of doctors	1832
Number of dentists	445
Number of lawyers	2362
Number of taxis	1203
Median household income	$49,678
Sister City	An San, South Korea

The festive Christmas season traditionally runs from the Friday after Thanksgiving through the big day itself. Purists will be horrified to note that Christmas decorations – and even sales – start appearing in September.

SPECIAL EVENTS

The months in which annual special events are held in Las Vegas can shift from year to year, and promoters have been known to move their 'shows' as finances dictate, so if an event is important to you, be sure to contact the **Las Vegas Convention & Visitors Authority** (☎ 702-892-7575, 800-332-5333; W www.vegasfreedom.com) to obtain dates and times.

January

Chinese New Year Day-long festivities involving entertainers from throughout Asia and Hawaii mark the beginning of the Chinese New Year. Held at the Asian Pacific Cultural Center (☎ 702-252-0400), 4215 Spring Mountain Rd.

OKC Gun Show One of the largest gun shows in the country (☎ 800-333-4867), held at the Cashman Field Center (☎ 702-258-8961), 350 N Las Vegas Blvd. Approximately 1500 sales and display booths attract more than 20,000 attendees each year. Admission is $10.

Super Bowl High Rollers Amateur bowlers compete for $1 million in prize money at this week-long tournament held at the Showboat Hotel (☎ 702-385-9150 to enter the contest, 800-257-6179 for reservations), 2800 Fremont St. The entry fee is $500 for one person, $750 for two or three people.

February

Las Vegas International Marathon This 26.2-mile event begins in Sloan and finishes at the southern end of The Strip. A half-marathon and relays are also run during the two-day event. Entry fees are $30 for the half-marathon and $40 for the big race. Call ☎ 702-876-3870 for details.

Mardi Gras A big Cajun buffet, ballroom dancing, and attendees in costumes make this festival a particularly good one to attend. Held at the Charleston Heights Arts Center (☎ 702-229-6383), 800 S Brush St, on the Saturday evening before Ash Wednesday.

March

Busch Grand National Nascar's Busch Grand National Series 300 runs at the 1.5-mile oval at Las Vegas Motor Speedway (☎ 702-644-4444, 800-644-4444), 7000 N Las Vegas Blvd. Tickets are priced at $15 for children and $45 for adults.

Corporate Challenge Twenty thousand amateur athletes compete on behalf of their companies in 27 sporting events held throughout town. The competition begins in mid-March and lasts through April. The entry fees are paid by the companies. Call ☎ 702-229-6706 for details.

Kite Carnival This popular event is held the first Saturday in March at Freedom Park, at the intersection of E Washington Ave and Mojave Rd. There's no entry fee and everyone's encouraged to help themselves to a free kite and fly it. Call ☎ 702-229-6729 for details.

St Patrick's Day Parade Downtown is the site of a raucous parade, replete with floats, every March 17. Notice the color of the beer in most of the casinos along Fremont St on this day: green. Yikes! The six-block procession starts at 8am and typically ends by 9:30am.

April

Earth Fair Held on the Saturday nearest Earth Day (April 22), Earth Fair draws 50,000 people. There are impersonators, a carnival for kids, and free plants and pine seedlings are given away. It's at Sunset Park (☎ 702-455-8206), 2601 E Sunset Rd, southeast of the airport.

Las Vegas Senior Classic Some of the top golfers on the seniors tour tee off for $1 million in prize money at the Tournament Players Club at The Canyons (☎ 702-242-3000), 1951 Canyon Run Dr. Tickets for the four-day event begin at $15 a day.

Mardi Gras Elaborate New Orleans–style carnivals featuring Cajun food, parades and stage shows take place in early April at the Rio (☎ 702-252-7777), The Orleans (☎ 702-365-7111) and Fremont Street Experience (☎ 702-678-5724).

World Series of Poker More than 4000 players match wits in 21 tournaments at Binion's Horseshoe (☎ 702-382-1600), 128 E Fremont St, from mid-April to early May to compete for $4 million in cash. Buy-ins cost $1000 for women, $10,000 for men. Public viewing is allowed.

May
AMA Supercross The top dirt-bike racers in the US rev it up every May at Sam Boyd Stadium Park (☎ 702-434-0848) at the end of E Russell Rd, past Boulder Hwy. General admission fees start at $10.

Cinco de Mayo On or near May 5, Mexicans celebrate Mexico's victory over French forces in 1862 at Puebla. (French reinforcements later crushed the Mexican army.) Day-long festivities at Freedom Park (☎ 702-649-8553) commemorate the anniversary.

Cinco de Mayo Dos Fremont Street Experience (☎ 702-678-5724) hosts a three-day celebration of Cinco de Mayo around May 5. The event features performances by a variety of Hispanic entertainers, including mariachis. Cinco de Mayo Dos is, basically, an excuse for a party.

Craft Fair and Rib Burnoff This self-explanatory mid-May event at Sunset Park (☎ 702-455-8206), 2601 E Sunset Rd, is a big crowd-pleaser. The featured attractions include handicrafts, country music, people having fun, and food – lots of food. Most meals run about $10.

June
Helldorado Days This four-day event at Thomas and Mack Center (☎ 702-870-1221 for Helldorado info, ☎ 702-895-3900 for the center), at Tropicana Ave and Swenson St, features nightly rodeos, barbecues and bull riding. Admission is $15 to the bull ride and $12 to the rodeo. Proceeds go to charity.

International Food Festival Culinary offerings from two-dozen countries highlight this delicious event held at Cashman Field Center (☎ 702-258-8961), 350 N Las Vegas Blvd. Cultural displays and ethnic dances add to the fun. Admission is $2; meals range from $5 to $10.

Winston Cup West Nascar racing returns to the Las Vegas Motor Speedway (☎ 800-644-4444), 7000 N Las Vegas Blvd, with this 150-mile race under the lights. General admission prices range from $15 to $45.

July
High Rollers This is the second (and the biggest) of three annual amateur-bowling contests held at the Showboat (☎ 702-385-9150, 800-257-6179), 2800 E Fremont St. More than $2.5 million is on the line. The entry fee is $1100. Spectators get in free.

The National Finals Rodeo is held in Las Vegas each December.

World Figure Skating Champions Some of the biggest names in ice-skating put on a summer show at the Thomas and Mack Center (☎ 702-895-3900), Tropicana Ave at Swenson St. Admission ranges from $20 to $30.

August
Kidzmania This two-day, air-conditioned event (☎ 702-233-8388) at Cashman Field Center (☎ 702-258-8961), 350 N Las Vegas Blvd, is geared for youngsters. The attractions include a petting zone, game shows and karate demonstrations. Admission is $5 for adults, and it's free for kids.

Police Olympics Cops from around the world compete in 22 events held at various Vegas venues during a five-day period. PO (☎ 702-259-6350) isn't likely to ever overshadow the real Games (one of the biggest events is a softball tournament), but it's fun and free to watch. Entrants pay $40.

Sundown Bluegrass Concerts Some of the best bluegrass music in the southwestern US fills the air at Jaycee Park (☎ 702-229-6511), 2100 E St Louis St, the first two Sunday evenings in August. Bring a picnic basket and come early. The entertainment is free.

September

Greek Food Festival The name says it all. Held late September or early October at St John's Orthodox Church (☎ 702-221-8245), 5300 El Camino Rd near W Hacienda Ave, this festival also features Greek music and dancing. Admission costs $2; dining is à la carte.

Las Vegas Cup Hydroplane Race Despite its name, this two-day event involving some of the world's fastest boats is held out front of Boulder Beach, Lake Mead. Some of the boats top 200 mph, and then break up! There's no charge to watch. Call ☎ 702-892-2874 for details.

October

Jaycee State Fair This six-day event (☎ 702-457-3247) held at Cashman Field (☎ 702-258-8961), 350 N Las Vegas Blvd, attracts some 65,000 visitors to a slew of exhibits, food booths and big-name bands playing rock, jazz and Latin music. Admission is $6 for adults, $4 for kids.

Las Vegas 500K Indy cars traveling in circles at high speeds for 500km are the centerpiece of this event, held at Las Vegas Motor Speedway (☎ 800-644-4444), 7000 N Las Vegas Blvd. Ticket prices range from $15 to $45.

Las Vegas Balloon Classic This three-day event at Sam Boyd Stadium Park (☎ 702-434-0848), at the end of E Russell Rd, past Boulder Hwy, features more than 100 hot-air balloons from around the world. Also displayed are vintage cars, handicrafts and antique machinery. Admission is free.

Rio's Italian Festival The Rio (☎ 702-252-7777), 3700 W Flamingo Rd, maintains a Carnaval theme all year except on the weekend preceding Columbus Day. Then, the Rio hosts a celebration of Italian food and entertainment. Entry is free. Dinner is à la carte.

November

Craftsman Truck Series These two Nascar races at the Las Vegas Motor Speedway (☎ 800-644-4444), 7000 N Las Vegas Blvd, involve 70 highly modified pickup trucks racing at speeds exceeding 150 mph. Tickets start at $25.

Thanksgiving Senior High Roller This weeklong holiday tournament attracts several hundred amateur bowlers over age 50, who pay a $400 entry fee and compete for $500,000 in prize money. It's held at the Showboat (☎ 800-257-6179), 2800 Fremont St.

December

Las Vegas Rugby Challenge Rugby teams from around the world vie for prize money at Freedom Park (☎ 702-656-7401), Washington Ave at Mojave Rd, during the first weekend of December. There's no charge for watching the two days of fun. Scrum!

National Finals Rodeo This hugely popular 10-day event features the top 15 rodeo performers in seven events, including steer wrestling and bull riding. Tickets to the rodeo, held at Thomas and Mack Center (☎ 702-895-3900), Tropicana Ave at Swenson St, are tough to obtain.

New Year's Eve Fremont Street Experience (☎ 702-678-5724) becomes a huge party scene every December 31, as thousands of celebrants turn out to hear live music, people-watch, and be dazzled by an overhead light show. Did we mention 'drink like fish'? They do that too. Admission is $15.

WORK

US law makes it difficult to work in the country without a prearranged permit from an employer. It is possible to overstay a J1 summer work visa, and thousands of students do this every year. But remember, the day the visa expires, you become an illegal alien in the eyes of US authorities.

If you're a visitor from abroad, word of mouth is usually the way to find out about working illegally at restaurants and bars. It helps if you do not have a discernible accent. Illegal white collar work is almost never available, since employers who hire undocumented workers are subject to big fines.

If you are caught working illegally, you will be immediately deported and barred from the US for at least five years. Gone are the days when US immigration agents gave

Bad Guys Need Not Apply

To work at any hotel-casino in Las Vegas, a prospective employee needs to obtain a 'sheriff's card' from the police department. The process starts with the applicant getting a signed referral from his or her prospective employer and presenting it and two photo IDs at the police department. The police department charges $5 for fingerprinting and running a background check, and $35 more for the card. The card is good for five years. Renewals are $20.

undocumented workers time to gather belongings and notify loved ones. Deportation now occurs the same day an agent finds you working without a green card or proof of citizenship.

If you have a green card or are a US citizen, it may interest you to know that, on average, 110 new jobs become available daily in America's fastest-growing city. To the disappointment of many people, most of those jobs pay only minimum wage. At the time of writing, that amount is $5.15 an hour. State law prohibits an employer from applying tips against the minimum wage.

RICHARD CUMMINS

RICHARD CUMMINS

RICHARD CUMMINS

Title Page: Las Vegas sings to the sound of poker machines (Photograph by Richard Cummins)

Top: A red-hot $1 poker

Middle: It's broken, I tell you! I keep putting the coins in this here hole but no can comes out.

Bottom: You gotta know when to hold 'em and know when to fold 'em

GAMBLING IN LAS VEGAS

Gambling can be an exhilarating experience – every lucky roll of the dice providing an electric rush of adrenaline – but when it comes to Vegas casinos, it's important to remember one thing: the house advantage. For every game except poker, the house has a statistical winning edge (the 'percentage') over the gambler, and for nearly every payout in nearly every game, the house 'holds' a small portion of the winnings. These amounts vary with the game and with individual bets, but they add up to what's referred to as a 'long-term negative expectation' – or the assurance that over the long haul, the gambler will lose everything.

As such, it's wise to approach gambling only as entertainment – one for which you pay a fee – and not as a way to fund your children's education. Understand the game you are playing, don't bet more than you are prepared to lose, and learn to leave when you are up. These three 'rules' are the best way to ensure that your time spent gambling will remain enjoyable and fun.

The Casino

The minimum age to enter the gambling pit is 18, but you must be at least 21 years old in order to play. The traditional casino games include baccarat, blackjack, craps, keno, the money wheel, poker, roulette, slot machines, the sports book and video poker. Each game has its own customs, traditions and strategies – the following sections give an overview of games played in Las Vegas' casinos. If you'd like to read more about the games you want to play beforehand, see Books in the Facts for the Visitor chapter for recommendations. Also check out the free gambling lessons at the large casinos.

It's acceptable to ask the dealer for help and advice. For instance, he or she should gladly tell you the odds on a particular bet at craps, or what the strategy is for the blackjack hand you've just been dealt. An entertaining dealer can make your time at the tables an unforgettable experience, so don't be shy about finding another table if your dealer is surly or unhelpful. It's also polite to 'toke,' or tip, your dealer if you are winning. Either place a chip on the layout (the area where you place your bet) for the dealer to collect, or place a side bet for the dealer, which he or she collects if it wins. Keno runners and slot attendants also expect a small tip.

Baccarat

Nothing conjures the image of high stakes, black tuxedoes and James Bond like baccarat, and yet, of the card games, it possesses the least strategy – none, in fact. The rules are quite fixed, the house edge is low, and there are no decisions for the player except for how to bet. The only thing special about the game, other than its mystique, is that minimum bets are usually $20 or $25, ensuring that only those with large bankrolls sit down to play. However, you can now often find less-formal minibaccarat tables near the blackjack pit with $2 to $5 minimum bets; these are good places to learn the game.

One player and the banker are each dealt two cards from a 'shoe' that contains eight complete decks of cards. The hand closest to 9 points wins. Aces through 9s count at face value; 10s and face cards are worth zero. If the cards exceed 10 points, only the second digit is counted. For instance, a king plus a 5 card equals 5; a 7 plus a 6 equals 3. A third card must be drawn under specific rules: a player must draw if the score of the two cards is 0, 1, 2, 3, 4 or 5; the player must stand with 6 or 7. Neither the player nor the banker can draw with a score of 8 or 9. If there's a tie, the hands are redealt. There are only three bets: on the bank, the player or a tie.

In baccarat, the 'bank' is passed around among the players; the player holds the shoe and continues as the banker as long as the bank hand wins. When the player's hand wins, the shoe is then passed to the next player, who then becomes the banker. A player can choose to pass the shoe. When you bet on the bank and the bank wins, you are charged a 5% commission that must be paid at the start of a new game or when you leave the table.

Blackjack

Blackjack is the most popular table game in Las Vegas because it is the one game bet against the house where the skill of the player affects the odds, and so it has become the most scrutinized and analyzed game of all – by both players and casinos. In fact, it's the only game where memory plays a role – where skilled card counters can track cards played and calculate the probabilities for future cards – and this has created a sometimes antagonistic relationship between players and pit bosses. However, even without card counting, it's possible to follow a basic strategy that can reduce the house advantage to almost nothing in certain situations.

Players bet against the dealer, and the object is to draw cards that total as close to 21 as possible without going over. Jacks, queens and kings count as 10, an ace is worth either 11 or 1 (the choice is yours), and other cards are counted at face value. The player places a bet and is dealt two cards. The dealer then gets two cards, one facing up and the other concealed. The player now has four choices: to 'stand' (take no more cards), 'hit' (take more cards, one at a time), 'double down' (double your bet and take one more card), or 'split' (in which, if you are dealt an original pair – such as two 8s – you create two new separate hands and play them individually).

Players draw cards until they stand on their total or 'bust' (go over 21 and lose immediately). The dealer then reveals the down turned card and must either hit on any total of 16 or less, or stand on any total of 17 or more – the house rules here are strict. If the player's hand is higher than the dealer's, he or she wins; if less, the player loses. Ties are called a 'push,' and no money changes hands. All wins are paid at even money, except 'blackjack' (a natural 21, when the first two cards are an ace plus a 10-value card), which pays 3 to 2 – or $3 for every $2 bet.

Many gambling books provide a chart of the 'basic strategy' that outlines the best percentage play for every single card combination, and it's perfectly acceptable to consult a copy of this chart at the gaming table. Basic strategy can be boiled down to a few general rules:

- If you have 12 to 16 and the dealer's up card is 2 to 6, stand
- If you have 12 to 16 and the dealer's up card is 7, 8, 9, 10 or ace, hit
- If you have 17 to 21, stand, no matter what the dealer's up card is
- Double down if you have 10 or 11 and the dealer's up card is 2 to 9
- Always split a pair of aces or 8s

Craps

Undoubtedly, the most fun and noise in a casino will be generated at a lively, fast-paced craps table – with players shouting, crowds gathering and everyone hoping for that lucky hot streak. Tossing dice is a completely random activity, but that doesn't stop people from betting  their 'hunches' and believing that certain numbers are 'due' – even though the odds are exactly the same on every roll. Craps can also be the most intimidating game to step up to for the first time, since the betting possibilities are very complicated, and shift as play continues. It's important to spend some time studying a betting guide and begin playing with the simplest wager (on the pass/don't pass line), which also happens to be one of the better bets in the casino.

To begin, the 'stickman' hands the dice to a player, who becomes the 'shooter' for that round. A 'pass line' bet means that on the first roll (the 'come-out' roll) the dice will total 7 or 11. If the dice total 2, 3 or 12 (called 'craps'), the player loses. Any other number becomes the 'point,' and the dice are rolled again until either a 7 or the point number comes up – if a 7 comes up first, the player loses; if the point comes up, the player wins.

A 'don't pass' bet is basically the reverse – if the come-out roll totals 7 or 11, the player loses; if it's 2 or 3, the player wins; 12 is a push. If a point is established, the don't-pass bettor wins on a 7 and loses if the point is rolled again. All these bets pay even money.

'Come' bets are placed after a point is established; 7 and 11 win, while 2, 3, or 12 lose. If none of these come up, the dice are thrown again until the point is thrown, and the player wins, or a 7 is thrown and the player loses. The don't-come bet is the reverse, except that 12 is a push. Come and don't-come bets also pay even money.

If you've already made a pass or come bet, and a point has been established, you can bet that the point will come up before a 7 is thrown. These bets pay off at a rate that is equal to the statistical chance of a win, so the house has no edge – this is called a 'free-odds' bet (or just an 'odds' bet), and it is the best chance you'll get in a casino. You don't have an advantage against the house, but the odds aren't against you.

There are even more betting options: 'place,' 'field' and 'buy' bets, and the one-roll 'sucker bets' – the big 6 or big 8, 'hard ways,' any 7 and any craps. Despite big payoffs, these last bets have long odds and a house edge between 9% and 17% – and are avoided by most craps players.

Keno

This slow-paced game with bad odds is a lot like lotto; there are 80 numbered squares on a card, a player picks from 1 to 15 numbers and bets $1 or so per number or number combination. You can bet straight, split, 'way' or combination. At the draw, the casino randomly selects 20 numbers, and winners are paid off according to how many of the winning numbers they chose, as shown on a 'payoff chart.' Payoffs range from $3 to $100,000. The amount paid off is distinctly less than the probability of selecting the numbers by chance, so the odds favor the house by over 20%. Keno runners circulate throughout the casino, and keno lounges serve refreshments while you watch the monitors.

The Money Wheel

Also known as the 'wheel of fortune' or 'big six,' this old carnival midway game is usually near the slot machines. Place your bet on one of 54 positions or slots, spin the wheel and, in most cases, lose your money. The prohibitive house advantage is only slightly less than at keno, making these lonely outposts.

Poker

Poker is unusual for casino games because players bet directly against one another. The house provides the table, the cards and the dealer, who sells the chips, deals the hands and collects a 'rake' from each pot. If you're not already a good poker player, don't even think about getting involved in a Vegas casino game. There are a number of different types of games, including high-low, seven-card stud and straight poker, but one of the most popular is hold 'em, in which five cards are dealt faceup on the table and two cards are dealt to each player. The person with the best five-card hand out of the seven cards wins.

Pai gow poker is a variation on regular poker: a joker is added to a regular 52-card deck, and players play against the bank. The joker is used as an ace, or to complete a straight or flush. Players are each dealt seven cards, which are then arranged into two hands. One hand contains five cards and is known as the 'high hand.' The second hand contains two cards and is the 'low hand.' The object of the game is to have both the high and low hands rank higher than the respective hands of the banker. The ranking is determined by traditional poker rules. If both hands rank lower, the wager is lost to the banker. If either hand wins while the other loses, this is a 'push,' and the wager is refunded. If either one of the player's hands ties the banker, then the bank wins. The house handles all bets and charges a 5% commission on all winning wages.

Roulette

This ancient game is easy to understand and often hypnotic to play. You can use either casino chips or special 'wheel chips,' which are dispensed at the roulette table and are a different color for each player. Roulette provides the most clear demonstration of the house edge. The roulette wheel has 38 numbers – from 1 to 36, plus 0 and 00. Half the numbers are colored red, the other half are black, while the two zeros are green. The table layout is marked with the numbers and the various combinations that can be bet.

You can bet that a result will be odd or even, red or black, high (19 to 36) or low (1 to 18). All of these bets pay off at even money, but the chances of a win are less than 50%, because the 0 and 00 don't count as odd or even, red or black, high or low. Your chances are 18 in 38 (47.37%), not 18 in 36.

Further, a bet on a single number (including the 0 and 00) pays out at 35 to 1, though true odds would be 37 to 1. You can also bet on pairs of numbers, or groups of 4, 5, 6 or 12 numbers, which all have a house advantage of 5.26% (the 5-number bet is actually slightly worse). These aren't the best odds in the casino, but they're far from the worst.

Slot Machines

The 'slots' are mind-numbingly simple – you put in a coin and pull the handle (or push a button) – but they are also wildly popular. Most machines take quarters, some take nickels or pennies and a few take tokens of $1, $5 and even more. Machines have various types of spinning wheels and payouts, but a player has no effect on the outcome. The probabilities are programmed into the machine, and the chances of winning are the same on every pull.

The only important decisions are which machine to play and when to stop. Some machines pay back a higher proportion of the money deposited than others (though, by law, slot machines must return at least 75%). Those that return a lot to the player, as much as 97%, are called 'loose' – hence the signs advertising 'the loosest slots in town.' Loose slots are more likely to be found in the highly visible areas of big casinos. Slots with a lower return, down to 84% or even less, are more common in impulse-gambling locations like waiting rooms, bars and bathrooms.

'Progressive slots' offer a jackpot that accumulates, and many slots are now linked in networks, to generate bigger jackpots. Often these pay off in the form of a new car, which is prominently displayed in the casino. The jackpots are factored into the payout percentage, so there's no extra statistical advantage to the player, except that a payout of a few thousand dollars may induce someone to quit while he or she is ahead, instead of putting all the winnings back into the slot.

The Sports Book

The bigger casinos usually have a 'sports book' room, where sporting events from around the country are displayed on video screens covering most of a wall. Players can bet on just about any ball game, boxing match, horse race or hockey game in the country, except for events taking place in Nevada. Sports books are best during major sporting events, when everyone is captivated by, betting on, and yelling about the same game.

Video Poker

Increasingly popular, video poker games are often built into a bar. Like regular poker, they deal you five electronic cards; you hold the cards you want and then draw again to complete a five-card hand. Quarter machines are common, though they can range from a nickel to $5 per bet. By employing correct strategy and finding machines with the best payout schedules, it's possible to improve your chances of winning and reduce the house advantage to nothing in some situations. Basically, make sure the machine you play pays back your bet for a pair of jacks or better, and has a one-coin payout of nine coins for a full house and six coins for a flush (a 9/6 machine). Much has been written recently about video poker strategy (since there is a modicum of player control), and it's worth reading if you enjoy these machines.

Getting There & Away

AIR
Airport

At the southern end of The Strip, **McCarran International** (☎ 702-261-5211; ⓦ *www .mccarran.com*) is the city's public airport, serving 36 million passengers annually. Although it's among the 15 busiest airports in the world, it's centrally located and extremely easy to navigate. The soaring popularity of Las Vegas as a vacation and business destination, combined with the tremendous growth of the local population, has put pressure on McCarran to expand rapidly. To meet the city's air-transportation needs, McCarran has been adding gates every year for the past decade.

McCarran consists of two terminals: Terminal 1 serves domestic flights, while the much smaller Terminal 2 serves international flights. Both terminals are reached from Paradise Rd. Terminal 1 is divided into four main wings, or gates, lettered A through D. Gates A and B are reached by walkways, and trams link gates C and D to the domestic terminal.

The ticketing counters, gates and baggage claim are easy to find. Departing domestic passengers who are already ticketed may check their bags at curbside and go straight to their respective departure gates for boarding passes. Departing international passengers must check their bags at their airlines' ticket counters before proceeding to the departure gates.

The Getting Around chapter has full details on the myriad options for getting from McCarran to your hotel.

Departure Tax

The airport departure tax is included in the price of your ticket.

Within the USA

The following is a partial list of domestic destinations served by nonstop flights from McCarran by scheduled carriers. Call the airlines for current prices and departure and arrival times. The McCarran International website (ⓦ www.mccarran.com) has a complete list of destinations receiving nonstop services.

Albuquerque Southwest Airlines
Atlanta America West Airlines, Delta Air Lines
Austin Southwest Airlines
Baltimore Southwest Airlines
Boston America West Airlines
Buffalo Southwest Airlines
Burbank Southwest Airlines
Charlotte US Airways
Chicago (Midway) American Trans Air, Delta Air Lines, Southwest Airlines
Chicago (O'Hare) America West Airlines, American Airlines, National Airlines, United Airlines
Cincinnati Delta Air Lines
Cleveland Continental Airlines
Columbus America West Airlines, Southwest Airlines
Dallas/Fort Worth America West Airlines, American Airlines, Delta Air Lines
Denver America West Airlines, Eagle Canyon Airlines
Detroit America West Airlines, Northwest Airlines

Grand Canyon Eagle Canyon Airlines
Houston Continental Airlines, Southwest Airlines
Indianapolis America West Airlines, American Trans Air, Southwest Airlines
Kansas City Vanguard Airlines, Southwest Airlines
Los Angeles America West Airlines, American Airlines, National Airlines, Delta Air Lines, Hawaiian Airlines, Southwest Airlines, United Airlines
Memphis Eagle Canyon Airlines, Northwest Airlines
Miami America West Airlines, National Airlines
Milwaukee Midwest Express
Minneapolis America West Airlines, Northwest Airlines
Nashville Southwest Airlines
New Orleans Southwest Airlines
New York (JFK) America West Airlines, National Airlines, Southwest Airlines
Newark America West Airlines, National Airlines, Continental Airlines
Oakland America West Airlines, Aloha Airlines, Southwest Airlines
Oklahoma City Southwest Airlines

Orlando America West Airlines
Palm Springs United Express
Philadelphia America West Airlines, National Airlines, US Airways
Phoenix America West Airlines, Southwest Airlines
Pittsburgh US Airways
Portland (OR) America West Airlines, Alaska Airlines, Southwest Airlines
Reno America West Airlines, Southwest Airlines
Sacramento America West Airlines, Southwest Airlines
Salt Lake City Delta Air Lines, Mesa Airlines, Southwest Airlines
San Antonio Southwest Airlines
San Diego America West Airlines, Southwest Airlines
San Francisco America West Airlines, National Airlines, United Airlines
San Jose America West Airlines, American Airlines, Southwest Airlines
Seattle Alaska Airlines, National Airlines, Southwest Airlines
St Louis American Airlines
Tampa America West Airlines, Southwest Airlines
Tucson America West Airlines, Southwest Airlines
Washington DC America West Airlines, United Airlines

Outside the USA

The following is a complete list of the airlines that provide nonstop service between Las Vegas and cities outside the US.

Frankfurt Delta Air Lines
Guadalajara Mexicana
Hermosillo AeroMexico
London Virgin Atlantic Airways
Mexico City America West Airlines
Tijuana Allegro Airlines
Tokyo Japan Airlines
Toronto Air Canada
Vancouver Alaska Airlines

If you'll be arriving from a foreign city other than those listed, or on an airline other than those specified, you must first clear customs elsewhere (in Houston, Los Angeles, Miami or New York, for example). After clearing customs, you can then board a domestic airplane bound for McCarran (see the boxed text 'Airlines Serving McCarran' for a complete list of airlines that have flights into and out of Las Vegas).

Airlines Serving McCarran	
AeroMexico	☎ 800-237-6639
Air Canada	☎ 800-776-3000
Alaska Airlines	☎ 800-426-0333
Allegiant Air	☎ 877-202-6444
Allegro Airlines	☎ 702-261-4430
Aloha Airlines	☎ 800-367-5250
America West Airlines	☎ 800-235-9292
American Airlines	☎ 800-433-7300
American Trans Air	☎ 800-435-9282
Aviascsa	☎ 888-528-4227
Comair	☎ 800-435-9282
Continental Airlines	☎ 800-525-0280
Delta Air Lines	☎ 800-221-1212
Eagle Canyon Airlines	☎ 702-736-3333
Hawaiian Airlines	☎ 800-367-5320
Japan Airlines	☎ 800-525-3663
Mesa Airlines	☎ 800-637-2247
Mexicana	☎ 800-531-7921
Midwest Express	☎ 800-452-2022
National Airlines	☎ 888-757-5387
Northwest Airlines	☎ 800-225-2525
Southwest Airlines	☎ 800-435-9792
United Airlines	☎ 800-241-6522
United Express	☎ 800-453-9417
Vanguard Airlines	☎ 800-826-4827
Virgin Atlantic Airways	☎ 800-862-8621

Services at McCarran

ATM Between esplanades E and W

Currency Exchange Arriving area, Terminal 2, and security checkpoint for departing passengers

First Aid South mezzanine above America West ticket counter

Fitness Center Below baggage claim in main terminal

Food 31 food and beverage outlets in the airport

Bank Just south of A-B security checkpoint

Gambling 571 slot machines inside airport

Information Gate C, esplanade east, rotunda, baggage claim

Lost & Found South mezzanine above ticketing

Notary Under the escalators between ticketing

Photocopiers Under the escalators between ticketing

Police South mezzanine above ticketing

Post Office 2nd level of main terminal, overlooking north baggage claim

Travel Insurance Under the escalators between ticketing

Western Union Under the escalators between ticketing

Flight schedules and ticket prices frequently change. If you're visiting Las Vegas from abroad, call several travel agents or ticket consolidators to obtain current air-route information and to get the best price. Check the travel sections of major newspapers or your local telephone directory for the details of consolidators nearest you.

Airline Offices

All of the airlines mentioned in the preceding pages have counters at the airport. If you need to purchase a ticket or make a change to an existing ticket while you're in town, either head out to the airport or see a travel agent; there's at least one travel agency in each megaresort. Citizens Area Transit (CAT) bus Nos 108 and 109 go to the airport.

BUS

The sole national bus company, **Greyhound Lines** (☎ 702-384-9561, 800-231-2222; W www.greyhound.com; 200 S Main St), has a station in downtown Las Vegas. The seats on most Greyhound buses are narrow but otherwise comfortable, the windows are big, and air-con/heating is switched on as needed. All buses are equipped with toilets.

Greyhound fares are low, and there are reduced seven-day advance-purchase fares between some cities. Buses to Los Angeles, for example, carry a one-way standard fare of $31 for the 301-mile trip, but a seat on the same bus purchased at least one week before departure is only $25. If you're in no hurry to reach Chicago, Greyhound will take you those 1937 miles for $129/79 standard/advance purchase.

In addition to the cities mentioned here, Greyhound's Las Vegas station also has non-stop service to Flagstaff, San Bernardino, Bakersfield, Fresno, Anaheim, Kingsman and numerous other cities. Call Greyhound or visit the company's impressive website for fares, schedules and discount information.

Following is a list of sample one-way standard/advance-purchase fares to/from Las Vegas: Barstow (159 miles, $31/29), Denver (1042 miles, $105/65), Kingsman (123 miles, $30/28), Needles (106 miles, $28/26), Phoenix (401 miles, $37/25), Salt Lake City (450 miles, $47/29), San Diego (426 miles, $46/30).

TRAIN

Freight trains connect Las Vegas with many other parts of the country, but passenger service was discontinued in 1996. At the time of writing, there was talk of reviving the service, but nothing concrete. Contact **Amtrak** (☎ 800-972-7245; W www.amtrak.com), the national rail passenger service, to inquire whether passenger service to Sin City has resumed.

At the time of writing, the closest Amtrak stations to Las Vegas were located in Needles, California (106 miles away), Kingsman, Arizona (123 miles away), and Barstow, California (159 miles away). Greyhound provides daily bus service between Las Vegas and all three cities.

CAR & MOTORCYCLE

Positioned in the center of a valley that's ringed by picturesque scenery, Las Vegas makes for a great road trip. The main roads into Las Vegas are Interstate 15, from the southwest and northeast, and US Highway 95 from the northwest and southeast. Chances are, if you'll be arriving by car or bus, you'll reach Sin City by either of these great spans of pavement. Avoid driving at night: you'll miss out on the scenery, and you could get very cold very fast if your car or motorcycle broke down on the open highway. Be advised that the mountains that surround Las Vegas Valley cause many vehicles to overheat during days when outside temperatures top 90°F. If you're heading into or out of Las Vegas on a hot day in a car or a truck, consider opening the windows and keeping the air-conditioning off, as it taxes the engine and increases the likelihood of overheating.

HITCHHIKING

Hitchhiking in America is dangerous and is no longer a common practice. It's a sad fact in the US that if you hitchhike, you expose yourself to the risks of robbery, sexual assault and worse. Most decent people are wary of hitchhikers, which can make the credibility of those who would stop extra suspect. Generally, truckers, once a hitchhiker's best friend, no longer stop for thumb-waggers.

That said, if you still insist on hitchhiking, it helps to follow a few guidelines. If you are a woman, even a group of women, just don't do it (you're right, that's not a guideline, just good advice). Some people in the US assume that a woman hitchhiker is asking for whatever she gets – rape and murder included. If you're a man, your chances of being picked up decrease with each additional person. Carry a neat destination sign and keep baggage to a minimum. Don't look like anyone you yourself wouldn't pick up.

ORGANIZED TOURS

There are many organized tours to Las Vegas. The vast majority appeal to senior citizens who enjoy gambling in Las Vegas for a couple of days at a time and prefer to leave the driving or flying to others. Typically included in the cost are transportation, accommodations and airport shuttle; meals are generally not included.

Some of these tours are led by a director; others are unaccompanied. The accompanied tours mostly consist of chartered bus travel from a retirement community. Round-trip transportation and two nights' stay can cost as little as $99.

Air travel is always a bit more expensive. At the time of writing, one unaccompanied tour offered round-trip travel on Southwest Airlines from Seattle, and two nights at the Sahara hotel-casino. The cost was $246 per person, double occupancy.

Among the many tours offered is one from the Los Angeles area provided by **L.A. City Tours** (☎ 888-800-7878, 310-581-0718; W www.lacitytours.com; 1021 Pico Blvd, Santa Monica). The company offers a 3-day, 2-night bus tour package that includes round-trip transportation from the City of Angels to Sin City in a first-class air-conditioned coach, with nightly casino hotel accommodations. It offers convenient pick-ups from most hotels in Hollywood, Santa Monica, Venice Beach, Marina del Rey, Los Angeles International Airport and downtown Los Angeles. Packages start at $129 per person based on double occupancy.

Tour Vacations To Go (☎ 800-338-4962, 713-974-2121; W www.tourvacationstogo.com; 1502 Augusta Dr, Suite 415, Houston, Texas), is one of many companies that book with Contiki. Contiki specializes in tours for budget-conscious travelers aged between 18 and 35. Contiki tours to Las Vegas are often booked around New Year's Eve, which is a particularly rowdy time to be in town. A typical Contiki New Year's Eve package might include two nights in Las Vegas and two in the Los Angeles area for $500. Lodging and ground transportation is included. Have a look at the **Contiki website** (W www.contiki.com) for further tours available.

B.H.Tour USA (☎ 626-712-5977; W www.bhtourusa.com; 1270 Rexford Ave, Pasadena, California), offers a 14-day, three-city tour that includes airport pickup, tours of Los Angeles, San Francisco and Las Vegas, ground and domestic-airline transportation, lodging and lots of attractions. Tour prices start at under $1200.

Getting Around

TO/FROM THE AIRPORT

Taxi, shuttle and limousine services are available at McCarran International Airport 24 hours a day. A taxi ride from McCarran to a hotel on The Strip typically costs between $10 and $20. A taxi ride to a downtown hotel generally costs $15 to $25. Taxis in Las Vegas are metered; in the extremely unlikely event that a driver claims his or her meter is broken, take another taxi. (See the Taxis section later in the chapter for further information.)

Airport shuttle service from the airport to a hotel on The Strip usually costs $4.50 per person. Add another $1 per person to reach a downtown hotel. **Bell Trans** (☎ 702-739-7990; ⓦ www.bell-trans.com) operates many of the airport shuttles. When leaving the baggage-claim area of the airport, exit through door No 12 and look for the shuttles. Call the company to book a return to the airport.

You can also take a limousine to and from the airport. A flat rate of $35 an hour or fraction thereof for a six-person limo applies. Since it rarely takes more than an hour to reach any hotel on The Strip or downtown from the airport, it will rarely cost more than this, unless there's heavy traffic. Bell Trans also provides a limousine service.

Another option if you are staying at the Sahara, Stratosphere or one of the downtown hotels – and if you don't mind walking a bit – is to board a No 108 Citizens Area Transit (CAT) bus for $1.25. From the airport, the No 108 bus proceeds north up Swenson St, then west on Sahara Ave to Paradise Rd. Here, you'd want to step off and walk the 150m or so to Sahara hotel-casino, or the 300m or so to the Stratosphere. This bus is useful for getting to USA Hostels – Las Vegas, a 15-block trek from the Stewart Ave stop. You can also take the No 108 bus back to the airport. The No 108 buses leave at 30-minute intervals from McCarran, beginning at 5:09am daily, with the last one departing from the airport at 1:34am.

If your hotel is in downtown, you could also hop aboard a No 109 CAT and ride it north along Maryland Parkway all the way to CAT's downtown station, at the corner of Casino Center Blvd and Stewart Ave. From there it's a short walk to most of the area's hotels. This bus also makes the return trip to the airport. The No 109 buses leave at 15-minute intervals and operate 24 hours a day. See the following Bus section for full details on bus services in Las Vegas.

The bus may not be the best option if you're weighed down with a lot of stuff; bus service isn't door-to-door service. If you're heavily packed, take a taxi or a shuttle, or inquire if your hotel offers airport shuttle service; several of the megaresorts do.

BUS

Citizens Area Transit (CAT; ☎ 702-228-7433; ⓦ www.catride.com) is the local bus company. CAT's general operating hours are from 5:30am to 1:30am, although service on some bus routes commences earlier than 5:30am, and is around-the-clock on the most popular routes. CAT provides excellent service along The Strip, downtown and the section between the two. At $1.25 ($2 for Strip buses) per ride, CAT's fares are a bargain. A 30-day unlimited-use CAT pass is available for $30; it can be purchased online or at CAT's downtown station.

If you're thinking of getting around town by bus, you'll want to visit CAT's impressive website, which contains everything you'd want to know about the bus service, from transfer information to downloadable route maps. Or, you can obtain a free CAT Guide, which includes all of CAT's timetables, route maps and a whole lot more. You can pick up a guide at most convenience stores in Las Vegas, at CAT's downtown station or from any CAT driver.

CAT has too many routes to describe here. But the five routes of primary importance to the tourist, by bus number and by unofficial name, are: No 108 (Paradise Rd/Swenson St), No 109 (Maryland Parkway), No 113 (N Las Vegas Blvd bus), No 202 (Flamingo Rd) and Nos 301/302 (The Strip).

The No 108 bus runs south from CAT's downtown station (at Casino Center Blvd on Stewart Ave) through Main St until it reaches Paradise Rd. From there, No 108 runs down Paradise Rd to McCarran Airport, where it loops through the pick-up area before heading north toward downtown. From the airport, No 108 proceeds north on Swenson St and Joe W Brown Dr, west on Sahara Ave to Main St, then north on Main St back to the station. The route is in service from 5:09am to 2:05am and departs every 30 minutes.

The No 109 runs east on Stewart Ave from CAT's downtown station, then south on Maryland Parkway for about 6 miles to Russell Rd, where it heads west into McCarran and loops through the airport's pick-up area. From the airport, No 109 doubles back on Russell Rd and Maryland Parkway. At Charleston Blvd it travels one block east, then continues north on 13th St to Stewart Ave, turns west and returns to the CAT station 12 blocks away. The route runs 24 hours a day and departs every 15 minutes.

The No 113 goes from the CAT downtown station north on N Las Vegas Blvd to the Las Vegas Speedway. These buses run every 15 minutes, 24 hours a day. Be advised that these buses are extremely popular on event days (such as a Nascar race), so leave yourself plenty of time to catch one.

Bus No 202 runs along Flamingo Rd from Cimarron Rd in the west to Jimmy Durante Blvd in the east. From The Strip, this is the bus you'd catch to go to the Palms, Rio or The Orleans hotel-casinos, to Pink E's bar/pool hall, or to a number of good restaurants on or near Flamingo Rd, west of The Strip. This route operates every 20 minutes, 24 hours a day.

Bus Nos 301 and 302 follow the same route along The Strip, but whereas the No 301 bus makes numerous stops, No 302 stops only at certain locations. Heading south from CAT's downtown station, they are: Fremont St, Charleston Blvd, Stratosphere, Circus Circus, The Mirage, Bellagio, Excalibur and Vacation Village. Heading north from Vacation Village, the No 302 bus stops only at Tropicana, Flamingo, Sands, Riviera, Stratosphere, Charleston Blvd, Fremont St and CAT's downtown station. Bus No 301 departs every 15 minutes, 24 hours a day. The No 302 bus operates every 15 minutes from 10am till 1am.

LAS VEGAS STRIP TROLLEY

Competing for a slice of The Strip's transportation action are numerous four-wheeled cable-car-resembling trolleys. These air-conditioned trolleys run the length of The Strip – from the Stratosphere at the northern end to Mandalay Bay hotel-casino at the southern end. They make only one digression from The Strip, to pick up folks at the Las Vegas Hilton on Paradise Rd. These trolleys operate every 15 minutes from 9:30am to 1:30am daily. The per-trip fare is $1.65, and exact change is required. Be advised that these vehicles are not wheelchair friendly.

The south-bound trolley starts at the Stratosphere on The Strip, and stops at the following hotel-casinos and malls: Circus Circus, Stardust, the Fashion Show Mall, The Mirage, New York-New York, Excalibur and Mandalay Bay.

Traveling north along The Strip from Mandalay Bay, the trolley stops at: Tropicana, MGM Grand, Bally's, Imperial Palace, Harrah's, the Fashion Show Mall (again), Riviera, the Las Vegas Hilton, Sahara and Stratosphere.

DOWNTOWN TROLLEY

Several trolleys make an endless loop on Ogden Ave, 4th St, a tiny stretch of Las Vegas Blvd, and Main St. These trolleys make it easy to get from the Fremont Street Experience in the downtown area to the Stratosphere at the northern end of The Strip, and vice versa. The Downtown Trolley operates at 20-minute intervals from 8am till 9:30pm daily, and costs 75¢ (35¢ for seniors and the handicapped).

CAR

Las Vegas is a very easy city in which to drive. The streets in the city follow a grid pattern – no simpler street pattern exists – and most motorists drive conservatively due to the presence of traffic cops and the steep fines they impose on law-breakers. Remember: in the US, pedestrians *always* have the right of way, many people react aggressively when honked at, and parking in a blue (handicapped) parking space carries a minimum $271 fine.

Drunk-driving violations are especially frowned upon, and they are punished by mandatory jail time, revocation of driving privileges, court fines, raised insurance premiums and lawyers' fees. Depending on your weight, as few as two beers consumed within an hour could bring your blood-alcohol content to the legally drunk level. If you're planning on going on the drinking binge to end all binges, be smart about it and take taxis.

Las Vegas has an exceptionally large number of jaywalkers. In fact, the number of people in Las Vegas injured by cars as they try to cross a street illegally is much higher than the number of motorists injured in automobile accidents in the entire Las Vegas Valley. If you're driving, overcome the temptation to view the attractions along The Strip; keep your eyes glued to the road ahead of you and the possible jaywalkers on it.

Rental

There are dozens of car-rental companies in Las Vegas. Rates vary, but typically start around $35 a day for an economy car. Most companies don't require insurance, but if you want a collision damage waiver, expect to pay an additional $10 per day. Most companies require a major credit card, and some require that the driver be at least 25

years old. The few rental-car agencies that accept cash deposits require customers to provide a round-trip ticket, a cash deposit of at least $250 and proof of employment.

In addition to the rental-car rates, a 7% sales tax (yes, *sales*, even though you're not buying the car) and a 6% license-tag fee are added to rental rates. On top of those costs, you'll be dinged a 10% airport surcharge if you pick up your car at McCarran. Many agencies maintain rental desks at the airport, including:

Avis	☎ 702-261-5595, 800-831-2847
Budget	☎ 702-736-1212, 800-527-0700
Dollar	☎ 702-739-8408, 800-800-4000
National	☎ 702-261-5391, 800-227-7368
Thrifty	☎ 702-896-7600, 800-847-4389

Dollar has counters at the following hotels.

Bellagio	☎ 702-693-8838
Circus Circus	☎ 702-369-9302
Excalibur	☎ 702-736-1369
Flamingo	☎ 702-732-4180
Four Seasons	☎ 702-632-5300
Golden Nugget	☎ 702-383-8552
Las Vegas Hilton	☎ 702-733-2171
Luxor	☎ 702-730-5988
Mirage	☎ 702-791-7425
Monte Carlo	☎ 702-730-7974
New York-New York	☎ 702-740-6415
Treasure Island	☎ 702-737-1081

Budget has counters at Stratosphere, Flamingo and Four Queens (☎ *702-736-1212 for all three*).

If you'd like to drive something exotic during your stay in Las Vegas, consider renting from **Rent-A-Vette** (☎ *702-736-2592, 800-372-1981;* Ⓦ *www.rent-a-vette.com; 5021 Swenson St*), near E Tropicana Ave. Among its wide selection are the Ferrari F355 Spyder ($749), Porsche 911 Cabriolet ($399), and Corvette convertible with 6-speed manual transmission ($269). Those prices are per *day*, not per week! A credit card in the driver's name and a valid driving license are required. Drivers must be at least 21 years of age. One additional driver is permitted free of charge. For weekend use, reserve at least two weeks in advance. Complimentary airport pick up and return are provided. In most instances, a car can be delivered to your hotel.

Don't like the look of those rates? Consider **Rent-A-Wreck** (R-A-W; ☎ 702-474-0037, fax 702-474-4679; 2310 S Las Vegas Blvd), which specializes in used cars no more than seven years old. Rates are as low as $25 a day with no daily mileage charge for the first 150 miles. Weekly rates are available and are as low as $140. Most of R-A-W's cars are compacts or mid-size sedans.

Buying

It's only worth your while buying a car if you are planning to spend a long time in the US (three months or more) and don't like public transportation. It's possible to buy a reliable used car for as little as $2000. If you choose to go this route, be sure to take the car you're considering to a mechanic to check it for major problems. Be advised that there are mandatory registration and insurance fees.

MOTORCYCLE

Motorcycles are great fun to ride in Las Vegas most of the year. The weather's generally fine, the streets are in great shape, and most of the drivers respect motorcyclists' right to share the road. Be advised that helmet use is required by law, as is a valid driving license with motorcycle endorsement.

There are lots of companies in Las Vegas that rent motorcycles. All rent helmets and provide free airport shuttle, and most can rent camping equipment. Typical company requirements: 25 years of age, a major credit card, proof of current auto insurance (the companies like to see that their customers are insurable) and proof of medical insurance for the rider and passenger.

Street Eagle (☎ 702-898-1050, 866-346-8490; ⓦ www.streeteagle.com/las_vegas/; 6330 S Pecos St) features a large variety of Harley-Davidson motorcycles. Rates are $120/139 plus tax for an eight-/24-hour period, regardless of the model selected. Rates include helmet use, basic liability insurance, all necessary locks and 250 free miles a day.

Las Vegas Motorcycle Rentals (☎ 702-431-8500, 877-571-7174; 2605 S Eastern Ave) has lots of new Harleys available for rent, starting from $75 a day for a Sportster to $195 a day for a V-Rod. The rates include unlimited mileage, helmet use and a rain suit. As with Street Eagle, weekly rates are available.

TAXI

If you don't want to do any more walking than you absolutely have to, you'll get by just fine in Las Vegas. For example, you can hail a cab at the entrance of every hotel-casino; you don't even have to go to the roadside to hail one. And taxis are reasonably priced on a per-trip basis. The entire length of The Strip, for example, is only 4½ miles long; a taxi ride from one end to the other runs about $10.

If there's a big convention at the hotel you're staying at, taxis could prove difficult to come by, and you may be better off asking the concierge or staff at the front desk to call a taxi for you. Otherwise, call one of the following companies:

Checker Cab	☎ 702-873-2000
Deseret Cab	☎ 702-386-9102
Star Cab Company	☎ 702-873-2000
Western Cab	☎ 702-736-8000

There are 19 cab companies operating more than 2000 taxis in the Las Vegas area. Standard rates, set by the meter, apply for all cabs in Las Vegas. To step into a cab costs $2.30, and each mile traveled is $1.80. When leaving McCarran, you will also be charged an airport tax of $1.20. The cost of having a taxi driver wait for you is 40¢ per minute. Sample fares include: downtown to the airport, $18 to $25; the airport to mid-Strip, $10 to $18; mid-Strip to downtown, $12 to $15; and downtown to the Convention Center, $12 to $15.

At the time of writing, none of Las Vegas' taxi companies accepted credit cards. By law, all of the companies are required to operate at least one van with a wheelchair lift. Star Cab Company has the greatest number of vans with wheelchair lifts.

BICYCLE

Although Las Vegas is very flat, and its streets are wide and in excellent condition, it's not the kind of place you really want to discover on a bicycle. For one thing, the city is hotter than nine kinds of hell for half of the year. Unless you're in peak Olympic condition, no matter how far you go in Las Vegas on a bicycle, you'll arrive sweating like some boiler-room grunt aboard a battleship in a WWII movie, your clothes clinging to you like wet gauze.

For another thing, most of the city's attractions are inside its hotel-casinos, and you can't simply park your bike beside the front door and saunter in; some valet parking attendant with token security-guard duties will (figuratively) throw a gasket if you try. Bikes, like cars, must be parked in garages, and that often means on the 3rd or 4th floor of a parking structure that's located well behind the hotel-casino. For a little money, a taxi will drop you at the front door. For even less money, a bus or trolley will drop you curbside.

Of course, riding a bicycle at night in a city where many of the motorists are at least mildly intoxicated and probably distracted by the sights is taking a really unnecessary risk. Other factors, such as the chance of rain or theft of the bicycle, should also be taken into account.

But if you're absolutely determined to ride a bike in Las Vegas, you can rent them from two companies in town. Prices start at $30 per day for a street bike and $35 for a mountain bike. Contact **McGhie's** (☎ 702-252-8077; W www.mcghies.com; 4503 W Sahara Ave, between Decatur Blvd & Arville St) or **Escape the City Streets** (☎ 702-596-2953, 800-596-2953, fax 702-838-6968; W www.escapeadventures.com; 8221 W Charleston Blvd).

See the Organized Tours section for information on organized bike tours in Las Vegas and surrounding areas.

WALKING

Often, the best way to get around Las Vegas is on foot. The city is flat and easy to navigate, and most tourists are interested in only two fairly small sectors: The Strip and, to a much lesser degree, downtown.

Most visitors see little reason to venture to 'the other side of town' – from downtown to The Strip, or vice versa – given all the things to do in each area. As such, *getting around* Las Vegas often means little more than trekking between three or four casino-hotels in a day.

Topping things off, the megaresorts on The Strip are making it increasingly easy to roam between them. One way the monoliths have done this is with trams. One tram links the Excalibur, Luxor and Mandalay Bay. Another links the MGM Grand with Bally's. A third tram connects Bellagio with the Monte Carlo. And still a fourth tram links Treasure Island with the Mirage. Others are planned.

Movable walkways have also greatly reduced the amount of walking required along The Strip. The Luxor, for example, is further connected to the Excalibur by a movable walkway called the People Mover. Also, it used to be that you had a 100-yard walk from roadside to the casino at Bally's; now a series of movable walkways carries you from the sidewalk right into the casino. There's another one at Caesars Palace.

If you're planning to make a lot of tracks, remember this: Las Vegas can get *extremely* hot, especially during the summer, so be sure to drink plenty of water.

ORGANIZED TOURS

Among the established companies offering tours of Sin City and its surrounds is **Gray Line** (☎ 702-384-1234, 800-634-6579, fax 702-632-2118; W www.pcap.com/grayline .htm; 4020 E Lone Mountain Rd). Gray Line offers a popular 3½-hour city night tour, starting at 6:30pm, that combines bus rides and walking; it costs $40 for adults and $30 for children aged three to 11. Another popular tour offered by Gray Line consists of an hour-long narrated helicopter ride over Sin City. The chopper departs at 6:30pm most of the year (8:30pm during summer months) and costs $75 per person. Gray Line also offers bus tours from Las Vegas to the Grand Canyon and back. A day trip to the canyon costs $150/130 for adults/children aged three to 11, while the Grand Canyon Overnighter costs $300/200.

For all you cyclists out there, **Escape Adventures** (☎ *702-596-2953, 800-596-2953, fax 702-838-6968;* W *www.escapeadventures.com; 8221 W Charleston Blvd)* offers some really cool bicycle trips to Bryce Canyon and Zion National Parks; Grand Canyon's north rim; Red Rock Canyon and Death Valley; and to many other fascinating places in a half-dozen or so states. Rates run from $85 for a half-day guided tour of Red Rock Canyon to more than $1000 for a five-night, six-day guided bike tour of Bryce Canyon and Zion National Parks.

If this sounds even remotely appealing to you, be sure to check out the company's website.

If climbing onto a bike sounds no more pleasant to you than having a tooth pulled, contact **Las Vegas Tour Reservations** (☎ *702-456-1419, 888-846-4747, fax 702-869-9992;* W *www.adventurelasvegas.com/tours/; 1930 Village Center Circle)* and inquire about its limousine tours. Picture this: yourself, driving past a gaggle of sweaty cyclists as you cruise along The Strip in a late-model limo fitted with leather seats, tinted windows, a CD player and TV, and in your hand is an ice-cold Bloody Mary (yes, there's a full bar, too, at no extra cost!). For just chump change, your own personal driver will take you on various tours, such as Red Rock Canyon ($350 per person), Hoover Dam ($325) or the Grand Canyon ($950), and you needn't leave the air-con vehicle when you reach the sights if you'd really rather not.

Things to See & Do

Las Vegas is a continuously evolving city. During the 1990s, the Fremont Street Experience converted downtown Las Vegas from an eyesore into a vibrant, open-air pedestrian mall with nightly light shows to stop visitors in their tracks. The downtown area has been further upgraded by the substantial improvements to three of the four major hotel-casinos along Fremont St and the total renovation of Main Street Station, an elegant Victorian-style resort just two blocks away. Today, Main Street Station is one of the classiest hotel-casinos in Las Vegas and possibly the best value for the money.

Meanwhile, The Strip has also undergone a transformation. The resorts that opened along S Las Vegas Blvd in the last decade or so emphasize themes, size, elegance, fine dining, upscale shopping and, of course, gambling. The trend started in November 1989 with the opening of The Mirage, which continues to wow crowds with its erupting volcano; glass-enclosed atrium filled with jungle plants; white tigers and bottle-nosed dolphins; a 20,000-gallon aquarium and spectacular shows.

Next up was the Excalibur, a gleaming white castle guarded by a moat and a fire-breathing dragon, with a medieval interior to match. Circus Circus, which scored high marks with parents when it brought big-top acts to The Strip in 1968, outdid itself in 1993 by opening a covered amusement park on five adjacent acres. Also debuting that year were the architecturally stunning Luxor, the MGM Grand hotel-casino-theme park, and Treasure Island with its daily pirate battles.

In the following years, the Hard Rock Hotel established Las Vegas as a major player with rock 'n' rollers, the Stratosphere took the city's skyline to new heights, and New York-New York opened with a fantastic array of attractions, including a world-class high-speed roller coaster. Many other theme-hotels opened during the late 1990s, including The Venetian, Paris-Las Vegas, the Rio, Mandalay Bay, Bellagio and The Orleans.

Las Vegas at its Best

Just as beauty is in the eye of the beholder, highlights are a matter of personal taste, but the places mentioned here are a good place to start.

- **Cirque du Soleil** *O* at Bellagio or Mystère at Treasure Island. Superb entertainment.
- **The Forum Shops at Caesars Palace** One of the most elegant shopping malls in the Americas (see the Shopping chapter).
- **Fremont Street Experience** A light show that always stops pedestrians in their tracks.
- **Guggenheims at The Venetian** Not one but two world-class museums under one roof.
- **Hard Rock Hotel** Not for everyone, but definitely for every hardcore rock 'n' roller.
- **Imperial Palace Auto Collection** Not just beautiful old cars, but historic ones to boot.
- **Luxor** Stunning re-creation of the wonders of ancient Egypt, without the hawkers.
- **Main Street Station** Lovely Victorian-era antiques abound in this classy downtown hotel.
- **Manhattan Express** The ride of your life at a marvelously impressive mini-Manhattan at New York-New York.
- **The Mirage** A volcano, white tigers, a huge aquarium and an indoor jungle. Wow!
- **O'Shea's Magic & Movie Hall of Fame** Possibly the best magic museum in the States.
- **Rio's Masquerade Village** Where Mardi Gras is celebrated with gusto all year long.
- **Siegfried & Roy** The world's greatest illusionists never fail to amaze their audiences in their secret garden at the Mirage.
- **Star Trek: The Experience** A motion-simulation ride for even the most critical Trekkie, at the Las Vegas Hilton.
- **Stratosphere Tower** For an aerial view of Las Vegas without the costly use of an aircraft.

All feature a variety of attractions not usually associated with casinos. The Venetian, for example, boasts two excellent museums; Rio hosts Mardi Gras–like parades six days a week; and Mandalay Bay is home to a nightclub that features the biggest names in rhythm & blues.

There's no shortage of things to see and do in Las Vegas. Rather, there's often not enough time to see and do everything. That's particularly true of The Strip, where the vast majority of Las Vegas' hotel-casinos can be found, and where the choice of attractions can be overwhelming at times.

In a very real sense, Las Vegas is two cities: the older, downtown Las Vegas, which attracts far fewer onlookers than The Strip, and is often preferred by gamblers who find white tigers, faux volcanoes and so on beneath them (*Real gamblers don't need to be entertained*, they snort). In substance, the downtown casinos have changed little over the years. Most are still low-ceilinged, with lots of cigarette smoke and only a modest effort at decor. As attractions, they have little to offer nongamblers.

Lady Luck Goes Digital

Slot machines, like everything else, have entered the digital age. Computer chips have almost completely replaced spring-driven reels, and the random selection of symbols now takes a split second – though the reels still spin suspensefully, delaying for a few moments the instantaneous result.

How else has the microchip changed the billion-dollar slot industry? For one thing, it allows slots to be networked, creating enormous combined jackpots that can reach tens of millions of dollars. It allows for slot club cards that reward regular slot players with prizes depending on how much money they bet. It also allows casinos to track their machines, individually and constantly, and to make them as entertaining as video games.

Indeed, some slot machines have even become 'cable ready,' allowing players to watch their favorite soap operas while they gamble.

Not every hotel-casino in Las Vegas is mentioned here, as quite a few are downright unattractive. They are places that should and will eventually be replaced, but so far are hanging on – buoyed by the success of the palaces around them. Also, the descriptions of the hotel-casinos here focus on their attractions, while their recommended restaurants can be found in the Places to Eat chapter, and descriptions of their hotel rooms and other guest-only amenities can be found in the Places to Stay chapter.

THE STRIP
Aladdin

The Aladdin (☎ 702-785-5555, 877-333-9474, fax 702-758-5558; ⓦ www.aladdin casino.com; 3667 S Las Vegas Blvd) opened on August 18, 2000, on the site of the original Aladdin hotel-casino of 1950s' fame that was imploded in 1998 to make way for its $1.4 billion incarnation. But only 13 months after opening, the owners of the new Aladdin filed for bankruptcy protection in court. By the time you read this, it is quite possible that the Aladdin will have been sold and its new owners will have dramatically changed the megaresort, which has been losing money almost from the day it opened. If changes aren't made, you can expect the following: an enormous square building with an appealing Moroccan facade, which houses a multilevel casino and a **Desert Passage** shopping and dining area, all gussied up in a strange mix of Middle Eastern themes.

Amazingly, despite the big bucks spent on the Aladdin, the decor seems to have been chosen from the least-expensive materials, with emphasis clearly placed on bulk rather than fine details. When compared to classy Bellagio or The Venetian, Aladdin is clearly sub-par. Its strengths are its entertainers – belly dancers, jugglers, musicians, acrobats and others who perform free of charge in the Desert Passage. Other parts of the Aladdin include a 100,000-sq-ft casino containing 93 gaming tables, 2800 slot machines, a keno lounge, and a race and sports book; a 16,000-sq-ft European-style gaming salon operated by London Clubs International and featuring 30 table games, including baccarat, roulette and blackjack; and 21 restaurants, seven bars, a full-service health spa, and a 7000-seat showroom. The hotel portion of the Aladdin contains 2600 guestrooms, notable mostly for their spacious bathrooms fitted with scads of marble.

Bally's Las Vegas

Bally's hotel-casino (☎ 702-739-4111, 800-634-3434, fax 702-967-3890; W www.ballyslv.com; 3645 S Las Vegas Blvd) opened in 1973 as the MGM Grand, which in 1980 was the site of the city's worst disaster – a fire that killed 87 people and injured 700. The resort has since undergone several renovations and today is one of the most cheerful on The Strip. Set back from Las Vegas Blvd, Bally's is reached by four 200ft people movers that transport visitors from The Strip, under a neon-lit canopy flanked by lush gardens. The moving walkway brings visitors to the entrance of a bright and inviting casino that features 100-plus table games, 1500 electronic and video slot machines, and a popular sports and race book. The high ceiling and space between tables and slots eliminates the sense of clutter found in many casinos.

There's no central theme to Bally's casino, unless that theme is 'big.' Everything in the one-room casino seems oversize – the chandeliers, the velvet chairs and the casino itself, which is about the size of a football field. *Big* also describes Bally's long-running production show, **Jubilee!** (see the Entertainment chapter for details), which is the largest in Las Vegas. Just how large? More than 1000 costumes are worn during the show; no fewer than 70 stagehands are required to operate the stage, sets, lights and sound equipment; and no less than 4200 pounds of dry ice are used each week to create the show's smoke effects. Also of note are Bally's 20 retail shops and the fanciful mural of celebrity faces behind the reception desk. A monorail links Bally's with Paris-Las Vegas.

Barbary Coast

The Barbary Coast hotel-casino (☎ 702-737-7111, 800-634-6755, fax 702-894-9954; W www.barbarycoastcasino.com; 3595 S Las Vegas Blvd) opened in March 1979 and has since undergone three major renovations. Today, it's a relatively intimate casino with a mere 550 slot machines, and contains a lavish display of intricately designed stained glass, stately Victorian-era chandeliers and lots of polished dark wood. Except for Main Street Station in downtown, no other gaming establishment in Nevada evokes the image of the West at the turn of the 19th century better than Barbary Coast.

The visual highlight of the hotel-casino is its Tiffany-styled stained glass: more than $2 million worth is lavished in the casino, in the hotel's restaurants (particularly in Michael's and Victorian Room) and in every one of its 200 guestrooms. The resort's showpiece is the **Garden of Earthly Delights**, a 30ft-by-5ft stained-glass mural on the casino's west wall, depicting a Victorian-era fantasy. Installed in 1984, the piece required 10 artists and took more than 10,000 hours to complete. Barbary Coast contends that it's the largest mural of its kind in the world. I wouldn't bet on that, but this hotel-casino is well worth a walk through.

Bellagio

Built on the site of the legendary Dunes hotel, and inspired by the beauty of the lakeside Italian town of the same name, the $1.6-billion Bellagio (☎ 702-693-7111, 888-987-6667, fax 702-693-8546; W www.bellagio.com; 3600 S Las Vegas Blvd) is the most opulent pleasure palace in Las Vegas. An 8-acre artificial lake lined with Tuscan architecture is quite different from what most people expect of Las Vegas; it is, in a word, elegant. The view from The Strip is one of a green-blue lake from which spring more than 1000 dancing fountains. At water's edge is a cluster of charming buildings that could have been plucked from Italy's lake district. Inside the butter-yellow, 36-floor hotel-casino behind the lake are 16 upscale restaurants (including the incomparable Le Cirque, imported from New York), an exquisite opera house, a highbrow shopping concourse and a European-style casino. The lobby is absolutely stunning, highlighted by an 18ft ceiling adorned with a backlit sculpture composed of giant glass flower petals in every vibrant color. The sculpture was produced by Dale Chihuly, whose work has been exhibited in many world-class museums. Real flowers, grown in a 90,000-sq-ft greenhouse behind the hotel, fill countless vases throughout Bellagio. Outside, there are six distinctive pool courtyard settings in Mediterranean style. Relaxing pools, soothing spas, garden-vista cafés and private cabañas are accented by artfully formed citrus and parterre gardens. Also at Bellagio is one of the most entertaining, unbelievable shows on The Strip (with prices to match), Cirque du Soleil's *O*. If you can, see it; you'll be glad you did. Be advised that baby strollers are not permitted in Bellagio, and the casino is strictly off-limits to persons under 21 years of age.

Caesars Palace

Caesars Palace (☎ 702-731-2222, 800-634-6661, fax 702-731-7172; ⓦ www.caesars.com; 3570 S Las Vegas Blvd) set the standard of luxury for Sin City's gaming industry when it opened in 1966. The Greco-Roman fantasyland captured world attention with its full-sized marble reproductions of classical statuary, its Strip-side row of towering fountains and its cocktail waitresses costumed as goddesses. Today, bar girls continue to roam the gaming areas in skimpy togas, and the fountains are still out front – the same ones Evil Knievel made famous when he jumped them on a motorcycle on December 31, 1967. Due to a $600-million renovation completed in 1997, Caesars Palace is more fantastic than ever. A 4000-seat showroom, modeled after the Colosseum in Rome, and under construction at the time of writing, will feature performances by Celine Dion, at least initially. Swimming pools inlaid with marble and granite have been added, gardens have been enlarged and facades have been given a cleaner, more modern look. Inside, cheesy mirrors and neon have been replaced with hand-painted murals; dark paint and carpeting have given way to tasteful earth tones. At the center of things are two casinos containing a total of 100 card tables and 1934 slot machines,

A Statue with Punch

Unique among the statues at Caesars Palace is one of former heavyweight boxing champion Joe Louis, the 'Brown Bomber' who did as much for destroying the race barrier in boxing as Jackie Robinson did for baseball. The statue graces the entrance of the sports book. Hewn from Carrara marble by Italian sculptors, it measures 7ft 6 inches high and weighs 4500 pounds.

After an incomparable professional boxing career that stretched from 1934 to 1951 and included a record 25 title defenses, Louis was for many years employed by Caesars Palace as a casino greeter, holding court with adoring fans at a favorite booth in the Café Roma and sitting ringside with customers during championship fights.

Following his death, a memorial service was held at Caesars Palace on April 17, 1981, at the request of his widow. The service was attended by a host of entertainment and sports celebrities, with eulogies delivered by legendary crooner Frank Sinatra and civil rights activist Jesse Jackson.

some of which accept $500 chips. Caesars Palace Race and Sports Book features 90 video screens and state-of-the-art electronic display boards. Other facilities include a movie theater with a dome-shaped screen, three live-entertainment lounges, a 3-D motion-simulated adventure called Race for Atlantis, a multichambered dining and magic experience and a phenomenal shopping concourse (see the Shopping chapter). With all of its attractions, Caesars Palace could be quintessential Las Vegas.

Caesars Magical Empire Caesars Palace opened this Empire (☎ 702-731-7333, 800-445-4544, fax 702-731-7643; show only adult/child 12 years & under $27/10, dinner & show $75/20) in 1996, replete with tunnels, grottoes, theaters and dining chambers – and an illusion around every corner. The adventure begins with guests being placed into groups of 24, each of which is then escorted through a maze of misty catacombs by Centurion guards to one of 10 private dining rooms. There, each group is treated to a magic show by its own private magician between servings of a three-course meal. Simple enough. However, most of the entertainment is not so straightforward. Nowhere in this Empire are things as they seem. Mysteries abound throughout the facility. You're not even safe in the bathroom, where ghosts appear in the mirrors! After dining, visitors are guided through more catacombs to the Sanctum Secorum, a seven-story magical realm with a broken bridge and a bottomless pit. Flanking Sanctum Secorum are two bars, one of which is home to two wisecracking skeletons (Habeus and Corpus), the other to a poltergeist who enjoys spooking guests with interactive magic. Highlighting the experience are two theaters where you can see more magic shows up close, and where there's a good chance you'll be asked to be in one. In generally impersonal Las Vegas, the Empire emphasizes audience participation in an intimate setting. Dinner seating starts at 4:30pm from Tuesday to Saturday, with the first show beginning at 5:15pm.

Race for Atlantis IMAX 3-D Ride This virtual-reality ride (☎ 888-910-7223; adult/ child 12 years & under $10/7; minimum height requirement of 42 inches; open 10am-11pm Sun-Thur, 10am-midnight Fri & Sat), to the lost city of Atlantis, is offered in a domed IMAX theater inside the Forum Shops wing of Caesars Palace. Cutting-edge sound engineering and high-tech motion-simulation equipment combine to immerse riders in a multisensory experience that brings the mythical kingdom of Atlantis to life. The attraction – which was the world's first giant-screen IMAX 3-D motion simulator ride when it opened on January 9, 1998 – begins with a brief walk through a stone hallway that leads to an underwater palace, of sorts. There, you board one of four 27-passenger motion simulators and, after enduring an obnoxious safety warning delivered in rap, your 'chariot' is sent racing toward the lost city in a flight to a finish that will determine the ruler of Atlantis for the next millennium. Each rider is issued a 3-D

The Best Tip Ever

Mr C, a very stylish and talented shoeshine at Caesars Palace, has been putting luster on fine footwear for more than 40 years. When asked recently who had given him the best tip since he'd been in business, Mr C didn't need to think hard: 'Sammy Davis Jr. Five hundred dollars – five $100 bills – for a pair of alligator boots. He was on his way to a $5000-a-plate awards dinner, and he wanted to look sharp. Sammy was always doing things like that – giving big tips, making people happy. He was very loved.'

---

visor that enables the illusion of debris hurtling past you. Fans and motion (your chariot jolts in all directions in synchronicity with the on-screen images) help create the deception that you're actually going somewhere. Although there is no age restriction, Caesars Palace asks persons with neck, back or heart problems to not race to Atlantis. Furthermore, if you have ever suffered motion sickness, you'd be wise to leave the riding to others. Although the ride lasts only 4½ minutes, that's more than enough time to empty your stomach's contents on 26 total strangers.

Circus Circus

Few people cruising The Strip overlook Circus Circus hotel-casino (☎ 702-734-0410, 800-444-2472, fax 702-734-2268; ⓦ www .circuscircus.com; 2880 S Las Vegas Blvd). You can't miss the enormous clown-shaped marquee out front and the tent-shaped casino under a pink-and-white big top. Granted, from outside the sprawling hotel-casino complex looks pretty cheesy, especially when compared to Bellagio or The Mirage, but under the big top there's plenty of fun to be had for people of all ages. As if you hadn't guessed, a circus-like environment exists inside – as it has since Circus Circus opened in 1968. The ground floor has two casinos containing a total of 2220 slot machines, 72 card tables and a 160-seat lounge. In keeping with its name, the decor is a carnival of colors, mainly pinks and oranges. Directly above the casino, and reachable by a circular ramp, is Midway, home to an arcade, games and free circus acts. On the center stage, animals, acrobats and magicians perform from 11am to midnight daily, with usually no more than 30 minutes between performances. Just come on in and take a seat; there's no admission charge or reserved seating. Nearby are lots of arcades – the video variety *and* old-fashioned carnival games. Among the latter: win a fuzzy space alien by tossing a whiffle ball into a basket, or by hitting a moving target with a cork gun. Another game involves striking a catapult with a wooden mallet, which flings a rubber chicken in the direction of a dozen pots placed on a rotating platform; if the chicken lands in a pot, you win. Circus Circus is a great place for kids and fun-loving adults.

Adventuredome At Circus Circus, Adventuredome (☎ 702-794-3939, 877-224-7287; W www.adventuredome.com; admission free; rides $3-5, all-day ride passes over 48 inches/ 33-48 inches/under 33 inches in height $19/ 14/free; open 10am-6pm Mon-Thur, 10am-midnight Fri & Sat, 10am-8pm Sun) is a fully enclosed, 5-acre amusement park packed with thrill rides. Amid a desert-canyon setting, replete with faux Pueblo cliff dwellings and an archaeological dig, are dozens of attractions. They include the only indoor, double-loop, double-corkscrew roller coaster in the US; a 20-seat, open-sided toboggan that makes a big splash after rocketing down a four-story slide; and a swinging pirate ship with a heart-pounding swoop.

Also popular are a bumper-car arena, a kiddy airplane ride, a Ferris wheel, a laser-tag center and a children's net climb/ ball crawl area. In the Extreme Zone are attractions for us older kids, including a four-story rock-climbing wall and a bungee-jumping area. Restaurants, video games and a carousel featuring live animals for your riding pleasure are also on the premises. And what would a Circus Circus amusement park be without clowns? Free clown shows are held throughout the day. While you're in Adventuredome, be sure to admire the 8615

panes of glass that fully enclose the theme park. Each pane weighs more than 300lbs!

Excalibur

According to legend, Excalibur was a magical sword embedded in stone. During post-Roman Britain, it was proclaimed that whoever could pull the sword from the stone would be crowned King of England. After gallant knights failed in their attempts to free the sword, Arthur, a mere squire, succeeded. The Arthurian legend forms the basis for much of the cheesy decor of the Excalibur hotel-casino (☎ 702-597-7777, 877-750-5464, fax 702-597-7040; W www .excalibur-casino.com; 3850 S Las Vegas Blvd).

The Excalibur epitomizes gaudy Las Vegas. With guestrooms in two nearby towers, the main structure is a caricature of a white castle, with bright orange- and blue-roofed towers and a faux drawbridge spanning a moat in front of the entrance. A mechanical fire-breathing dragon does mock battle with Merlin here every hour on the hour from dusk till midnight. Inside the castle, which contains a casino, restaurants and shops, the walls are adorned with coats of arms – cheap stained-glass art of valiant knights, with neon knights on neon horses. Excalibur could have been done up in good taste, resembling an elegant English castle, but its owners apparently decided to go the cheap, kitschy route (which, to be sure, is just fine with most families). Even Excalibur's dinner show, **King Arthur's Tournament**, is more like a demolition derby with hooves and armor than a flashy Vegas production. Excalibur is connected to the luxurious Luxor (a classy must-see) by a covered people mover, making it easy to zip over to Excalibur, if only for the snicker factor.

Court Jesters Stage Excalibur is owned by the same folks who own Circus Circus, which has had phenomenal success due, in no small part, to the free high-quality circus acts that perform there. Following the same winning formula, the management of Excalibur established Court Jesters Stage, where a variety of acts can be seen free of charge

Touring Vegas on Foot

There's lots to see and do in Las Vegas, but unless you've got at least a week in town you must plan ahead to experience the best of Sin City. Due to the deceptively large distances between the city's major sights – the hotel-casinos – and the size of the properties, most visitors are unable to visit more than four or five in a day. Each of the following walking tours takes six to eight hours (including a lunch break).

Venice to Bellagio

Explore the two fine museums and exquisite shopping arcade, and take a romantic canal ride at The Venetian before crossing S Las Vegas Blvd to Treasure Island. Watch a late afternoon mock pirate battle, then take a tram to The Mirage, taking in the faux volcano, white tigers and Siegfried & Roy's Magic Garden. From here, head to Caesars Palace to peruse The Forum Shops, Race for Atlantis and Caesars Magical Empire before winding up at Bellagio, with its elegant gaming areas, upscale shops and dancing fountains.

Paris to Egypt

Start at Paris-Las Vegas, ascend Eiffel Tower, and cruise by lovely bistros and shops. Take the tram to MGM Grand for its captivating lion habitat and glamorous casino before delving into the World of Coca-Cola. Pick up the pace at New York-New York, exploring its wonderful NY-theme gaming areas and unforgettable roller-coaster. Hop on the tram to Mandalay Bay, bask on the sand-and-surf beach and visit the Shark Reef before taking another tram to the marvelous Egyptian-themed Luxor casino, which houses King Tut's Tomb museum.

Thrill Rides to the Station

Soak up the endless views and two incomparable thrill rides at Stratosphere, then take a taxi downtown to Golden Nugget (Hand of Faith Nugget) and Binion's Horseshoe ($1 million in cash). Stroll pedestrian-only Fremont St between Main St and Las Vegas Blvd – these five blocks are the original Las Vegas Strip. Round out your day with a visit to Main Street Station, home to many historical artifacts. Enjoy!

---

every day. On the 2nd floor of the casino, a short distance from the people mover to Luxor, the stage boasts a cast of 30 performers dressed in medieval costumes, each giving contemporary as well as traditional performances. There are musicians, for example, who play period instruments such as the mandolin, flute and harp, as well as magicians performing feats that medieval alchemists never would have imagined. There are also jugglers and puppeteers. The shows are great fun for everyone, and as with the performances at Circus Circus, you can't beat the price. Performances begin at 10am and continue on the half-hour until 10pm from Monday to Thursday, and until 1am on Friday and Saturday; there are no shows on Sunday. Acts average 10 minutes.

Flamingo

When it opened in 1946 with 105 rooms and an elegant casino, the Flamingo (☎ 702-733-3111, 888-308-8899, fax 702-733-3353; W www.flamingolasvegas.com; 3555 S Las Vegas Blvd) was the talk of the town. It was by far the biggest hotel-casino in Las Vegas, and the most expensive; its owners – all members of the New York mafia – shelled out an unprecedented $6 million to build a tropical gaming oasis in the desert. It was prime gangster Americana, initially managed by the infamous mobster Ben 'Bugsy' Siegel. He didn't manage it for long. Siegel died in a hail of bullets at his girlfriend's Beverly Hills home soon after the Flamingo opened, the victim of a contract killing ordered by the casino's investors; the Flamingo had gotten off to a slow start and the investors believed the Flamingo would fail, so they 'took care of business.' With Siegel, the investors made a business mistake: not only did the Flamingo survive, but it's continued to thrive.

In 1970, Hilton purchased the hotel-casino and has expanded it regularly over the years; today it has an incredible 4000 rooms. The casino itself has been remodeled many times since 1946 and it no longer resembles the elegant original, nor does the casino try to evoke images of a tropical paradise or theme – other than a few pink-and-orange neon lights that kind of resemble flamingo feathers. However, just outside the gaming area are the Flamingo's gardens, and they are magnificent: 15 acres of pools, waterfalls and waterways; ponds filled with swans, ducks and koi; and no fewer than 2000 palm trees and jungle plants everywhere you look. Sadly, the flamingos from Florida and the African pigeons that used to inhabit little islands are gone, the result of too many inconsiderate visitors who found joy in feeding them chewing gum and cigarette butts. The Flamingo isn't what it was in the days when even its janitorial staff wore tuxedos, but its gardens *are* a sight to behold.

GameWorks

GameWorks (☎ 702-597-3122; www .gameworks.com; 3769 S Las Vegas Blvd; admission free; open 10am-1am Mon-Thur, 10am-2am Fri & Sat, 10am-midnight Sun) is a high-tech entertainment center intended for teens and adults. If you enjoy video games, virtual-reality experiences or just hanging out in places where lots of hip people are having fun, GameWorks is the place for you.

The center has an impressive Hollywood pedigree: GameWorks was conceived by film director Steven Spielberg and created by the entertainment company DreamWorks SKG, along with high-end video game maker SEGA Enterprises and Universal Studios. GameWorks consists of one large underground room containing a popular restaurant, full bar, 75ft climbing wall, intimate

pool hall and *lots* of state-of-the-art video and virtual-reality games. One of the more popular games is **Vertical Reality**, in which eight to 12 players are strapped into seats and divided into groups. The players race the clock to rid a skyscraper of criminals – actually ascending up to 24ft as they succeed, and descending in a controlled 'free fall' as they get hit. Vertical Reality might be the only game of its kind in which players experience physical consequences based on their actions. Also popular is a Jurassic Park attraction that pits groups of four heavily armed players against flesh-eating dinosaurs. Yes, it *is* as fun as it sounds. As GameWorks was designed for social interaction (the best games involve numerous participants), the best time to go is at night, when the facility is most crowded. Expect to pay $25 or more for two hours of play.

Harley-Davidson Café

The Harley-Davidson Café (☎ 702-740-4555; www.harley-davidsoncafe.com; 3725 S Las Vegas Blvd; open 11am-11pm Sun-Thur, 11am-midnight Fri & Sat) is mostly a restaurant (and a surprisingly expensive one for a pseudo-biker hangout; see the Places to Eat chapter), but it's also a shrine to all things Harley, and that makes it an attraction. Just as the menu jacket states, the café highlights years of Harley-Davidson culture, history and motorcycles – not to mention many of the enthusiasts who have made H-D legendary. A conveyor belt carries a dozen Harley 'hogs' overhead (among which are always the seven most recent models), and the walls are covered with photos of Harley racers and celebrities beside their Harleys. *Easy Rider* star Peter Fonda poses in a black leather jacket, looking oh so cool as he stares way, way off into the distance while seated on his – yes! – Harley. Beside Peter are the words: 'A man went looking for America. And he couldn't find it anywhere...' Somehow the words ring with much greater force when you're reading them in the office-worker-turned-weekend-biker capital of Las Vegas. Or perhaps they just need to be accompanied by the juicy aroma of BBQ ribs, the tinkling of beer glasses and the sounds of people having fun. Found throughout the friendly establishment are dozens of beautifully painted Harley gas tanks, each signed by a celebrity (Goldie Hawn, Sting and Caroll Burnett among them). There's even an adjacent store carrying lots of Harley-Davidson merchandise (which can also be ordered online). Gamblers won't find a single slot machine at this Strip stop, just Harley diehards in Hog Heaven.

Harrah's

When it opened in 1973, Harrah's (☎ 702-369-5000, 800-427-7247, fax 702-369-5500; W www.harrahs.com/our_casinos/las/; 3475 S Las Vegas Blvd) was a Holiday Inn property with a riverboat theme. It wasn't until 1992 that the hotel-casino we know today received its present name and dropped the riverboat look in favor of a whimsical facade and interior reminiscent of Carnival and Mardi Gras. Those changes took place during a $200-million renovation and expansion that turned a mostly forgettable Strip joint into the fun attraction it is today. Unlike some megaresorts that make a half-hearted effort at a theme (Bally's rushes to mind), the decorators of Harrah's clearly enjoyed their work. Everywhere the visitor looks there's something playfully suggestive of Carnival in Venice or Mardi Gras in New Orleans.

Among the attractions at Harrah's is an enormous backlit mural over the main entrance, featuring the greatest Las Vegas entertainers of all time. Photographers will want to see the mural at night, when light passing through the glass mural produces a captivating artwork. Inside, the 103,325-sq-ft casino (one of the city's largest) is nearly always swarming with gamblers who appreciate the bright and uplifting decor, not to mention its great variety of games: 1460 slot machines, 300 video poker machines, 51 blackjack tables, eight roulette wheels, eight craps tables, two keno lounges, four minibaccarat tables, a race and sports book, red dog, eight poker tables, four Pai Gow poker tables, three Caribbean stud tables and four Let It Ride games. The facility is also home to a popular lounge, a comedy club, seven restaurants and 2579 guestrooms.

Holiday Inn Casino Boardwalk

This Holiday Inn hotel-casino (☎ 702-733-2400, 800-635-4581, fax 702-730-3166; W www.hiboardwalk.com; 3750 S Las Vegas Blvd) is like any other Holiday Inn, except that on The Strip it had to have a theme, and so it chose to call itself the 'Coney Island of Las Vegas' and run with that proposition. The facade sports a faux roller coaster, a giant clown's face and the like, while inside a small but bright and pleasant casino (featuring 20 state-of-the-art table games, 600 slot and video games, and a full-featured race and sports book) goes heavy on clown objets d'art. Unfortunately for the Holiday Inn, the colossal New York-New York opened up a short distance away with Coney Island Emporium, a family entertainment center that's vastly superior to the mild attractions offered by the Holiday Inn (namely, free magic shows in the lounge every afternoon and evening). Still, after spending time in the casinos of the megaresorts, it's refreshing to wander into this bright, airy and cheerfully colored hotel-casino and play a few slots.

Imperial Palace

The Imperial Palace hotel-casino (☎ 702-731-3311, 800-634-6441; W www.imperial palace.com; 3535 S Las Vegas Blvd) has 2700 rooms and turns to the Orient for its inspiration. Though the small, blue-roofed pagoda at the front of the hotel is a bit hokey, the Oriental theme within (lots of wind-chime chandeliers and faux jade, bamboo and curved wood accents) is quite alright. The popular 75,000-sq-ft casino is tastefully decorated in bamboo and rattan furnishings under a dragon-motif ceiling, and it's packed with 1844 slot and video machines, 26 blackjack tables, four crap tables, three roulette tables, a keno lounge, a big wheel, minibaccarat, a race and sports book, two Pai Gow poker tables, three Let It Ride tables and two Caribbean Stud tables. Special features include an impressive auto collection (see following), men's and women's health clubs, and an Olympic-size pool with waterfall and heated spa. Imperial Palace also has the best celebrity impersonator show on The

Strip, **Legends in Concert**. Imperial Palace doesn't have the wow factor of, say, The Venetian or Bellagio, but if you happen to be strolling by and aren't in a hurry, it certainly warrants a look inside – especially if you're an auto aficionado.

Imperial Palace Auto Collection At the back of the hotel-casino, the Imperial Palace Auto Collection (✆ 702-731-3311; 5th floor; admission free; open 9:30am-9:30pm daily) is one of the largest privately owned auto collections in the world. A full description of each of the more than 200 cars on display would fill this guide, and serious car buffs could easily spend several hours here. Among the wonderful vehicles on hand are Marilyn Monroe's pink 1955 Lincoln Capri convertible; an armor-plated 1939 Mercedes-Benz 770K convertible used by Adolph Hitler during parades; a 1982 Range Rover 'Popemobile,' custom-built at the factory for the papal visit to the United Kingdom; a 1936 V-16 Cadillac limousine used by Franklin D Roosevelt, US president from 1933 to 1945 (it is the only unrestored vehicle on display); and a 1981 Zimmer Golden Spirit owned by Liberace, whose 1966 Rolls-Royce Silver Shadow is on display in a plush, gallery-like setting on the 5th floor of the Imperial Palace parking facility. You will also find a gorgeous, guacamole-colored 1929 Duesenberg Murphy convertible coupe, a red 1958 Porsche 356A Speedster, a 1925 Studebaker paddy wagon that was used by the Los Angeles Police Department, and a 1935 Packard formerly owned by Emperor Hirohito. The gift shop features a wide selection of automobile memorabilia and books. Visitors are welcome to take photos of the vehicles.

Luxor

Named after Egypt's splendid city of antiquity, Luxor hotel-casino (✆ 702-262-4000, 800-288-1000, fax 702-262-4452; ⓦ www.luxor.com; 3900 S Las Vegas Blvd) has the greatest wow factor of Las Vegas' many megaresorts. That's not simply because Luxor houses the world's largest atrium, has 120,000 sq ft of smartly arranged

casino space and hosts a stunning array of attractions. Rather, it's that the resort's designers chose a theme that easily could have ended up a pyramid of gaudiness, but instead succeeded in creating an elegant shrine to Egyptian art, architecture and antiquities. This Luxor evokes the same awe-inspiring sensations as Egypt's Luxor, the site of grand temple monuments on the east bank of the Nile. From an architectural standpoint, Luxor is the most unique resort in town. Built in 1993, the hotel-casino consists of a 30-story pyramid cloaked in black glass from base to apex: in all, there are 26,783 glass plates totaling 570,000 sq ft. The atrium is so voluminous it could accommodate nine 747 jetliners stacked one atop another and still have room for 50 Cessnas. At its apex, a 40-billion-candlepower beacon – the world's most powerful – sends a shaft of blue-white light 10 miles into space.

Out front of the pyramid is a 10-story-high crouching sphinx and a sandstone obelisk etched with hieroglyphics. The pyramid's interior is tastefully decorated with giant Egyptian statues of guards, lions and rams; sandstone walls adorned with hieroglyphic-inscribed tapestries and grand columns; a stunning replica of the great Temple of Ramses II; and a pharaoh's treasure of polished marble. There's a casino, of course, featuring 2530 slot and video machines, 116 gaming tables, poker, keno and a state-of-the-art race and sports book; a museum devoted to King Tutankhamun (see following); and for entertainment Luxor offers the **Blue Man Group** (see the Entertainment chapter for details).

King Tut's Tomb & Museum When legendary English archaeologist Howard Carter first peered into the tomb of King Tutankhamen in Egypt's Valley of the Kings in 1922, he gazed upon a collection of antiquities representing the finest works of ancient craftsmanship. Today, Luxor's visitors can see exquisite reproductions of the same artifacts Carter discovered on his apocryphal descent into the fabled tomb of an obscure Egyptian dynasty (circa 1350 BC). The museum (admission $5; open 9am-11pm

Sun-Thur, 9am-midnight Fri & Sat) contains authentic reproductions of more than 500 items discovered in Tutankhamen's tomb, positioned exactly as they were found according to records maintained by the Carter expedition. Dr Omar Mabreuck, a renowned Egyptologist, oversaw the production of the museum pieces, which required 50 people over six months to assemble. Among the exhibits: King Tut's innermost gold-leaf coffin, decorated with ornate hieroglyphics and thousands of simulated precious stones; the antechamber, which contains three wooden and gold funerary beds carved in the form of animals; and the treasury, which in addition to golden treasures, also contains several miniature wooden boats intended to carry Tutankhamen on his voyage to the afterworld. A 15-minute, self-guided walking tour of the museum allows visitors to view treasures reproduced using the same gold leaf and linens, precious pigments, tools and original 3300-year-old Egyptian methods. If you haven't been to Egypt's famous antiquities museum and don't plan to visit it anytime soon, this attraction provides an excellent reproduction of what you would see there.

IMAX Theater at Luxor Unlike some other IMAX theaters, which project movies against a curved overhead screen, the IMAX Theater at Luxor *(☎ 702-262-4555; 2-D/3-D movies $8/9)* projects its movies the old-fashioned way: on a flat, wall-mounted screen. However, the films shown here employ a technology that permits the projected images to be 10 times more detailed than conventional movies. With such increased detail, a much larger screen can be used without compromising clarity. As a result, the screen at Luxor's theater is nearly seven stories high, although the theater contains only 312 seats. The consequence of this is that you feel *very* close to the action. You don't so much watch the movie as experience it. A 15,000-watt sound system grabs your ear loud and clear. About half of the films shown at Luxor are two dimensional (like regular movies), but the other half are designed to convey three dimensions. Watching a 2-D IMAX film on a huge screen

takes film viewing to a new level, but watching a 3-D IMAX film on a huge screen is a galactic leap. The 3-D experience requires you to wear a headset that features 3-D viewing technology (without it, the movie's just a blur). The headset also contains an eight-channel, digital surround-sound system to further immerse you in the film.

M&M's World

M&M's World *(☎ 702-736-7611; 3769 S Las Vegas Blvd; admission free; store open 10am-midnight Sun-Thur, 10am-1am Fri & Sat; 3-D movies 10am-6pm Sun-Thur, 10am-8pm Fri & Sat)* is dedicated to the famous candy. Though primarily intended for kids, it's quite entertaining for adults as well. Unlike the neighboring World of Coca-Cola (see later in the chapter), which is both amusing and educational, M&M's World isn't really meant to be taken seriously. For starters, visitors follow a walkway through a 'candy factory' that's a whole lot more like a fun-house corridor than any real factory. Giant brightly colored gears turn, lights flash and bells go off – and absolutely no candy is manufactured. But kids like it, and that's the intent. After the 'factory,' visitors attend a phony class at 'M&M's University,' where a spunky 'professor' lectures about the history and the making of M&M's. It's a whole lot of amusing nonsense. Minutes later, visitors are ushered into a theater to watch a complimentary short 3-D movie about a candied peanut who lost his 'M' at a craps table, and his travails to get his letter back. If you've never seen a 3-D movie before, you're in for a treat. The 25-minute tour ends at an M&M's gift shop, where M&M's and promotional materials are on sale. M&M's World is probably most appreciated by children aged between five and 11.

Mandalay Bay

Las Vegas casinos have long sought to increase their appeal by placing under their roofs popular chain restaurants and restaurants managed by celebrated chefs. The $950-million Mandalay Bay *(☎ 702-632-7000, 877-632-7000, fax 702-632-7013; ⓦ www .mandalaybay.com; 3950 S Las Vegas Blvd)* is no exception. Among its 15 restaurants is one managed by chef Wolfgang Puck, of Spago fame (Trattoria del Lupo), and another managed by chef Charlie Palmer (Aureole). But when Mandalay Bay made its debut in April 1999 with a special concert performance by legendary tenor Luciano Pavarotti, it carried the bundling strategy two steps further by opening a House of Blues on its premises and by renting its 35th through 39th floors to the super-luxurious Four Seasons Hotel. That's right, an upscale hotel within an upscale hotel – a Las Vegas first. In addition to 424 guestrooms, the Four Seasons features a spa and five-star dining.

Among the Mandalay Bay's various attractions is Shark Reef (see following) and two very impressive aquariums (one near the registration desk, the other inside the Coral Reef Lounge). The quality of attractions and cuisine that Mandalay Bay offers compliments the attention to detail that went into this tropically themed resort. Gamblers will appreciate the vast and classy casino, home to 122 gaming tables, 2400 slot machines and a race and sports book. The Salon Privé caters to high-stakes games. The resort's premiere bar, **rumjungle**, features walls of fire at its entrance, ceiling-to-floor cascades inside, Latin jazz most nights of the week, a salsa dance floor and more than 100 rums ready to sample. Outside, an 11-acre garden includes a sand-and-surf beach (open spring and summer and featuring actual surfing competitions), a lazy-river ride, a variety of pools and a jogging track. Adding to Mandalay Bay's appeal is its proximity to the must-see Luxor.

Shark Reef This place (☎ 702-632-7000, 877-632-7000; adult/child 5-12 years/child 4 years & under $15/10/free; open 10am-11pm daily, last visitors admitted at 10pm) isn't your typical aquarium. For starters, the attraction features numerous enormous aquariums holding an awesome 1.6 million gallons of water and no fewer than 2500 specimens. While the largest of the aquariums contain large and small sharks, others highlight the beauty of jellyfish, moray eels and stingrays. There's even a petting zoo of sorts, where visitors are encouraged to touch

stingrays and pint-size sharks as the creatures swim in a shallow, supervised pool. Part of the attraction of Shark Reef is that it allows visitors to experience an undersea environment on many levels, viewing exhibits from various angles. Guests are able to see rays resting on the ocean floor and then look up and watch a school of fish swim overhead. In addition to the aquariums, there are smartly designed compounds crawling with golden crocodiles, water monitors and other rare and endangered toothy reptiles. Despite billboards around town advertising Shark Reef with an image of a great white shark looking oh-so menacing, you won't see any great whites at Mandalay Bay. In all, Shark Reef is a bit overpriced, but it's also the best shark exhibit you're ever likely to see.

MGM Grand

With 5034 rooms, the $1-billion MGM Grand (☎ 702-891-1111, 800-929-1111, fax 702-891-1112; W www.mgmgrand.com; 3799 S Las Vegas Blvd) is the largest hotel in the world. Despite its size, the shimmering emerald-green City of Entertainment – as MGM Grand bills itself – has done a superb job of making its attractions seem intimate. The megaresort has accomplished this feat by embracing not one but many themes taken from Hollywood movies. The most obvious example of this is the resort's dance club, Studio 54 (of New York nightclub and motion-picture fame). The adjacent casino consists of one gigantic, circular room with an ornate domed ceiling and replicate 1930s glamour, replete with bandstand (live swing and jazz plays every night, free of charge). At 171,500 sq ft, MGM Grand's casino floor is equal in size to four football fields, and

Spare Change

When the MGM Grand opened on December 18, 1993, $3.5 million in quarters were needed for its slot machines, and to provide change. Thirty-nine armored cars were used to transport the 14 million coins, which were delivered in 3600 sacks. Each sack weighed 60lb.

offers the full spectrum of table games (around 165) and slots (a whopping 3724) as well as a race and sports book, a poker room and a keno lounge. Other attractions include two shopping concourses, a 17,157-seat special events center that often facilitates mega-concerts and championship boxing bouts, the very saucy 'La Femme' topless revue, and an array of culinary choices with an impressive celebrity chef lineup. For theatrical amusement, MGM Grand offers **Rick Springfield in EFX Alive**, which is one of the top production shows in Las Vegas (see the Entertainment chapter). With so much to do in MGM Grand, many guests choose to spend all of their time in Las Vegas here.

MGM Grand Lion Habitat In July 1999, MGM Grand opened a $9-million, 5345-sq-ft Lion Habitat (☎ 702-891-1111; admission free; open 11am-11pm daily). This swank enclosure showcases up to six adult lions daily, including Goldie, Metro Jr and Baby Lion, three direct descendants of MGM Studios' famous signature marquee lion, Metro. The MGM owns 18 of the magnificent big cats, but for the comfort of the animals and the safety of their trainers, no more than two are allowed in the enclosure simultaneously. One of the treats of the Lion Habitat is its see-through walkway tunnel, which allows the lions to roam above, below and around their onlookers. At times, the lions sleep atop the tunnel, separated from their admirers only by a sheet of Plexiglas and a couple of feet of air.

No doubt aware that their cat house would be compared to the tiger exhibit at The Mirage, the executives at MGM Grand really went to town with their multilevel lion home; it definitely warrants a stop. While they're not cared for by a pair of well-known illusionists, the cats' caretaker, Keith Evans, has been working with big cats for more than three decades and lives with 22 big cats on 8½ acres just outside town. He and other trainers can often be seen inside the Lion Habitat, engaged in tug-of-rope with the large and playful felines. Next to the spacious compound is a retail shop with loads of lion-related souvenirs.

The Lion's Share of Bronze

The front entrance of MGM Grand features the largest bronze statue in the United States – a 45ft tall, 100,000-pound bronze lion statue, perched atop a 25ft pedestal and ringed by lush landscaping, water fountains and Atlas-themed statues. MGM Grand contains no less than 18,000 doors, 7778 beds, 18,000 tons of air-conditioning equipment and 93 elevators. Just like home, eh?

The Mirage

When the Mirage opened in 1989, owner Steve Wynn told reporters his goal was to build a hotel-casino 'so overriding in its nature that it would be a reason in and of itself for visitors to come to Las Vegas.' The Mirage (☎ 702-791-7111, 800-627-6667, fax 702-791-7446; W www.mirage.com; 3400 S Las Vegas Blvd) is such a place. The $730-million megaresort enraptures guests in its tropical setting, replete with a huge atrium filled with jungle foliage, picturesque cascades and meandering creeks. Woven into this waterscape are scores of bromeliads enveloped in sunlight and moistened by a computerized misting system.

Circling most of the atrium is a Polynesian-themed casino that incorporates the unique design concept of placing gaming areas under separate roofs to invoke a feeling of intimacy. Tropical plants add to the splendor of the elegant casino. The registration area features an awesome 20,000-gallon aquarium that's filled with sharks, pufferfish, angelfish and other tropical fish. World-famous illusionists Siegfried & Roy perform in a theater designed just for them. Nearby is a spacious open-air enclosure where white tigers play. Special slanted glass permits gamblers a glare-free view of the big cats, which are rotated among several lovely habitats throughout the day. The Mirage features an elite collection of fine boutiques presenting men's and women's sports, casual and formal wear. Fine dining is available in five international restaurants. Family dining is featured in four additional restaurants, including a 24-hour coffee shop. At the front, a lagoon contains a faux volcano that erupts with a roar, steam and fireballs every 15 minutes from 6pm until midnight. Few people leave The Mirage unimpressed.

Secret Garden of Siegfried & Roy Illusionists Siegfried & Roy and their white tigers have been performing most nights to sell-out crowds in a theater adjacent to The Mirage's casino since their debut in 1989. How the men spend their days is anyone's guess, but the big cats can almost always be found at one of four locations, including the Secret Garden behind the casino. There, visitors can expect to see a black jaguar, snow leopard, white lions, white tigers, orange tigers and an Asian elephant named Gildah. The cats are among the 50-plus felines owned by Siegfried & Roy, some of which are used in the duo's extraordinarily popular show. Cats are nocturnal animals, which means they don't move about much during the day. Since the Secret Garden is closed at night, the best time to visit is late afternoon. It's then that the cats start thinking about dinner and are most alert, often chasing one another and otherwise being frisky.

Audio guides are available free of charge, and there's a gift shop selling lots of Siegfried & Roy souvenirs. The price of admission allows visitors access to the adjacent Dolphin Habitat, which consists of two huge pools in which eight bottle-nosed dolphins spend their days swimming, leaping and interacting with their keepers. Be sure to visit the underwater viewing rooms, where you can get the best look at the playful small-toothed whales (yes, dolphins are whales). The Secret Garden and Dolphin Habitat *(☎ 702-791-1111; adult/ child under 10 years $10/free; open 11am-4:30pm Mon, Tues, Thur & Fri, 10am-5pm Sat & Sun)* keep later hours during summer. Children under 10 years of age must be accompanied by an adult.

Monte Carlo

The Monte Carlo hotel-casino *(☎ 702-730-7000, 800-311-8999; W www.monte-carlo .com; 3770 S Las Vegas Blvd)* is a joint venture between the owners of Bellagio and Circus Circus. The product reflects the European elegance of the former and the entertainment orientation of the latter. The resort, which debuted in June 1996 at a cost of $344 million, is fronted by Corinthian colonnades, triumphal arches, dancing fountains and allegorical statuary. A gorgeous entryway opens onto a bustling and tastefully appointed casino, just as you'd expect from an establishment trying to reproduce the grandeur of its namesake in Monaco.

Behind the casino stands a stately tower containing 3002 guestrooms and a magnificent marble-floored, crystal-chandeliered lobby, evocative of a European grand hotel. Palladian windows behind the registration desk overlook the hotel's 2½-acre pool area, replete with a 5000-sq-ft wave pool for body surfing, an artificial river for tubing, waterfalls and swimming pools. Other amenities include a unisex styling salon, a full-service spa, a fully equipped exercise room and lighted tennis courts; ah, but these things are only for guests. Open to everyone is a shopping concourse (see the Shopping chapter), seven restaurants, and a spacious casino with 97 table games, 2092 slot machines, a high-limit gaming area and a race and sports book. For entertainment, Monte Carlo presents the excellent **Lance Burton: Master Magician** (see the Entertainment chapter for details), who is believed by many to be the best illusionist in Vegas. Monte Carlo is definitely worth a look.

New York-New York

New York-New York hotel-casino *(☎ 702-740-6969, 800-693-6763; W www.nyny hotelcasino.com; 3790 S Las Vegas Blvd)* is a $485-million must-see. Its facade re-creates the Manhattan skyline, complete with 12 New York–style skyscrapers. These interconnected structures are approximately one-third of the actual size of New York City's architecture. The tallest tower replicates the Empire State Building at 529ft (47 stories). Other icons include a 150ft replica of the Statue of Liberty; a Coney Island–style roller coaster called Manhattan Express; a 300ft-long (or one-fifth size) replica of the Brooklyn Bridge; and replicas of the Chrysler,

AT&T and CBS buildings. Design elements throughout the property also reflect the history, color and diversity of Manhattan. The 84,000-sq-ft casino is a true marvel of design. Its 71 gaming tables and 2400 slots are set against a rich backdrop of famous New York landmarks, and its race and sports book offers electronic satellite wagering.

Ringing most of the stunning casino is a wide array of restaurants and retail shops behind colorful facades that resemble businesses found along Park Avenue, in Greenwich Village and at Times Square. **The Bar at Times Square**, which features live 'dueling pianos' each evening, is particularly popular with the thirtysomething crowd (see the Entertainment chapter). **Coyote Ugly**, a bar and dance saloon that takes its cue from the movie of the same name, opened in late 2001 and has been popular ever since (see the Entertainment chapter). The attention to detail at New York-New York is remarkable, down to the whiffs of steam that rise from the faux sewer covers along the path to the Chrysler elevator. Not only that, this version of New York can be just as, or even more, crowded with tourists: for instance, whereas a mere 178,000 pedestrians stride Manhattan's Brooklyn Bridge annually, more than 5 million people each year cross Las Vegas' Brooklyn Bridge. New York-New York claims to be the 'greatest city in Las Vegas.' The folks at The Venetian, The Orleans and Paris-Las Vegas beg to differ. Decide for yourself. You'll have great fun in the process.

Manhattan Express Within New York-New York is the Coney Island Emporium, a family entertainment center that re-creates the aura of the Coney Island amusement park in the early 1900s. The 28,000-sq-ft facility features the latest arcade attractions, but the *pièce de résistance* is **Manhattan Express** *(ME; rides $8; open 10am-10pm Sun-Thur, 10am-11pm Fri & Sat)*. ME is the world's first roller coaster to feature a heartline twist-and-dive maneuver, and only the second heartline coaster to operate in the world. For the uninitiated, a 'heartline roll' is similar to the sensation felt by a pilot during a barrel roll in a fighter plane, when the center of rotation actually becomes the same as the passenger's center of gravity. In the twist-and-dive portion of the 230-second ride, the train rolls 180 degrees, suspending its riders 86ft above the casino roof, before diving directly under itself. To embark on the hair-raising ride, board one of the five four-car, 16-passenger trains from inside the casino. The train's first move is to ascend 203ft. Height and speed characterize the first half of the ride. The initial drop of 75ft is just a warm-up for the 55-degree, 144ft, 67mph second drop that passes within a few feet of the hotel's valet entrance. Continuing beside Tropicana Blvd, the train ascends to 152ft above street level, banks left, and then climbs onto the casino roof. Here, riders encounter a dizzying succession of high-banked turns, camel-back hills, a vertical loop, a 540-degree spiral, and finally, the sensational heartline twist and dive. As the train nears the end of its 4777ft of track, the coaster disappears through the casino roof and returns to the station. Riders must be at least 54 inches tall.

Paris-Las Vegas

Like so many Las Vegas hotel-casinos, the $785-million, 34-story Paris-Las Vegas *(☎ 702-946-7000, 888-266-5687, fax 702-967-3836; ⓦ www.parislasvegas.com; 3645 S Las Vegas Blvd)* strives to capture the essence of an international, exotic locale by re-creating its landmarks – in this case, fine likenesses of the Arc de Triomphe, Champs-Élysées, Paris Opera House, Parc Monceau and even the Seine River. The signature attraction of the resort, like the signature attraction of the French capital, is a 50-story (half-scale) Eiffel Tower, where visitors can dine in a gourmet restaurant overlooking The Strip or travel in a glass elevator to an **observation deck** *(adult/child 6-12 years/child 5 years & under $9/7/free; 10am-midnight daily)* for a panoramic view of Las Vegas Valley. Just how authentic is the tower? Gustave Eiffel's original drawings were used to re-create this Eiffel Tower. The Vegas version is welded together rather than riveted like the original, but the designers added cosmetic rivets to the tower for authenticity.

Also unlike the original, the Paris-Las Vegas landmark is fireproof and able to withstand a major earthquake. Paris-Las Vegas is adjacent to Bally's and the two are connected by an extension of the Rue de la Paix, a Parisian street known among jet-setters for its chi-chi French boutiques and restaurants. Paris-Las Vegas features no fewer than 11 French restaurants and 31,500 sq ft of upscale French retail shopping set along quaint cobblestone streets and winding alleyways. Surrounded by street scenes of Paris, the 85,000-sq-ft casino contains 100 table games, 2200 slots and a race and sports book. Le Cabaret Lounge features live French- and English-style entertainment, while Napoleons showcases jazz and popular-music bands nightly.

Riviera

The Riviera (☎ 702-734-5110, 800-634-6753, fax 702-794-9451; W www.theriviera.com; 2901 S Las Vegas Blvd) was the first high-rise on The Strip, rising to a then-impressive nine floors when it opened on April 30, 1955, with Liberace doing the ribbon-cutting honors and Joan Crawford delivering opening remarks. The hotel-casino has been renovated numerous times over the years and today boasts one of the largest casinos in the world (albeit a dimly lit and confusing one) at an even 100,000 sq ft. When the Riviera opened, it contained a mere 18 gaming tables and 116 slot machines. Today, it has 1576 slots and video machines, 21 blackjack tables, four craps tables, two roulette wheels, a keno lounge, a wheel of fortune, and race and sports books; there's also one baccarat, two Pai Gow poker, Sic-Bo, two Caribbean stud and five poker tables. There are several dozen retail shops on the premises, a handful of restaurants (not including a fast-food center called Mardi Gras Food Court) and a lounge with nightly entertainment. One thing to keep in mind about this surprisingly popular hotel-casino is that it's got spicy ads all over the place for its three adult-theme shows, **Crazy Girls**, **Splash**, and **An Evening at La Cage**. If you don't want little Johnny or Suzy seeing some butt-glorified ads, don't bring them into the hotel-casino. The ads are pretty hard to miss.

Sahara

Along with the Stardust and a couple of downtown hotel-casinos, Sahara (☎ 702-737-2111, 888-696-2121, fax 702-791-2027; W www.saharavegas.com; 2535 S Las Vegas Blvd) is one of the few old-Vegas resorts to have survived ownership changes and an onslaught of keen competition from newer gaming houses. Over the years, Sahara has undergone many changes, some better than others. The marquee now features a gaudy caricature of a camel's face. The Sahara strengthened its Moroccan theme with a vastly improved Strip-side entrance that features several dozen royal palms, an arched dome with lots of marble, golden chandeliers, tiny dark-blue tiles and other Arabian Nights details. The Moroccan-desert theme continues inside, where the casino is guarded by a row of sultan statues.

The replacement of tack with elegance is very apparent to any longtime visitor. Improvements include gold-painted ceilings, molded columns laced with colorful vines and jeweled lattice-work soffits. Outside, toward the towers that contain more than 2000 guestrooms (which have been renovated as well), is a lovely 5000-sq-ft heated swimming pool adorned with Moroccan mosaic tiles and ringed by lots of tanning decks. There is also **Speed – The Ride** (rides/all-day unlimited pass $8/13; open noon-9pm Sun-Thur, noon-midnight Fri & Sat), an awesome roller coaster with a top speed of 70mph. If you make it to Sahara, be sure to pass by the resort's **Congo Room** to see who's performing; the Congo has showcased entertainers from Mae West to The Beatles since the Sahara first opened its doors in 1952, and it's continuing to draw big names.

Las Vegas Cyber Speedway The vastly improved Sahara is the brainchild of developer Bill Bennett. Soon after buying Sahara in 1995, Bennett decided Sahara could benefit from a state-of-the-art motion-based simulator attraction, and he called upon the wizards at Illusion Inc to create a field of Indy-car simulators so real they'd excite actual Formula 1 drivers. Illusion Inc, which developed the simulators that trained US

Keep an eye on Vegas' sharks; Mandalay Bay

The ups and downs of life at New York-New York

It's just like the real New York, only smaller; New York-New York

I just pulled it from a stone...

'Beam me up, Scotty, there's no intelligent life down here…' Starship Enterprise departs from the Hilton.

The Great Sphinx sees all at the Luxor

tank troops for Desert Storm, was up to the task. Two years and $15 million later they presented Speedworld, later renamed Las Vegas Cyber Speedway (☎ 702-737-2750; rides $8; open 10am-8pm Mon-Thur, 10am-10pm Fri & Sat). Cyber Speedway consists of 24 simulators at three-quarters of the size of actual Indy cars. Each of these faux racers is bolted to a computer-controlled hydraulic platform, and each is fronted by a 20ft, wrap-around screen that projects a virtual replica of the Las Vegas Motor Speedway. When the virtual-reality experience begins, drivers compete in a computer-synchronized race that's simply scary in its realism. When, for example, you turn your steering wheel too abruptly and begin sliding, unless you're able to regain control of your race car the image in front of you will quickly be one of a fast-approaching wall. If you brake hard to avoid it, your car will dip suddenly and speakers all around you will squeal with tires skidding. Most drivers exit their cars sweating and breathing heavily. They are then given a detailed printout showing individual lap record speeds, braking performances and assorted other factors. Pass on Cyber Speedway if you have a heart condition or suffer from motion sickness. It's that intense.

Stardust

When it was completed in 1958 at a cost of $10 million, the Stardust (☎ 702-732-6111, 800-634-6757, fax 702-732-6257; W www .stardustlv.com; 3000 S Las Vegas Blvd) was the most spectacular hotel-casino in town. With its 1065 guestrooms, it was also the world's largest resort complex (at least by room count). While the Dunes hotel-casino had brought bare-breasted showgirls to The Strip with its *Minsky Goes to Paris* revue, the day the Stardust opened, it brought actual French showgirls with its *Lido de Paris* revue, in a display of one-upmanship. No question about it, the Stardust was a 'real class joint' back then, as mobsters used to say. Today, *Lido de Paris* is gone and Stardust's entertainment consists chiefly of Wayne Newton and a stellar lineup of performers, including the great jazz-rock group

Chicago and comedians Don Rickles and Andrew 'Dice' Clay. Other quality acts appear in the Starlight Lounge. By sticking to its roots (Wayne is a throwback to the Vegas of old), Stardust has acted wisely; Stardust guests aren't, by and large, big fans of pop culture, but they are big fans of the Vegas of yesteryear. Stardust was also wise to keep its landmark 188ft starry sign, and not so long ago added a much-needed 1500-room tower and expanded its casino to 100,000 sq ft. Still, compared to new beauties such as The Venetian and Paris-Las Vegas, there's absolutely nothing spectacular about Stardust, except maybe for the high level of second-hand cigarette smoke that abounds in its casino. In terms of a theme, Stardust has a dull pseudo-tropical thing going on that's not much of a drawcard. Nevertheless, Stardust continues to see as much action as ever, thanks to its legendary status and the fact that its sign appears in every Vegas establishing shot called for by movie directors. For what it's worth, The Strip won't be the same when Stardust inevitably becomes Earth dust. Maybe that's reason enough to see it while you can.

Stratosphere Tower

Las Vegas has many buildings exceeding 20 stories, but only one tops 100 stories. At 1149ft, the white, three-legged Stratosphere Tower (☎ 702-380-7777, 800-998-6937, fax 702-383-5334; W www.stratosphere hotel.com; 2000 S Las Vegas Blvd) is the tallest building in the western US. At its base is a casino that's got all the usual trappings of a sprawling Vegas gaming room, but little in the way of a theme, and the several dozen retail shops one floor up leave a lot to be desired. However, it's what's atop the elegantly tapered $550-million tower that people have been coming to see since it opened in 1996, and here you'll find a revolving restaurant, a circular bar, an indoor viewing deck and above it an outdoor viewing deck, affording spectacular views in all directions. To get you there, the Stratosphere has the fastest elevators in America: they ascend and descend at 20.5mph, or about three times the speed of regular elevators, taking

THINGS TO SEE & DO

Las Vegas Free & Fun

Some of the best things in Vegas don't cost nothin'. If you're counting your copper coinage for the penny slots, it may interest you to know that many of Sin City's best attractions are also free.

- **Battle for Buccaneer Bay** High-seas hijinks have never been so much fun to watch.
- **Brilliant Light Show** When the Fremont Street Experience is on, all eyes look toward heaven.
- **Gold & $1 Million** Golden Nugget has a mega-nugget and Binion's Horseshoe flashes big cash.
- **Lofty Lounge Acts** Every major hotel-casino has got them, and most are excellent entertainers.
- **Mardi Gras Celebrations** In Rio's Masquerade Village several times a day, six days a week.
- **Roar like a Lion** Roar with MGM Grand's signature animal at its amusing Lion Habitat.
- **Shrine to Rock Stars** Hard Rock's casino is a temple to the gods and goddesses of rock 'n' roll.
- **Spectacular Floral Arrangements** Flower lovers will appreciate Bellagio's lobby and casino.
- **Stage Performances** Acrobats, animals and clowns at Circus Circus, court jesters at Excalibur.
- **Tigers and a Volcano** The Mirage is a feast for the eyes and ears. That's the volcano rumbling.
- **Up with Nature** The Flamingo's 15 acres of gardens and Tropicana's Wildlife Walk.
- **Window Shopping** Million-dollar necklaces in Bellagio's shops and high fashion at Caesars.

you 108 floors in a mere 37 ear-popping seconds. Once you've recovered from that ride, head for the world's highest roller coaster, just above the outdoor observation area. Just how high is the High Roller? A whopping 110 stories! And rising above that thrill ride is a second, the Big Shot consists of 16 completely exposed, outward-facing seats that zip up and down the steel spire that forms the pinnacle of the tower. The Big Shot is like a glass elevator, only there's no glass, and riders are strapped into plastic seats instead of standing. On top of that, instead of ascending and descending at a barely discernible speed, the Big Shot rockets riders 160ft in 2.5 seconds, producing a blood-rushing, fighter-aircraft-mimicking four Gs of force. Leave it to Las Vegas to reduce Disneyland to kid's stuff. The **rides** *(people over/under 3 years return $7/free, tower & High Roller $5, tower & Big Shot $8, tower & High Roller & Big Shot $20; open 10am-1am Sun-Thur, 10am-2am Fri & Sat)* do not operate when there's strong wind or rain. Not to be forgotten, the Stratosphere has two good production shows: **American Superstars** and **Viva Las Vegas** (see the Entertainment chapter). And, new in 2001, the resort added a 3606-seat outdoor events center that features rock concerts and championship boxing.

Treasure Island

Although the officials at Treasure Island (☎ 702-894-7111, 800-944-7444, fax 702-894-7446; ⓦ www.treasureisland.com; 3300 S Las Vegas Blvd) insist the theme of their hotel-casino is strictly 'elegant Caribbean hideaway,' the similarities between it and Disneyland's famous Pirates of the Caribbean ride are too great to be coincidental. The mock sea battle that takes place at Treasure Island's entryway is ripped straight from Disneyland's how-to book of popular attractions – and that's not necessarily a bad thing, if you're young at heart. From The Strip, the pirate-themed resort announces its presence with a 60ft-high skull-and-crossbones sign. Coming from Las Vegas Blvd, visitors enter Treasure Island via a drawbridge-style approach that spans artificial Buccaneer Bay, beside which is a replica of an 18th-century sea village. In the bay, two ships – a pirate vessel and a British frigate – set the stage for scheduled mock sea battles. The pirate theme continues inside the resort, with black carpeting emblazoned with colorful images of gold coins, enormous jewels, and the like. The walls and ceilings of the casino are covered with paintings of piracy. The casino's one-armed bandits (slot machines) are tightly grouped, but no-one seems to mind – the sprawling, 75,000-sq-ft casino with 2002 slots and 82 gaming tables is usually packed. Equally popular is Treasure Island's awesome production show, **Mystère**, which is performed by the French-Canadian performing troupe Cirque du Soleil (see the Entertainment chapter). Numerous restaurants such as the popular Lookout Café and a shopping promenade with stores such as Damsels in Dis'Dress are very popular. It's hard not to be swept away by Treasure Island. Easing the journey there or away is a monorail ride to The Mirage, which shares a 100-acre site with Treasure Island.

Cool Pools

If you intend to spend much of your time in town at poolside, it might interest you to know that Las Vegas is home to some truly spectacular swimming pools, which are open to guests during spring and summer. The following are among the better ones.

- **Garden of the Gods** With its gorgeous lawns, its Corinthian columns, magnificent palms and marble-inlaid pools, Caesar Palace's stately Garden is a divine sight to behold.
- **Goony Over Lagoons** At The Mirage, guests can explore the wandering, interconnected lagoons on foot or submerged.
- **Mandalay Beach** Mandalay Bay's wave pool features 1700 tons of sand, 1.6 million gallons of water and waves large enough to support surfing competitions. Need we say more?
- **Oahu, Vegas-style** Hard Rock Hotel's très hip pool area features a crater-like swim hole with sandy beaches, piped-in underwater music and a jungle of lush vegetation.
- **Taste of the Tropics** For tropically landscaped grounds, head to Tropicana, home of a 12,000-sq-ft pool ringed by a lagoon, a picturesque waterfall and 60 varieties of trees.

Battle for Buccaneer Bay A full-scale battle between Treasure Island's pirates and British naval officers takes place no fewer than five times a day at Buccaneer Bay, located between The Strip and the resort's can't-miss casino. From the road you'll spy the two wooden ships and the nearby viewing platforms for bystanders, and like the volcanic eruptions at The Mirage, no tickets are needed for the show, which involves 30 stunt performers and actors, and a hefty amount of gunpowder. Just saunter up to the viewing area and watch the drama unfold. It all begins when the British frigate, the HMS *Brittania*, rounds Skull Point and spies the pirate ship *Hispaniola* unloading its booty. Great pirate antics and a spectacular pyrotechnic war ensues, including cannon shots that snap a mast, set buildings aflame and force combatants on both sides to hurl themselves into the sea. Showtimes are 4pm, 5:30pm, 7pm, 8:30pm and 10pm, Sunday through Thursday, with an additional performance at 11:30pm Friday and Saturday.

Tropicana

Built in 1957, the Tropicana hotel-casino (☎ 702-739-2222, 888-826-8767, fax 702-739-2469; ⓦ www.tropicanalv.com; 3801 S Las Vegas Blvd) has had lots of time to lose its luster, lose its crowds and go the way of the Dunes and the Sands – ashes to ashes, dust to dust. Instead, after more than 40 years, the Tropicana has never looked better. Thanks to a major renovation in 1995, the Trop's entryway resembles a festive Caribbean village, sporting two three-story likenesses of Maori gods, a waterfall, a lagoon, outrigger canoes and a Polynesian longhouse that often hosts Hawaiian musicians. The tropical-paradise theme virtually disappears in the casino, except for a few flower prints and a few exotic plants here and there. Still, the casino is roomy, bright and otherwise appealing. The resort's 1900 recently remodeled rooms reside in two towers, between which are five acres of swimming pools, five spas, a 110ft waterslide, thousands of tropical plants, a lovely waterfall and two lagoons that are home to flamingos, swans and ducks. A very popular section of the Tropicana is **Wildlife Walk**, which is a wide, elevated hallway with views of the pools and gardens below. At one end of the walk, resting in a little inside garden of their own, is a clutch of exotic birds, including a blue-and-gold macaw, an umbrella cockatoo, a green macaw and a sulfur-crested cockatoo, among others. Entertainment offered at the Trop includes the long-running production show **Folies Bergère**, the Comedy Shop comedy club and the **Casino Legends Hall of Fame**. Pedestrian skywalks link the Tropicana with MGM Grand, Excalibur and Luxor.

Casino Legends Hall of Fame The 'World's Largest and Most Unique Gambling Museum' *(admission $4; open 7am-9pm daily)* lives up to its billing, offering

---

Size Matters

In Vegas, size matters. Here are some current records Vegas holds.

- **World's biggest hotel** MGM Grand, with 5032 rooms
- **World's largest atrium** Luxor
- **World's biggest gold nugget** Hand of Faith at the Golden Nugget
- **World's highest roller coaster** High Roller at the Stratosphere
- **World's first heartline roller coaster** Manhattan Express at New York-New York
- **World's largest public wine collection** The Wine Cellar at Rio
- **World's most powerful beacon** Luxor
- **World's largest race and sports book** Las Vegas Hilton
- **World's largest carved emerald** The 430-carat carved Moghul Indian Emerald at the Fred Leighton store inside Bellagio
- **North America's largest bowling alley** Showboat
- **Fastest elevator in the United States** Stratosphere
- **Tallest building in the western United States** Stratosphere

---

terrific value and a wonderful trip down memory lane for Vegas old-timers. Here, you'll marvel at the attention to detail paid to a recreation of a showgirl's dressing room, you'll hear rare interviews with Vegas notables, watch a captivating video of megaresorts exploding, gaze upon some classic photographs of legendary Vegas performers, and scan more than 8000 gambling chips in denominations ranging from $0.01 to $100,000. This is a must-see for history buffs and Vegas lovers alike.

The Venetian

A gondola-filled lagoon and full-scale reproductions of Venetian landmarks abound at The Venetian *(☎ 702-414-1000, 888-283-6423, fax 702-733-5190; W www.venetian .com; 3355 S Las Vegas Blvd)*. Graceful arched bridges, actual flowing canals, vibrant piazzas and welcoming stone walkways really do capture the spirit of Venice in faithful detail. Sheldon Adelson broke ground with this $1.5-billion, 35-story megaresort shortly after closing the 44-year-old Sands Hotel Casino in 1996. The Venetian is being developed in two phases on the old Sands site – Phase 1 opened in 1999 with 3036 roomy suites, an elegant 120,000-sq-ft casino and a 500,000-sq-ft shopping area known as the Grand Canal Shoppes. The casino is linked to the 1.15-million-sq-ft Sands Expo and Convention Center, which features state-of-the-art facilities located at the heart of the ever-popular Strip. This fantastic hotel-casino also has a large health spa and fitness club, 15 restaurants, and two Guggenheim museums. The **Guggenheim Hermitage** *(☎ 702-414-2440; adult/student/child 6-12 years $15/ 11/7; open 9am-11pm daily)* features rare artworks from both the Guggenheim in New York and the State Hermitage Museum in St Petersburg, Russia; and, the **Guggenheim Las Vegas** *(☎ 702-414-2440; adult/student/child 6-12 years $15/11/7; open 9am-11pm daily)*, features annual exhibits.

Phase 2 of The Venetian's construction, which was scheduled for completion in late 2000 but postponed indefinitely when the US economy tanked, will add 3000 more suites to the site. With more than 6000 suites in all,

The Venetian will be the world's largest hotel. Even if you've had the good fortune of strolling the cobblestone pathways and plying the romantic canals of the one-and-only Venice, you won't want to miss the Las Vegas version. In a city filled with spectacles, this is surely one of the most spectacular.

Wet 'n' Wild

The coolest place on The Strip during the hot period is the 26-acre Wet 'n' Wild water park (☎ 702-871-7811; W www.wetnwild.com; 2601 S Las Vegas Blvd; adult/child 3-10 years/child under 3 years $25/20/free; open 10am-6pm daily, May-Sept). Wet 'n' Wild offers kids and adults alike more than a dozen slides, chutes and floats refreshed by 1.5 million gallons of constantly filtered water. You may have made a splash at a water park before, but it's unlikely you've ever been to one like this. Among the many attractions are **Raging Rapids**, a simulated white-water rafting adventure on a 500ft-long river; **Blue Niagara**, a dizzying six-story descent inside intertwined looping tubes; **Willy Willy**, a monstrous whirlpool that propels riders around and around on inner tubes in a circular pool; **Surf Lagoon**, a 500,000-gallon wave pool that's popular with body surfers; **Bomb Bay**, a bomblike enclosure 76ft in the air that sends its occupants on a vertical flight into a sparkling pool target; and **Banzai Banzai**, a rollercoaster-like ride in which riders atop plastic sleds swoosh down a chute at a 45-degree angle into a pool, where they skip like stones for more than 100ft. There is a leisurely float trip as well, but most of what Wet 'n' Wild has to offer was designed for the wild, not the mild. The park has plenty of food concessions and even a swimwear store. Open hours often stretch to 8pm or later during heat waves.

World of Coca-Cola

The official museum of the world's leading soft-drink maker, World of Coca-Cola (☎ 702-597-3122; 3769 S Las Vegas Blvd; adult/child under 6 years $7/free; open 10am-midnight Sun-Thur, 10am-1am Fri & Sat) is an excellent attraction that takes the visitor well beyond who invented Coke and why (which in itself is pretty interesting stuff). You will not be privy to the Coca-Cola recipe – the exact ingredients and process used in making Coca-Cola is a closely guarded secret. Only five people are in the know, and the only written record of how to make the sweet dark syrup that's at the heart of the beverage is kept in a vault in Atlanta. Among the many displays at the World of Coca-Cola is a counter where a soda jerk stirs up a glass of Coca-Cola the old-fashioned way. There are also human-sized (and bigger) samples of Coca-Cola bottle art from international competitions; a theater where guests can watch Coca-Cola commercials from the 1950s, '60s and '70s; Coca-Cola advertisements from the 1930s; beautiful Coca-Cola refrigerators; and early bottle-dispensing machines. At the sampling station, visitors can try 30 beverages produced by the Coca-Cola Company worldwide, including Krest Ginger Ale from Mozambique, Guaraná Tai from Brazil, and Lychee Mello from Thailand. The requisite gift shop contains *lots* of high-quality Coca-Cola promotional products, such as black leather jackets with an eye-catching Coca-Cola Las Vegas patch on the back. The museum is a very pleasant surprise.

EAST OF THE STRIP
Hard Rock Café & Hotel

The Hard Rock Café & Hotel (☎ 702-693-5000, 800-473-7625, fax 702-693-5010; W www.hardrockhotel.com; 4455 Paradise Rd) is the world's first rock 'n' roll casino, and it includes the most impressive collection of rock memorabilia ever assembled under one roof. The facility consists of a restaurant and a hotel-casino, with several acres of free parking in between. The restaurant varies little from Hard Rocks scattered across the planet, but the hotel-casino is really something special. The entryway opens up to a roomy circular casino around which you find bars, a concert hall, a bank, a sports book and a retail store. Throughout the hotel-casino are the clothes, tools and toys of rock stars. Among the priceless memorabilia: concert attire worn by Elvis,

Madonna and Prince; a drum kit used by Alex Van Halen; a custom motorcycle that was originally owned by the Hell's Angels and donated by Nikki Sixx of Mötley Crüe; a 5m-by-3m display case filled with Beatles memorabilia; dozens of jackets and guitars formerly owned by the biggest names in rock 'n' roll; and Jim Morrison's handwritten lyrics to one of The Doors' greatest hits, 'The Changeling.' The list could fill 10 pages, and each item is smartly displayed. Grab a hotel-casino guide and foldout map, containing detailed information about every piece of memorabilia on the premises, from the reception desk. This place is a must-see for rock 'n' rollers.

Las Vegas Hilton

The enormous popularity of the Las Vegas Hilton (☎ 702-732-5111, 888-732-7117, fax 702-732-5790; ⓦ www.lvhilton.com; 3000 Paradise Rd) with business travelers is in no small part due to its proximity to the Convention Center. Being off The Strip, it does not attract nearly as many glassy-eyed slot jockeys and slobby low-rollers as the casinos on Las Vegas Blvd. The casino, which has been used in many films including *Diamonds Are Forever* and *Indecent Proposal*, is roomy and tastefully appointed; there's nothing phony about the Austrian-crystal chandeliers or the Italian-marble columns. Off to one side is the $17-million **SuperBook**, the largest race and sports book in the world. **The Nightclub** at the Las Vegas Hilton hosts numerous big-name performers (see the website for a calendar of upcoming acts). Out-of-this-world entertainment is on the ground floor of the Hilton's North Tower; that's where you'll find the $70-million interactive attraction **Star Trek: The Experience**.

The Las Vegas Hilton has a number of fine restaurants, including one that specializes in seafood, another in French cuisine and a third in gourmet Chinese. There's an 8-acre rooftop recreation deck that features a heated pool and a spacious whirlpool spa. A health club on the 3rd floor offers steam rooms, saunas, treadmills and tanning booths, along with weight training equipment and cardiovascular facilities. A massage, manicure, facial and/or body wrap is a phone call away. No wonder so many guests view the Hilton as mixing business with pleasure.

Star Trek: The Experience The highlight of *Star Trek: The Experience* (☎ 702-732-5111; ⓦ www.startrekexp.com; motion-simulator rides $25; casino & bar open 24hr, voyages 11am-11pm) is a 22-minute motion-simulated voyage through space at warp speed aboard – what else? – the starship *Enterprise*. The attraction also includes a complete re-creation of the promenade from *Star Trek: Deep Space Nine*, where guests can dine in Quark's Bar & Restaurant, choose from the largest selection of *Star Trek* merchandise in the known universe, and even converse with a variety of interplanetary visitors. State-of-the-art video games are also on the premises. Did I mention gambling? The gateway to *Star Trek: The Experience* is the 20,000-sq-ft, very futuristic SpaceQuest Casino, where guests step aboard a simulated spaceship that is constantly circling the Earth from an orbit of 1500 miles. The focal points of this casino in space are three 10ft-by-24ft 'space windows' above the gaming area, which create the illusion of a genteel passage around our happy planet. There's no cost to enter the casino, to investigate the *Star Trek* merchandise or to saunter up to Quark's Bar and be treated just like any other Earthling. The motion-simulation ride begins with a really cool museum-like exhibit featuring authentic *Star Trek* costumes, weaponry, makeup, special effects and props used in the four *Star Trek* television series and eight motion pictures. Be advised that if you suffer from motion sickness, the motion-simulation ride is instead your ticket to Puke City.

Liberace Museum

Known and loved throughout the world as 'Mr Showmanship,' Liberace was honored during his lifetime with two Emmy Awards, six gold records (each signifying 1 million in record sales) and two stars on the Hollywood Walk of Fame. Following his death in

1987, the late great entertainer was posthumously honored with the creation of this off-Strip museum (☎ 702-798-5595; Ⓦ www.liberace.org; 1774 E Tropicana Ave; adult/child $12/8; open 10am-5pm Mon-Sat, 1pm-5pm Sun), which houses the most outrageous rhinestone-studded costumes and some of the most ornate cars you'll ever see. While audiences enjoyed listening to Liberace's exuberant keyboard artistry, they were also amazed and amused by his outlandish style. Liberace's favorite stage pianos are not to be missed – a rhinestone-encrusted Baldwin and a concert grand covered in mirror squares are a visual feast. Many rare pianos are on display as well; among them are a hand-painted Pleyel on which Chopin played, and a Chickering grand once owned by George Gershwin. Liberace's car gallery includes a hand-painted red, white and blue Rolls-Royce convertible, a Rolls-Royce clad entirely in mirror tiles, and a 1934 Mercedes Excalibur covered in Austrian rhinestones. Among the many pieces of outlandish jewelry on display is Liberace's trademark candelabra ring, complete with platinum 'candlesticks' and diamond 'flames.' Many visitors favor the Liberace wardrobe exhibit, where feathered capes, rhinestone-studded costumes, and million-dollar furs make for fun viewing. The Liberace Museum is a Las Vegas must-do.

San Remo

The often-overlooked San Remo hotel-casino (☎ 702-739-9000, 800-522-7366, fax 702-736-1120; Ⓦ www.sanremolasvegas.com; 115 E Tropicana Ave) is a great find for party-hearty budget-conscious gamblers. While the San Remo isn't quite on The Strip, it's only a short walk from it. Its convenient location – behind the Tropicana, across the street from the MGM Grand and a hop, skip and a jump from the Bellagio and Caesars Palace – is one of its attractions. Many Vegas regulars like to stay at the San Remo because it's in the thick of things, yet the room rates are generally much less than those on The Strip, and the lovely swimming pool out back is heated all year. The San

---

Marriages Made in Heaven

Heaven might not be your word choice, but 'Marriages Made in Las Vegas' definitely doesn't have the same magical ring to it. Then again, there must be something magical about it, since more than 300 couples a day tie the knot in Sin City.

The reasons people cite for getting hitched here are countless, but the low licensing fee ($35) and the absence of waiting-period and blood-test requirements are often mentioned. The services themselves can range in quality from a 10-minute drive-thru to a big 'do' at a hotel-casino (12 resorts contain wedding chapels).

If you're thinking of 'making it official' in Las Vegas and want to know what's required, call the **County Clerk's Office** (☎ 702-455-3156, 200 S 3rd St). Be advised that New Year's Eve and Valentine's Day are crush times for Vegas wedding chapels; plan ahead if you want to have your big day on either of these days.

Among the scores of celebrity couples who have exchanged vows in Las Vegas are Whoopi Goldberg and David Claessen, Jon Bon Jovi and Dorothea Hurley, Melanie Griffith and Don Johnson, Richard Gere and Cindy Crawford, Bruce Willis and Demi Moore, and Clint Eastwood and Dina Ruiz.

Remo's medium-size casino isn't much to look at – it has low ceilings, a bad floral theme, gaudy chandeliers and lots of second-hand smoke – but (and this is a big *but*) the San Remo pours free champagne in the slot areas around-the-clock, has a two-for-one drink deal from 4pm to 6pm daily, and its slot club is one of the most generous in the city. Given these alcoholic and budgetary attractions, it's easy to see why so many people overlook the cheap flower murals and claustrophobic ceiling. Of course, if you feel the need to breathe, a few minutes out by the pool will usually set you right. Not only is the pool ringed by mature palm trees and a flowering desert landscape, but when it's hot out, frozen drinks are brought to you poolside.

WEST OF THE STRIP
Elvis-A-Rama Museum

You'd think a museum devoted to The King would simply be 'too much,' but that's not the case with Elvis-A-Rama (☎ 702-309-7200, fax 702-307-3584; W www.elvisarama.com; 3401 Industrial Rd; adult/child 12 years & under $10/free; open 10am-6pm daily). There are 2000 personal items that once belonged to that big hunk o' love, for which the museum's fanatical owner paid a whopping $5 million. On display are such nifty collectibles as Presley's army uniform, a love letter to a girlfriend, his little black book of phone numbers, even his Social Security card.

Unfortunately, all too often the items aren't accompanied by information signs and their significance is anything but obvious. Moreover, there's very little history on display about the man who sang so wonderfully about hound dogs, teddy bears and a certain hard-headed woman; it's assumed you knew all about his life when you walked in, which is a big assumption. The stuff on display is pretty cool, that's for sure, but suspicious minds are left muttering in the dark too often. The lack of information gets a lot of visitors all shook up. They look around the museum and feel it's now or never, and they see plenty of The King's good luck charms, but the lack of context leaves many visitors with a feeling of surrender. If you picked up on the 15 references in this paragraph to number-one hits of the man who popularized 'Jailhouse Rock' and 'Don't,' you'll probably leave Elvis-A-Rama sated. If you didn't note at least 10 of the references, well, hopefully you won't be lonesome tonight or otherwise feel a need to be loved tenderly. The cost of admission includes a 15-minute Elvis impersonator show, held seven times a day.

Gold Coast

The chief selling points of the Gold Coast hotel-casino (☎ 702-367-7111, 888-402-6278, fax 702-365-7505; W www.goldcoast casino.com; 4000 W Flamingo Rd) are its relatively inexpensive rooms, its 72-lane bowling center, 774-seat bingo parlor, and plain-but-high-ceilinged and easily navigated casino (which makes up in size what it lacks in decor). And while it might not be much, there are two features of the Spanish-facade Gold Coast casino you'll find at no other large casino in town: it has windows and it has more video poker machines than it has slot machines. You read it here first! A hit with visitors and locals alike are the Gold Coast's two no-cost lounges, which offer a variety of sounds from Dixieland jazz to rock 'n' roll, and its colossal Country & Western dance hall, the largest in Nevada. Bowlers will appreciate the Brunswick 2000 equipment and automatic scoring system at the bowling center, open 24 hours, which is a favorite of families. Amenities include a pro shop with instructor, bumper bowling for kiddies and a pizza parlor. Also popular with families are the Gold Coast's Twin Theaters, which show first-run movies (the popcorn is drenched with real butter!). The Gold Coast combats its distance from the ever-popular Strip by offering free shuttle service to and from its sister hotel, the Barbary Coast on Las Vegas Blvd; the service operates every 15 minutes from 9:30am to 12:30am daily.

The Orleans

One mile west of The Strip, The Orleans (☎ 702-365-7111, 800-675-3267, fax 702-365-7535; W www.orleanscasino.com; 4500 W Tropicana Ave) is a New Orleans–themed hotel-casino that has done only a so-so job of re-creating the Big Easy. Regardless, The Orleans has been a crowd-pleaser since it opened on 88 acres in 1997. Its popularity is due mostly to the fact that its room rates tend to be significantly lower than those at Strip-side hotels, but The Orleans isn't devoid of attractions either. Among its most popular are the 70-lane bowling alley, 14-plex movie theater, selection of seven restaurants, video arcade, swimming pool complex with a bubbling spa, and numerous specialty bars. The 112,000-sq-ft, first-floor casino consists of one bright and airy rectangular room with a high ceiling. On balconies along the edge of the room are costumed mannequins resembling Mardi Gras celebrants. On the casino floor are more than 2100 slot machines, 60 card tables, a 20-screen race and sports book, a 20-table poker room and a 60-seat keno lounge. Near the gaming area is the Bourbon Street Cabaret, which features free live entertainment nightly. There is also an 827-seat showroom that has spotlighted performers like Willie Nelson and Ray Charles. The decor at The Orleans isn't as magical as it could be, but in many minds its attractions more than make up for its visual shortcomings. The Orleans provides free shuttle service to and from The Strip and the airport.

The Palms

New in December 2001, the Palms hotel-casino (☎ 702-942-7777, 866-725-6773; ⓦ www.thepalmslasvegas.com; 4321 W Flamingo Rd) offers an eclectic mix of restaurants and bars, a spa and a salon, 14 movie theaters, the only off-Strip IMAX theater, an arcade and a 1200-seat showroom. The 95,000-sq-ft casino has 2400 slot machines, 55 table games, keno, poker and a race and sports book. Topping off its venues (literally) is **Ghost Bar**, located on the roof of a 40-story tower containing 455 guestrooms. Its upscale and smart, and the Ghost Bar provides a fantastic view back on The Strip. What's special about the Palms is that everything is done right, due in part to Raymond Visan, creator of the wonderful Buddha Bar in Paris, Andre Rochat, one of Las Vegas' most revered French restaurateurs, and other developers of the Palm's many venues.

No expense has been spared in the creation of this resort, which along with neighbors Rio and Gold Coast have combined to make a very appealing off-Strip district. Foodwise, Garduño's Mexican Restaurant, twice voted the Best Mexican Restaurant in the *Las Vegas Review-Journal's* annual poll, and Blue Agave Oyster & Chilé Bar offer the visitor lots of great eats (there are several other notable restaurants at the Palms as well). As for the theme – every Vegas hotel-casino has to have a theme, right? – the Palms really doesn't have one. Instead, there's a subtle, somewhat Mediterranean feel to the place that is very welcoming and unpretentious, and offers a nice detour from the gaudiness so often found in Vegas.

Rio

The name of this wildly popular hotel-casino says a lot about Rio (☎ 702-252-7777, 888-684-3746; ⓦ www.playrio.com; 3700 W Flamingo Rd), which offers only suites and has a Mardi Gras theme. The Rio is a strenuous walk from The Strip, and when it opened in January 1990, a lot of people thought it wouldn't survive. They said it was simply too far from Las Vegas Blvd, and tourists wouldn't make the effort. They were wrong. By 1997 the Rio was running so strong that its owners added a 41-story tower and the enormously festive **Masquerade Village**, which is now the center of the action and a big hit with tourists and locals. The 'village' occupies the first two floors of Rio's twin towers and offers a hearty mix of food, shopping and gaming choices, as well as loads of free entertainment, which all adds up to an ongoing party atmosphere. Occupying most of the village is a huge, 120,000-sq-ft casino decked out with a color-filled Rio-esque motif. The casino features 1710 slot machines, 71 table games, a poker room and a full-service race and sports book.

Ringing the ground-floor casino are two dozen upscale retail shops and the two best buffets in town – one offering international cuisine, the other seafood. Every even hour from 4pm to 10pm (except Wednesdays), sets modeled after Mardi Gras floats, and suspended from tracks in the ceiling, parade above the gaming tables; costumed performers dance on the floats and lip-synch to Motown songs. (Yes, Motown, and it *is* a bizarre choice.) Other performers simultaneously appear on a stage that rises from the casino's basement. There's no Ipanema at Rio, but guests will find a beach beside one of the resort's three pools. Fifty floors above the village, atop one of Rio's towers (and reached by an exhilarating glass elevator ride) is the VooDoo Lounge, which is a great place to enjoy a drink (see the Entertainment chapter for details). Also, one floor below the village, in an easy-to-overlook cellar, is the world's largest collection of fine wines (see the Shopping chapter). Not only that, Rio offers excellent evening entertainment with *The Scintas*, a terrific comedy/variety musical foursome (see the Entertainment chapter for details). In short, Rio's not on The Strip but it's well worth the trip. The free shuttle service to and from Harrah's, right on The Strip, makes it easy. A shuttle departs every 15 minutes, from 10am till 1am daily.

Scandia Family Fun Center

This family amusement center (☎ 702-364-0070; 2900 Sirius Ave; admission free; open 10am-11pm daily, occasionally later), a few blocks west of The Strip, features three 18-hole miniature-size golf courses, bumper boats, batting cages, midget Indy cars and more than 200 video arcade games. There is a variety of pricing plans from which to choose, including the Unlimited Wristband, which costs $16 and entitles its wearer to unlimited miniature golf, Lil' Indy Raceway rides and bumper boat rides, and 10 arcade tokens or 10 batting-cage tokens. The Super Saver option costs $11 and entitles the wearer to 18 holes of miniature golf, a Lil' Indy Raceway Ride, a bumper boat ride and five arcade tokens or five batting-cage tokens. Eighteen holes of miniature golf for the little one will set you back $6 (children 5 years of age and younger play for free with a paying adult). Turns at the Lil' Indy Raceway and the bumper-boat attraction cost $4 each (raceway drivers must be 54 inches tall; bumper boat drivers must be 46 inches tall). The batting cage has 18 automated pitching machines in all, tossing hardballs or softballs depending on the hitter's preference. The cost to use a machine is $1.25 for 25 pitches; discounts are available for 15, 30 and 60 minutes of use.

DOWNTOWN
Arts Factory Complex

Las Vegas' art scene received an enormous lift in June 1997 when commercial photographer Wes Isbutt, somewhat by accident, created the Arts Factory Complex (☎ 702-676-1111; W www.theartsfactory.com; 101-109 E Charleston Blvd). Isbutt was looking for space for his photographic business, **Studio West Photography** (☎ 702-383-3133; 107 E Charleston Blvd), when he came across a block-long 1940s structure that he liked.

Although he hadn't set out to establish an art colony in Las Vegas, that's exactly what he did. Isbutt bought the entire building and made most of its space available to local artists as well as galleries exhibiting works mostly by local artists. In a short time a burgeoning arts community developed. Today the building's two floors house several art galleries, an architecture firm, several individual artists' studios, two graphic design firms and other businesses, including a tattoo parlor. While the quality of some of the art is debatable, talent is clearly evident in many of the pieces on display. Anyone interested in art by Las Vegas residents or art of Las Vegas should definitely pay a visit to the Arts Factory Complex. The various businesses do not keep the same hours, and they frequently change (artists, you know). At the time of writing, most of the businesses were open noon till 5pm Monday, Tuesday, Thursday and Friday. You'd be wise to call ahead.

California

At many Vegas hotel-casinos, the lucky spin of the slot will earn you a new BMW Z3, a convertible Jaguar or a red-hot Dodge Viper. At the 'just-call-me-Cal' California (☎ 702-385-1222, 800-634-6255, fax 702-388-2610; W www.thecal.com; 12 E Ogden Ave), one very lucky nickel player will someday ride home in a – drumroll please – VW Beetle! That simple fact tells you a lot about the 781-room Cal, built in 1975 and lightly attired in tropical apparel – even the casino dealers wear Hawaiian shirts (mainly because 85% of the Cal's guests hail from Hawaii). In 1998, around the time the Bellagio opened a $300-million gallery of fine art (now gone) and Paris-Las Vegas broke ground on the world's second Eiffel Tower, the Cal issued a press release: 'Coin-free Penny Slots come to the Cal!' Beneath that banner headline appeared this riveting subhead: 'New multi-denominational machines bring lots of options.' Sure enough, on the mezzanine level of the Cal is a bank of penny slot machines that accept $1, $5, $10 and $20 bills. But wait, there's more! Instead of paying out a hopper full of coins, the Cal's newest slots pay in vouchers, which can be redeemed for cash at the change cage. Yippee! Okay, enough poking fun. Fact is, penny slots offer superior time-on value (the amount of time a player is able to stay on a machine with a small amount of money), and the Cal's casino, though small by Vegas standards, offers all the usual table games and has more than 1000 slots, video poker and video Keno machines. Few hotel-casinos can boast two $1-million-plus slot wins only a week apart; the Cal can. The Cal can also boast seven jackpots in only four days. Not very many casinos can claim that. There's nothing spectacular about the Cal, but it does make cents. Lots of cents.

Fremont

The legendary Fremont hotel-casino (☎ 702-385-3232, 800-634-6182, fax 702-385-6229; W www.fremontcasino.com; 200 E Fremont St) has been packin' 'em in since 1956, when it opened as downtown's first high-rise. Also separating it from the pack in 1956 was its wall-to-wall carpeting; at the time, every other downtown casino had sawdust-covered floors in its gaming area. It was here, too, that famous lounge singer Wayne Newton began his career (he's a fixture at Stardust these days). Despite these firsts, the Fremont has since slipped into mediocrity in most regards – its very good restaurants being the major exception. Like its sister hotel-casino, the California – both are owned by Boyd Gaming, which also owns Main Street Station and Stardust – it serves a large contingent of travelers from Hawaii, and has a weak tropical-island motif. The casino is nothing special, but its location at the heart of the Fremont Street Experience and its wide variety of gaming options has made it a favorite with many gamblers. The Fremont's casino covers 32,000 sq ft, which means that it's much smaller than those found on The Strip. There are more than 1000 machines to choose from at the Fremont, which features Keno and video poker machines. Most of the table games permit bets ranging from $20 to $1000. The slot lineup includes denominations ranging from 5¢ to $5. Although the casino is smoky, non-smoking tables are available.

Fremont Street Experience

Ten years ago, downtown Las Vegas had lost nearly all of its tourists to the rapidly developing Strip. With the opening of each new megaresort on Las Vegas Blvd, older downtown hotel-casinos such as Fitzgerald's, Golden Nugget and Binion's Horseshoe lost their luster. With no end to the development of The Strip in sight, something had to be done, or downtown was destined to become a ghost town (wandering homeless people not withstanding). The city and the area's businesses came up with a plan, which was realized in December 1995: a $70-million, five-block-long pedestrian mall called Fremont Street Experience that is topped by an arched steel canopy filled with computer-controlled lights. The canopy is 1386ft long and 90ft high, and it runs the length of Fremont St from Main St to Las Vegas Blvd; its belly is covered from edge to edge with no fewer than 2.1 million multi-colored lights, which are controlled by 31 computers. Suspended from the giant light board are 208 concert-quality speakers. Five times nightly (on the hour, every hour, from 8pm till midnight), the canopy becomes a six-minute light show enhanced by 540,000 watts of wrap-around sound and music.

When the lights come on, they usually stop people in their tracks. The shows are quite remarkable, as their 73 programmers have no fewer than 65,536 color combinations of light with which to be creative. Has it helped pick up business downtown? Absolutely. Although the casinos along Fremont St generally aren't as nice as the newer ones on The Strip, their proximity to one another is a real plus, and a misting system built into the canopy provides welcome relief on hot days.

Hand of Faith

No, Hand of Faith is not the title of a life-affirming religious group, nor is it a brand of dishwashing detergent. Rather, it's the name of the largest single gold nugget in the world, weighing a massive 61lb and 11oz. Along with another nugget weighing 13lbs and a treasury of 26 smaller chunks of the most valuable, ductile yellow metallic element known to humankind, Hand of Faith is on

Huge Nugget Found in Backyard

The 61lb Hand of Faith nugget on display at the Golden Nugget hotel-casino was found in October 1980 near Wedderburn, Australia, by a man using a metal detector. The man, who has chosen to remain anonymous, was prospecting behind the modest trailer home he shared with his wife and four children when he made the spectacular discovery. The meteor-resembling nugget was in a vertical position a mere six inches below the surface when it was found.

display under glass at, appropriately enough, the **Golden Nugget** (☎ 702-385-7111; 129 E Fremont St at 1st St). Although picture taking is generally not permitted in Las Vegas casinos for security reasons, the management of the Golden Nugget smiles upon visitors who snap away at the mighty rocks. And why not? It's not like any of the other casinos in town can claim to possess the heftiest hunk of gold ever found. Viewing is available 24 hours a day.

$1 Million in Cash

In the grand Las Vegas tradition of one-upmanship, Binion's Horseshoe hotel-casino (☎ 702-382-1600; 128 E Fremont St) responded to the Golden Nugget's display of precious yellow rocks by offering its visitors a chance to drool over $1 million in rare $10,000 bills. There are 100 of them in all, kept under glass in a display case shaped, appropriately enough, like a horseshoe. And guess what? You can take as many photographs of the money as you like; you just can't leave with any of it. However, you *could* leave the casino with your own million dollars, at least in theory: a no-limit gambling policy has been a fixture at Binion's for years. That's one of the reasons the blackjack tables are usually filled day and night. The horseshoe of cash is at the back of the ground-floor casino, to the right of the long bar. The casino is directly across Fremont St from the Golden Nugget, so you could see the gold and see the cash in just a matter of minutes.

Jackie Gaughan's Plaza

Built on the site of the old Union Pacific Railroad Depot, the Plaza (☎ 702-386-2110, 800-634-6575, fax 702-382-8281; W www .plazahotelcasino.com; 1 Main St) doesn't look like it's changed much since it opened in 1971. Like most hotel-casinos back then, its casino is jammed with slot and video machines – nearly 1600 in a 57,120-sq-ft area – and its decor is limited mostly to thousands of tiny recessed lights and mirrors designed to give the illusion of space. Also in the room are 19 blackjack tables, 12 poker tables, five craps tables, three roulette wheels, two keno lounges, minibaccarat, one Pai Gow poker table and a race and sports book. The decor doesn't seem to correspond to a theme, unless the theme is *cheap*. Even the chandeliers – and there are chandeliers – look cheap. And that's just fine with the Plaza's gamblers, many of whom are attracted to the casino because of its penny slots and $1 blackjack tables.

The Plaza's room rates are lower than most, and its location – at the western end of Fremont Street Experience – is ideal for an old-Vegas (pre-megaresort) casino like this one. The Greyhound bus depot is next door and the public train station is actually inside the Plaza, though it's been dormant since Amtrak stopped service to Las Vegas a few years back. Like most of the hotel-casinos downtown, the Plaza is intended for hardcore gamblers; it leaves the Parisian, Venetian and New York themes to others. Here, you'll find dealers and cocktail waitresses who treat people well. What the Plaza lacks in elegance, it makes up for in warmth and value. Which goes a long way in explaining why it's seemingly always filled with people.

Las Vegas Motor Speedway

There's something going on every week of the year at the Las Vegas Motor Speedway (☎ 702-644-4444, 800-644-4444; W www .lvms.com; 7000 N Las Vegas Blvd). It hosts a variety of motor races on a 1.5-mile super speedway, 2.5-mile road course, 4000ft dragstrip, and paved and dirt short-track ovals; there are also facilities for motorcross and even go-cart competitions. Annual events

Getting Hitched in Vegas: A True Story

We knew we wanted to get married in Vegas, nowhere else, but apart from booking the flights and our first night's accommodation, we decided to put no planning into the actual day. We just wanted to turn up (from Britain) and do it.

We made a point of flying United – when you get married, little things like the name of an airline seem important. The next morning, we had breakfast in our wedding outfits (cream dress for me, old shorts for Simon) and walked the length of The Strip, checking out the Little Chapel of the West, the Hitching Post, the Little Chapel of Love and many others. To be truthful, the more we saw, the less we were inclined to entrust them with the happiest day of our lives. Many were pretty tacky, full of plastic flowers, fake stained-glass windows and doll's house pews.

We went to get our State of Nevada marriage license at the County Court. As the clerk was typing it up, she recommended we try the registry office across the road. Las Vegas seems a long way to come to be married in a registry office, but local advice is usually worth heeding, so we had a look. Though the building itself was positively ugly, we were won over by Flora, a friendly, heavily made-up grandmotherly type who, for US$35, would perform the ceremony – no appointment necessary. A lady was summoned from the typing pool to perform as both witness and official photographer.

Twenty minutes later we emerged newly wed and headed straight for Binion's Horseshoe Casino – not for a gamble but for a tipple. The place was dimly lit, packed with punters and buzzing with atmosphere. We got our picture taken next to its claim to fame – an illuminated horseshoe stacked with a million dollars' worth of real paper bills.

Outside, we were surprised to find the Moscow State Circus performing a free show. As we ooed and aahed with the crowd, I fingered my new Russian wedding ring, trying not to attach too much significance to this post-Soviet coincidence.

Finally, as the sun set, we strolled back down The Strip. Outside Treasure Island, we jostled with parents and children to witness its life-size sea battle. Among the fireworks, the screams, the cannon-fire and the thickening smoke, we slurped champagne straight from the bottle. We walked next door, where the fake volcano at the Mirage Hotel was rumbling and simmering, readying itself for another volcanic eruption. The lava ran, the sky lit up, and we looked at each other. In a Las Vegas sort of way, the earth was moving for both of us.

Charlotte Hindle

at the $100-million, state-of-the-art racing complex include Indy car, Nascar, dwarf car, classic car, truck, sprint car, dragster and sand-pull competitions. Call for a schedule of upcoming events, or visit the speedway's website. Tickets generally cost between $10 and $15, but can go much higher for certain competitions. Facilities include a restaurant and gift shop.

Las Vegas Natural History Museum

If you've ever been to a really good natural history museum, you won't be wowed by this one – but your kids might. That's because the Las Vegas Natural History Museum (☎ 702-384-3466; 900 N Las Vegas Blvd; adult/child 4-12 years $5.50/3; open 9am-4pm daily, closed Thanksgiving Day & Christmas Day) has lots of things youngsters love, but the exhibits aren't well done enough to impress most adults. The museum is divided into five main rooms, each about the size of a standard living room and each with a different theme. The international wildlife room contains two dozen or so stuffed exotic animals rather weakly displayed and the marine-life room contains several aquariums and about a dozen stuffed sharks suspended from the ceiling. Stuffed state residents of the nonhuman variety are featured in the Nevada *au naturel* room, and there's animated dinosaurs and fossils in the dinosaur den. The young scientist center is a popular interactive area for children of all ages and allows kids to touch lots of cool stuff such as fossils, the leg bone of a dinosaur and a stuffed bobcat (its fur is wearing thin, but kids still pet it with glee). A particularly good exhibit is a sandbox containing a mastodon's tooth, a T-rex tooth and so on. Kids are encouraged to play archaeologist and uncover the items, and when they do there are brushes available for sweeping the objects clean for further investigating. This last exhibit must appeal to some basic human urge – parents can often be seen 'helping' their children play one Leaky or another.

Lied Discovery Children's Museum

Directly across the street from the Natural History Museum is the Lied Discovery Children's Museum (☎ 702-382-3445; 833 N Las Vegas Blvd; adult/child 2-17 years $5/4; open 10am-5pm Tues-Sun), which houses exhibits designed for kids between three and 12 years of age. Unfortunately, most of the dozen or so exhibits are either too complex for children to understand or operate successfully, or they are too simple and therefore boring. For example, The Pathway to Music exhibit consists of 13 squares placed on the ground, each representing a musical note that will chime when stepped on. Four kids following precise instructions and acting in unison can play 'Twinkle, Twinkle Little Star' by stepping on specific squares in a specific order. It's a smart exhibit, but that level of coordination is beyond many youngsters. It's never used, except by the hyperactive visitors who like to stomp and make noise. In contrast, the Bubble Art exhibit allows participants to pull a rope that raises a bar from a trough of bubble solution and – voila! – create a large bubble. There's no real scientific lesson here, just an activity most kids find amusing for a few minutes. It's a shame, but the Lied's interactive exhibits leave many kids either confused or bored.

Main Street Station

This 'old fashioned' hotel-casino recreates Victorian opulence with unique design,

detailed craftsmanship and an extensive collection of antiques, architectural artifacts and collectibles. Main Street Station (☎702-387-1896, 800-713-8933, fax 702-386-4466; W www.mainstreetcasino.com; 200 N Main St) is not only the most beautiful of the downtown establishments, but it is also the most historically interesting. Throughout the lovely 420-room hotel-casino are notable objets d'histoire, most keeping to the turn-of-the-19th-century theme. Then there are the other pieces of history, such as a large graffiti-covered chunk of the Berlin Wall that now serves as one of the walls supporting the urinals in the gentleman's restroom.

Other artifacts on display at Main Street Station are the private rail car Buffalo Bill Cody used to travel the US with his Wild West Show from 1906 until his death in 1917; three exquisite bronze chandeliers above the casino's central pit, which were originally installed in the Coca-Cola Building in Austin, Texas, in the 1890s. The ornate mahogany woodwork that now graces the casino entry, hotel registration desk and the Company Store, was removed from a 19th-century drugstore in Covington, Kentucky. Additionally, the gorgeous Pullman Grille dining room was built around an ornate carved oak fireplace and wine storage cabinets taken from Preswick Castle in Scotland (the unique sideboard niche includes panels that depict characters and morals of Aesop's Fables). Main Street Station has old-fashioned elegance and historic treasures almost everywhere you look. The registration desk dispenses free copies of Guide to Artifacts, Antiques & Artworks, which identifies and describes the historic attractions in the hotel-casino. Also worth checking out is its adjacent **Triple 7 Brew-Pub**, which makes its own beer and features excellent music several nights of the week.

Old Las Vegas Mormon Fort State Historic Park

The remains of the Las Vegas Mormon fort (☎ 702-486-3511; 908 N Las Vegas Blvd; adults/child 6-12 years $2/1; open 8:30am-4:30pm daily) are unspectacular, but this is where it all started in the 1850s. An adobe quadrangle provided a refuge for travelers along the Mormon Trail, between Salt Lake City and San Bernadino. Some of the original walls still stand, and a three-room display shows artifacts and photos from the early days. Outside, there are sample fields of the first crops grown here and an archaeological dig.

ACTIVITIES
Bowling
Bowling is very big in Las Vegas, and most bowling centers are in hotel-casinos where you can work on your glide and release at any time. The bowling centers mentioned here are in hotel-casinos and all rent top-of-the-line equipment. Fees vary but are about $2 per game and $1.50 for shoe rental. Occasionally a facility will be closed for league bowling. If bowling in Las Vegas is a priority to you, call ahead to avoid any unpleasant surprises.

Gold Coast (☎ 702-367-4700, 4000 W Flamingo Rd) 72 lanes, a pro shop, a resident professional and especially low fees on weekends and holidays

Santa Fe (☎ 702-658-4995, 4949 N Rancho Dr, Business Hwy 95) 60 lanes, a pro shop and Bowlervision, which tracks the speed and path of the ball from the time it leaves your hand

The Orleans (☎ 702-365-7111, 4500 W Tropicana Ave) 70 lanes and a pro shop. Beware: there's league play nightly at 5:30pm and 9:30pm; lanes can be unavailable then

Gambling
The chief tourist activity in Las Vegas is gambling. There isn't a city in the world that compares to Las Vegas in terms of the variety and quantity of games. See the 'Gambling in Las Vegas' special section for descriptions of the games themselves. Anyone intending to do a significant amount of gambling in Las Vegas should consider doing the following three things.

Join a Slot Club You receive a plastic card that you insert into a machine before you begin play. You are awarded points by how much money you put into the machine, and those points are redeemable

at the hotel-casino for cash, merchandise or 'comps' (complimentary meals, rooms, limousine rides and so on), or a combination of the three. Membership is free, but you must be at least 21 years old and have a photo identification. All of the megaresorts and some of the smaller casinos have slot clubs – just go to the main change cage inside the casino where you'll be doing your gambling and ask to join their slot club. You'll have your slot-club card within minutes.

Ask to Be Rated If you play the tables, ask the pit boss to rate your play. Why? Because each year the city's casinos give out more than $500 million in comps to rated players (unrated players get nothing). Generally, if you are playing between $5 and $10 per hand, you can expect to be comped breakfast and/or lunch at the casino's coffee shop. Between $10 and $25 per hand, expect a free meal and a heavily discounted room rate. Between $25 and $100, expect free show tickets, free gourmet meals and a free room. Between $100 and $250, you needn't concern yourself with your room, food or drink bills – the casino will gladly pay them and give you any show tickets you might want. If you're gambling $250 or more per hand, the casino will typically pay for your suite, food, drinks, limousine service, greens fees and even airfare.

Take Some Gaming Lessons Unless you know how to gamble intelligently, and most people don't, consider getting some free instruction from professionals. Most dealers are happy to explain the ins and outs of a game or give you a guide that shows you how to play the game, but many casinos go a big step further: they offer free lessons from professional gambling instructors. Among the hotel-casinos that offer free instruction at scheduled times are Bally's, Caesars Palace, Circus Circus, Excalibur, Flamingo, Harrah's, Imperial Palace, Lady Luck, MGM Grand, Riviera, Sahara, San Remo, Stardust and Tropicana. This list is by no means conclusive. Call the hotel-casino that most interests you for class times and other details.

Golf

There are dozens of golf courses in Las Vegas Valley, most within 10 miles of The Strip. Generally, reservations for tee times should be made at least a week in advance. Following is a partial list of golf courses in the Las Vegas area. Among the courses that do not appear here are those belonging to private country clubs, where membership fees of $30,000 up front plus $350 a month are common; privately owned courses that are limited to residents of a particular gated community; and one golf course where play is limited to the 51 members of the Las Vegas Paiute tribe. Call for greens fees, tee times and directions.

Angel Park Golf Course (☎ 702-254-4653, 100 S Rampart Blvd) A 36-hole Arnold Palmer-designed municipal golf course

Badlands Golf Club (☎ 702-363-0754, 9119 Alta Dr) Designed by US Open Champion Johnny Miller amid spectacular terrain

Desert Rose Golf Course (☎ 702-431-4653, 5483 Clubhouse Dr) Municipal course with moderate length, wide fairways and fast greens

Highland Falls Golf Club (☎ 702-254-7010, 10201 Sun City Blvd) Designed by course architect Greg Nash and golfer Billy Casper

Las Vegas Golf Club (☎ 702-646-3003, 4300 W Washington Dr) Inexpensive municipal golf course with lots of trees and little water

Legacy Golf Club (☎ 702-897-2187, 130 Par Excellence Dr) One of the top 100 golf courses in the US, located in nearby Henderson

North Las Vegas Golf Course (☎ 702-633-1833, 324 E Brooks Ave) A night-lighted municipal course for nine holes on 18 acres

Wildhorse Golf Club (☎ 702-434-9000, 2100 W Warm Springs Rd) An 18-hole semi-private course in nearby Henderson

But surely we must be in Paris…

Soothing spas at the Bellagio

The towering Eiffel

… or Venice perhaps

The stunning opulence of the Venetian's interior lobby

RICHARD CUMMINS

'Chariot! Oh, ahem… taxi!'

NEIL SETCHFIELD

The Bellagio rises from the legendary Dunes Hotel's ashes

LEE FOSTER

When you stop seeing stars, explore virtual reality at Gameworks

RICHARD CUMMINS

The sculpted gardens of Caesars Greco-Roman fantasyland

Places to Stay

There's no shortage of places to stay in Las Vegas, and room options range from filthy wham-bam-thank-you-ma'ams east of downtown to exquisite suites overlooking The Strip. Rates range from as little as $12 a night at one of the youth hostels to $10,000 or more a night for a penthouse suite at one of the glamorous megaresorts on South Las Vegas Blvd.

Las Vegas room rates vary with demand, and they vary wildly. A standard room at the Bellagio, for example, usually goes for $169 a night, Sunday through Thursday. However, the same room will cost $499 when there's a big convention in town. That very same room will carry a $2000-a-night price tag on New Year's Eve.

In addition, during slow periods many of the hotel-casinos try to lure customers with discounted room rates. These rates are often advertised in the travel sections of major US newspapers. Occasionally, the discounted rates involve two companies working together. At the time of writing, for example, the Las Vegas Hilton was offering standard rooms for $29.95 to people possessing Bank of America Visa cards. The regular rate for the same room was $69.95.

What all this means is that the rates shown here should be viewed only as approximate. The amounts you are quoted by the hotels could be substantially higher; it's unlikely they will be substantially lower, as the rates shown here are the standard rates – when it's not a recognized holiday and there are no big conventions in town. As with so many things in life, timing is everything, particularly when it comes to Las Vegas room rates.

Another thing to remember is that some hotel-casinos on The Strip can offer rooms for the same price as a dumpy joint on Fremont St in downtown. That's because the big hotel-casinos make their big bucks in their gaming areas, whereas the dumpy joint hasn't got a casino to recoup room losses. With Las Vegas, it's wrong to assume that

Room Rate Categories

Budget	$40 and under
Mid-Range	$41 to $70
Top End	$71 and above

nice, centrally located accommodation must be much pricier than rooms in a poorly situated, unappealing little place.

If you'll be visiting Las Vegas on a tight budget, or if you're simply determined to get the best value you can find, be sure to contact at least a handful of hotels, as you never know who will be running a special when you visit. It takes less time than you might think, and if you're calling from the US or Canada, you can usually use a toll-free number. Most of the hotels also have websites that allow you to check room rates and availability.

Whatever you do, don't arrive in Las Vegas without a reservation. There are more than 100,000 hotel rooms in Sin City, but you'd be shocked and amazed how often every standard room in town is occupied. If you simply show up at a hotel-casino and ask for a room, you may find the only one available is a two-bedroom suite with a nightly rate exceeding most mortgage payments.

THE STRIP

As mentioned earlier, room rates fluctuate with demand, and nowhere is this more true than the hotels along The Strip. The room prices shown here are standard midweek rates, and they do not include the 9% hotel tax. Expect to pay a little more on weekends, a lot more during popular events such as National Finals Rodeo, and even more during hotel-filling conventions such as the Comdex consumer electronics trade show, which attracts 2200 exhibitors and more than 200,000 delegates each November. See the 'Major Convention Dates' boxed text in the Facts for the Visitor chapter for details on other conventions.

For more information about the hotel-casinos on The Strip, be sure to see the Things to See & Do chapter.

Places to Stay – Budget

Barbary Coast (☎ 702-737-7111, 800-634-6755, fax 702-894-9954; W www.barbary coastcasino.com; 3595 S Las Vegas Blvd; rooms from $39) is an excellent mid-Strip hotel-casino. Great care has been taken to ensure that the charming Victorian-era decor found elsewhere in the establishment carries through to its 400 rooms as well. Guestrooms have half-canopied brass beds, lace-curtained windows, attractive floral carpets, quaint sitting areas and gaslight-style lamps. It shares an intersection with Caesars Palace, Bally's Las Vegas and Bellagio.

Circus Circus (☎ 702-734-0410, 800-444-2472, fax 702-734-2268; W www.cir cuscircus.com; 2880 S Las Vegas Blvd; rooms from $39) has 3612 standard rooms and 132 suites which, like clowns, come in all shapes and sizes. There are two-story suites, minisuites, parlor suites, Jacuzzi suites and so on. The very popular standard rooms come with sofas, balconies or patios, and desks, and are all 460 sq ft in size. The color scheme varies, but is generally a tasteful gray-blue or mauve, and the rooms are very well maintained. These appealing rooms have an attractive price much of the time. Don't let the name fool you, either: Circus Circus, like the vast majority of Las Vegas' hotel-casinos, has spent millions of dollars in recent years replacing the kitsch with class. Most rooms are desinated nonsmoking, 45 were designed for the hearing impaired and 122 are wheelchair accessible.

Imperial Palace (☎ 702-731-3311, 800-634-6441; W www.imperialpalace.com; 3535 S Las Vegas Blvd; rooms from $39, suites from $69), looking only slightly like a Japanese temple, is a hotel-casino offering 2700 rooms, including 225 suites, situated in a 19-story tower. The standard rooms are nothing special, and at 280 sq ft are smaller than most, but they all have air-con, satellite TV and even balconies. Given the hotel's mid-Strip location and often low rates, these

A Casino with a Heart

The Imperial Palace has always made a point of hiring people with disabilities, who make up 13% of its staff. This fact was little known until 1991, when the hotel-casino was named Employer of the Year by US President George Bush's Committee on Employment of People with Disabilities.

Two years later, the Imperial Palace was widely recognized when it opened the Resort Medical Center, a 24-hour medical facility serving hotel employees, their families, and guests of the Imperial Palace and other area hotel-casinos.

The Imperial Palace also hosts a special Christmas party at which low-income seniors and nonambulatory convalescent-center residents are treated to a complimentary dinner and show. The party, the hospital and the drive to hire people with disabilities were all initiated by Ralph Engelstad, the sole owner of this major Las Vegas hotel-casino.

rooms are an awfully good value. At even better value are the much larger Luv Tub suites. Each features a spacious bedroom with an ego-stroking mirror over a king- or queen-size bed and a 300-gallon sunken 'luv tub' in an oversize, heavily mirrored bathroom.

Sahara (☎ 702-737-2111, 888-696-2121, fax 702-737-2027; 2535 S Las Vegas Blvd; rooms from $39) has been renovated in a relentless Moroccan theme that is either cheerful or gaudy, or both, depending on one's taste. The carpeting and drapes are tan, the upholstery appears in earth tones, and each room comes with a wooden desk topped with a brass lamp. Tame enough, classy even. But the rest of the 2035 guestrooms are done up in a mix of stars and stripes and vivid colors that are a bit too much for some people. On the one hand, the Moroccan overkill adds to the festive ambience that pervades the Sahara, which has gone to great lengths to provide a substantial wow factor, but on the other hand, as an authentic reproduction of another place the Sahara scores a big fat 'F.'

Places to Stay – Mid-Range

Excalibur (☎ 702-597-7777, 877-750-5464, fax 702-597-7040; W www.excalibur-casino .com; 3850 S Las Vegas Blvd; rooms from $49) has an Arthurian motif that appears in all of the public areas and doesn't end at your guestroom door. There's a total of 4032 rooms within the Excalibur's two 28-story towers, and all contain walls papered to resemble the interior of a castle. Hung on the walls are prints of knights jousting. The bedspreads have a fleur-de-lis theme, the mirrors are flanked by sconces and the oak furnishings are heraldically embellished. Nonsmoking rooms, rooms with extra-wide doors for wheelchair accessibility, and Jacuzzi suites are available. While some hotel-casinos don't welcome kids, the Excalibur is clearly child-friendly. Children aged under 17 can stay for free in their parents' room.

Flamingo (☎ 702-733-3111, 888-308-8899, fax 702-733-3353; W www.flamingo lasvegas.com; 3555 S Las Vegas Blvd; rooms from $39) is centrally located, and underwent a $130-million renovation and expansion some years ago. The addition of a 612-room sixth tower raised the total number of guestrooms at this legendary hotel-casino to 3642, including 36 parlor suites and 150 minisuites. Although each standard guestroom is a mere 333 sq ft in size, the closet and bathroom are undersize and one wall of the bedroom is a floor-to-ceiling window, so the rooms seem much more spacious than they actually are. They are certainly pleasant to return to at the end of the day, in no small way because of the attractive color scheme: soft blues and peach, watercolors of tropical scenes, and light-colored wood furnishings. The Flamingo has lots of faithful customers, and for two good reasons: location and price.

Holiday Inn Casino Boardwalk (☎ 702-733-2400, 800-635-4581, fax 702-730-3166; W www.hiboardwalk.com; 3750 S Las Vegas Blvd; rooms from $39) has the distinction of being the world's largest Holiday Inn, as well as the world's most bizarre (how else can you account for the enormous fake roller coaster and the enormous fake Ferris wheel out front?). For better or worse, there's nothing unusual about this Holiday Inn's 655 guestrooms, the majority of which are in a newish 16-story tower. Except for the vibrant colors and prints of Coney Island, the tower's guestrooms are typical Holiday Inn fare – quite all right but nothing to get excited about. A minority of the hotel's rooms are pleasantly presented in pastels.

Luxor (☎ 702-262-4000, 800-288-1000, fax 702-262-4452; W www.luxor.com; 3900 S Las Vegas Blvd; standard rooms from $49, jacuzzi suites from $99, other suites from $500) has 4467 rooms which are possibly the most distinctive of all of the rooms in Las Vegas. They range in size from 465 sq ft for a standard to 4800 sq ft for the penthouse. All rooms feature art deco and Egyptian furnishings, and the marble bathrooms contain phones, vanity mirrors and hair dryers (but usually only a shower). Facilities available to guests include the 12,000-sq-ft Oasis Pool and Spa with hot whirlpool, steam bath, dry sauna, facials, massages, five body-wraps (volcanic salt and honey, herbal, aroma, steam and aloe), aromatic sea-salt scrubs and soaks, hair and nail salon and a complete fitness center. By the way, the Luxor's unusual high-speed elevators are called 'inclinators,' since they must travel at a 39-degree angle to ascend the Luxor's pyramid shape. You must be a guest to ride in one.

MGM Grand (☎ 702-891-1111, 800-929-1111, fax 702-891-1112; W www.mgm grand.com; 3799 S Las Vegas Blvd; standard rooms from $69, suites from $99, suites with jacuzzi from $119) has rooms which, like the rooms at Luxor, aren't punched from a cookie cutter, despite the fact that there are so many of them (exactly 5032, including 751 suites, housed in four 30-story emerald-green towers). Each of the 446-sq-ft standard guestrooms is done up in what the hotel-casino seriously refers to as a *classic motif* – 'Wizard of Oz,' 'Hollywood,' 'Southern' or 'Casablanca.' The Oz rooms have tasseled green drapes, emerald-green rugs and upholstery, and wallpaper emblazoned with silver and gold stars. The Hollywood rooms feature gold-flecked walls hung with prints of Marilyn Monroe, Humphrey Bogart and other icons of the silver screen, beds backed by mirrors, lots of gilded moldings and maple-on-cherrywood furniture. The Southern rooms feature faux 18th-century Old South furnishings and faux-silk beige damask walls hung with prints from *Gone With the Wind*. The Casablanca rooms contain satiny fabrics amid earth tones and prints of Moroccan market scenes. Large bathrooms with drop-dead-lovely marble tubs are standard. The Luxurious Suites range in size from 675 to 6040 sq ft and include multiple bathrooms and outdoor patios with whirlpool.

The Mirage (☎ 702-791-7111, 800-627-6667, fax 702-791-7446; W www.mirage .com; 3400 S Las Vegas Blvd; rooms $69-399, suites from $259) has three 30-story towers containing a total of 3044 rooms. There are one- and two-bedroom suites, as well as eight villa apartments and six lanai bungalows, each with a private pool. The standard guestrooms, at 360 sq ft, are smaller than many found elsewhere along The Strip, but all of the rooms at The Mirage are quite attractive. Gone are the original tropical colors; in their place are subtle color schemes of taupe, beige and peach with black accents. All of the standard rooms have marble entryways and a canopy over

the headboard. The bathrooms are adorned with plenty of marble but are rather small. If space is a big consideration, you could do better elsewhere for the price. On the other hand, The Mirage is centrally located and has a white tiger's share of attractions. And the rooms, though small, *are* elegant.

Monte Carlo (☎ 702-730-7000, 800-311-8999; W www.montecarlo.com; 3770 S Las Vegas Blvd; standard rooms from $59, suites from $139) offers 3014 rooms decorated in traditional European style, with beige wallpaper, cherrywood furnishings, floral-print fabrics and fleur-de-lis friezes. The standard rooms are only standard size (406 sq ft), but they are lovely retreats and the large marble tubs lend themselves extremely well to long, therapeutic soaks. In 2002, The Spa at Monte Carlo received $3 million in upgrades and is really quite something to behold, with marble from China, stone from India, porcelain from Italy, ceramics from Indonesia, and granite from Saudi Arabia. The hotel's Monaco suites received $2 million in improvements at about the same time.

New York-New York (☎ 702-740-6969, 800-693-6763; W www.nynyhotelcasino .com; 3790 S Las Vegas Blvd; standard rooms from $69) has nothing to dislike except the lack of elbow room in some of its standard guestrooms. These range in size from 300 to 400 sq ft and vary enormously in layout (there are 63 layouts in all, a product of the hotel's peculiar shape). If you happen to get one of the 300-sq-ft rooms, you'll know it; they feel terribly small. However, all 2033 of the guestrooms at New York-New York are done up splendidly in art deco. Even the bathrooms, most with black marble-topped sinks, are impressive. For only $15 above the standard-room rate, you can get a Deluxe Room with a minimum of 450 sq ft of space. The hotel's Marquee Rooms range in size from 500 to 600 sq ft and usually cost $35 over the price of a standard room. For $75 above the standard rate, you can get (if available) a Jacuzzi Room, which spreads over 600 to 700 sq ft. There are no suites to be had, unless you're a big spender; those that exist – and plenty *are* located in the towers – are allocated to high rollers.

The Great Room-Rate Game

It often pays to call the hotel where you'll be staying a week or so in advance to see if the rates you were quoted when you booked a room have changed. If they've fallen, you can keep the difference if you ask that your quoted rate be changed. The savings can be substantial: let's say, for example, that you booked a room at the Flamingo on July 1 for the first week of August, at a cost of $89 a day. On July 21, you call the Flamingo and learn that the rate for a room for the first week of August is now $69. If you tell the Flamingo reservations agent that you reserved a room for that week at $89 a night and want your rate changed to $69, the agent will make the adjustment – and you'll save $140. If you don't ask, you will be charged the higher rate.

Riviera (☎ 702-734-5110, 800-634-6753, fax 702-794-9451; W www.theriviera.com; 2901 S Las Vegas Blvd; standard rooms from $40, suites from $250) has 2075 guestrooms, including 156 suites and 37 rooms that are specially designed to accommodate wheelchair patrons. The rooms are typical hotel fare – soft floral decor, cable TV, in-room safes, nothing fancy – but then there's usually nothing fancy about the rates, either: during a very quiet time (the first week of August, for example), it's often possible to obtain a standard room at the Riviera for as little as $40 a night. That same room will rocket up to $159 or more during a hotel-filling event or convention. Suites are considerably bigger and have a living room that's completely shut off from the bedroom.

Stardust (☎ 702-732-6111, 800-634-6757, fax 702-732-6257; W www.stardustlv.com; 3000 S Las Vegas Blvd; standard rooms from $60, suites from $175) has 1500 rooms that aren't going to appear in *Architectural Digest* anytime soon. There's nothing terribly wrong with them; they just seem to have been stamped from the same inexpensive mold. However, in the same way that a cheap dress with a floral design can be pretty, so too are these rooms. The general color scheme is peach carpeting with light-colored walls, black accents and floral-print bedspreads. There's little attention to detail, and the hotel staff, perhaps cognizant that their rooms don't measure up, won't divulge square footages. However, the dimensions of one of the bedrooms are a mere 308 sq ft (14ft by 22ft); if you add another 40 sq ft for the bathroom and 16 more for the closet, the estimated square footage of a standard room at Stardust is 364 – or well below the norm. The suites are much bigger and nicer.

Stratosphere (☎ 702-380-7777, 800-998-6937, fax 702-383-5334; W www.stratospherehotel.com; 2000 S Las Vegas Blvd; rooms from $69) has 1500 rooms which are not in the neck-craning tower, but rather in a much smaller building at the base of the spire. The rooms are standard size but more handsome than most, containing cherry-wood furniture with black lacquer accents, matching carpet and drapes, and abstract paintings. In-room safes, large-screen TVs, phones with data ports, and hair dryers are standard. The main drawback to staying at Stratosphere is the fact that it's far from most of the other megaresorts on The Strip. The nearest hotel-casino is Sahara, and even that is a fair walk away, and on the other side of a busy intersection.

Treasure Island (☎ 702-894-7111, 800-944-7444, fax 702-894-7446; W www.treasureisland.com; 3300 S Las Vegas Blvd; standard rooms from $69, suites from $149) has public areas which maintain the theme of an elegant Caribbean hideaway, including the hotel-casino's three 36-story towers with a total of 2900 rooms (among which are 212 suites). All of the rooms are decorated with light-colored carpeting, white-washed wood furnishings, brass fixtures and copies of 18th-century nautical paintings. Floor-to-ceiling windows make the average-size rooms seem more expansive than they really are.

Tropicana (☎ 702-739-2222, 888-826-8767, fax 702-739-2469; 3801 S Las Vegas Blvd; standard rooms from $49, suites from $149), world famous from the day it opened (April 4, 1957), contains a total of 1884 guestrooms in twin towers, including 120 suites and 80 minisuites. The rooms in the Island Tower conform to a Polynesian theme (wood-and-bamboo furnishings, tropical pastel pinks and greens, and colorfully pleasing bedspreads). The rooms in the Paradise Tower, far from adhering to a tropical theme, are decorated in a French provincial style; unlike the rooms in the Island Tower, these rooms contain refrigerators, hair dryers, irons and ironing boards. The drawback to all of the standard rooms at the Trop is size: the Island Tower rooms are only 350 sq ft; those in the Paradise Tower only 360 sq ft. Mostly, the bedrooms are a decent size, but the bathrooms are a bit cramped. Suites start at 600 sq ft. Most of the rooms have floor-to-ceiling windows.

Places to Stay – Top End

Aladdin (☎ 702-785-5555, 877-333-9474, fax 702-758-5558; W www.aladdincasino.com; 3667 S Las Vegas Blvd; standard rooms from $99) boasts 2600 guestrooms, the most basic of which contain nothing more than you'd expect to find at a top-end resort (TV with pay movies, hair dryer, iron and ironing board, safe). For an additional fee, you can have high-speed Internet access in your room. Despite their cost, the rooms themselves are nothing special, and the overwhelming color is orange-brown (no, not very attractive). The bathrooms contain plenty of marble and space, but for the price you can do better elsewhere. Aladdin was swimming in a sea of debt at the time of writing. If sold, it's possible (and hoped) that the new owners will lower the costs of the rooms and suites, and convert their color schemes.

Bally's Las Vegas (☎ 702-739-4111, 800-634-3434, fax 702-967-3890; W www.ballyslv.com; 3645 S Las Vegas Blvd; standard rooms from $99, suites from $300) has two 26-story towers containing a total of 2814 guestrooms, including 265 suites. The standard guestroom measures 450 sq ft, which is larger than average, while the suites range from 900 to 2600 sq ft. All of the rooms are pleasantly decorated in earth tones, and all contain sofas and TVs. Special guest offerings include a full-service health club, private poolside cabanas, eight tennis courts and video rental.

Bellagio (☎ 702-693-7111, 888-987-6667, fax 702-693-8546; W www.bellagio.com; 3600 S Las Vegas Blvd; rooms from $169, suites from $1155), a spectacular hotel-casino, has accommodations ranging from 510-sq-ft standard guestrooms to 2055-sq-ft penthouse suites. Surprisingly, while the guestrooms are tastefully appointed with custom European-style furnishings and soothing earth tones, they actually appear smaller than, say, the 333-sq-ft guestrooms at the much less expensive Flamingo. That's because the bathrooms and closets in Bellagio guestrooms are oversize, and the guestrooms contain more furniture than most. The bathrooms are luxurious, featuring Italian-marble floors and surfaces, plush robes and soaking tubs. If 'soaking tubs' sounds good to you, be sure to investigate Bellagio's fabulous spa; it offers luxurious body-care treatments in the European tradition.

Caesars Palace (☎ 702-731-2222, 800-634-6661, fax 702-731-7172; W www.caesars.com; 3570 S Las Vegas Blvd; standard rooms from $99, suites from $450) offers some of the most lavish standard guestrooms in town. The vast majority (1134 out of a total of 2471) are in the 29-story Palace Tower. There are five floor-plans in all, ranging in size from 550 to 750 sq ft. All have 9-ft ceilings, which enhance the feeling of spaciousness, and subtle design elements such as wall mirrors framed in ancient-coin patterns, wood cabinets trimmed in Greek key designs and wall treatments inspired by Pompeian murals. All feature whirlpool tubs, superior custom furnishings, two-line telephones with data ports, ironing boards, irons, hair dryers, safes, small refrigerators, TVs with video-checkout services, and generous closets. The older rooms in the three smaller towers are just as lovely and include even more Greco-Roman touches, such as Roman columns, pilasters and (occasionally) classical sculptures in niches.

Four Seasons Hotel (☎ 702-632-5000, 800-332-3442, fax 702-632-5195; W www.fourseasons.com; 3950 S Las Vegas Blvd; standard rooms from $225, deluxe rooms from $250, premier The Strip view rooms from $300, suites from $350) is a service-oriented, nongaming hotel occupying the 35th through 39th floors of the Mandalay Bay hotel-casino. It contains 424 rooms, all of which are spacious, tastefully appointed and filled with the usual amenities. The standard rooms have an average size of 500 sq ft and feature lovely views, and oversize marble bathrooms replete with a large vanity, a deep-soaking tub, a glass-enclosed shower stall and a toilet with telephone. Also available are 810-sq-ft executive suites, one- and two-bedroom suites, special suites and presidential suites. The Four Seasons emphasizes comfort, quiet and service. Services include a 24-hour business center, a 24-hour concierge, voice mail and multiline telephones, high-speed in-room Internet access, complimentary use of the extensive health and fitness facilities, a full-service spa and a free-form swimming pool. There's also 24-hour dining service, an all-day restaurant, express check-in and check-out, an early-arrival and late-departure lounge, no-smoking rooms and twice-daily housekeeping. In case you were wondering, Four Seasons guests are whisked to their hotel via three private elevators; they do not have to share elevators with Mandalay Bay's guests.

Harrah's (☎ 702-369-5000, 800-427-7247, fax 702-369-5500; W www.harrahs .com/our_casinos/las; 3475 S Las Vegas Blvd; standard rooms from $85, superior rooms from $115, junior suites from $135, executive suites from $275) has 2699 guestrooms, including 108 suites that have been decorated in a pleasing color scheme that evokes the ambience of Mardi Gras. All contain a table with two chairs, a full-size armoire with his-and-her chests, a large-screen TV with Nintendo and pay-per-view movies.

Standard rooms have either a king-size bed or two double beds; superior rooms have two queen-size beds; and suites generally have one king-size bed, although a few have two queen-size beds. The standard room is a typical 336 sq ft, while the superior room is 372 sq ft and also comes with a hair dryer, a work desk, a larger TV, two telephone lines, an iron and ironing board, and a bathroom with a marble countertop and marble floor.

The neatest thing about the superior rooms is that they are located in the Carnival Tower, which overlooks The Mirage and its erupting volcano. Watching the volcano at night from the comfort of your cozy hotel room is very cool. The junior suite is a very spacious 558 sq ft, and has a separate seating and work area and a couch that can fold out into a bed, but it does not have a separate bedroom. The executive suite provides 800 sq ft of living space, including a bedroom with walk-in closet that's separate from the seating and work area. Guests have free access to a swimming pool, Jacuzzi, health club and arcade.

Mandalay Bay (☎ 702-632-7777, 877-632-7000, fax 702-632-7013; W www.man dalaybay.com; 3950 S Las Vegas Blvd; standard rooms $99-139, suites $149-649) has ornately appointed rooms designed by award-winning interior designer Anita Brooks (who also decorated the rooms at the Monte Carlo). Each large standard guestroom (515 sq ft) boasts a tasteful tropical motif and features a floor-to-ceiling window, a 27-inch TV in an armoire, a lighted closet and a desk. Both bedroom phones have data ports. Standard bathrooms include separate tub and shower, twin vanities, a makeup mirror, a third telephone, a blow dryer, imported-stone floors and surfaces, and an enclosed toilet. Suites, in addition to the amenities found in the standard guestrooms, have an imported-stone entry, wet bar with refrigerator, spa tub, powder room, big-screen TV, brand-name spa products, and a dining set in one-bedroom suites and anything above.

Paris-Las Vegas (☎ 702-946-7000, 888-266-5687, fax 702-967-3836; W www.paris lasvegas.com; 3645 S Las Vegas Blvd; standard rooms from $119, deluxe rooms from $139, superior rooms from $159, premier rooms from $219) has elegantly appointed rooms in a 34-story tower modeled after the famous Hôtel de Ville. The 2916 guestrooms are a very comfortable 450 sq ft and feature custom-designed furnishings, crown moldings and rich French fabrics. The stately armoire serves as the closet, enhancing the European feel of each room. The bathrooms are spacious and contain lots of marble, a separate bathtub and shower with authentic European fixtures, linen hand towels, a large vanity with shelves, hair dryers and a makeup mirror. Like everywhere else in Las Vegas, the room rate varies with availability. Unlike everywhere else in Las Vegas, prices also vary depending on which floor you're on. Starting rates apply for standard rooms up to and including the 16th floor. Deluxe rooms are on floors 17 through 23, superior rooms occupy floors 24 through 29, and premier rooms occupy floors 30 through 34. Rooms facing the half-scale Eiffel Tower and the dancing fountains of Bellagio across the street cost more than those facing the back of Paris-Las Vegas' property.

The Venetian (☎ 702-414-1000, 888-283-6423, fax 702-733-5190; W www.venetian .com; 3355 S Las Vegas Blvd; Standard rooms from $169, Piazza suites $650, Renaissance suites $1500, Doge suites $5000, Penthouse suites $10,000) opened in 1999 and it leaves a spectacular impression upon the throngs of visitors who have since crossed its graceful arched bridges and flowing canals. The Venetian's 3036 'standard' guestrooms are anything but standard. Every one of these rooms is a 700-sq-ft suite, with crown molding, wrought-iron railings, baseboards and a marble foyer entrance. The 130-sq-ft bathrooms are finished in fine Italian marble and appointed with a lighted, magnified make-up mirror, hair dryer and telephone. The canopy-draped bedchamber has a spacious closet and a Venetian floral armoire containing a safe and TV, and there's a sunken living-room salon with an entertainment center and second TV. Other facilities include a minibar, a fax machine with copier and computer printer capabilities, a separate phone line, a convertible sofa that opens to a queen-size bed, two upholstered chairs, a coffee table, writing desk and game table. The Venetian also offers 318 Piazza, Renaissance, Doge and Penthouse suites ranging in size from 1330 to 5000 sq ft.

EAST OF THE STRIP

See the Things to See & Do chapter for further descriptions of the east-of-Strip hotel-casinos.

Places to Stay – Budget

Motel 6 Tropicana (☎ 702-798-0728, 800-466-8356, fax 702-798-5657; W www .motel6.com; 195 E Tropicana Ave; singles/ doubles from $34/40) is one of the great budget bargains in Las Vegas and has 608 rooms. It's also less than a half-mile from The Strip and easily reached by bus (just hop on any westbound CAT No 201 bus). The rooms are nothing spectacular, but are quite comfortable in a mostly pink-and-gray color scheme. Each room contains a queen-size bed (two doubles are also available), dresser, table and chairs, large TV (with a free movie channel) and a shower (some have a tub as well). There are two swimming pools on the premises (but no Jacuzzi), free parking outside your door and local calls are free.

Places to Stay – Mid-Range

Super 8 Motel (☎ 702-794-0888, 800-800-8000; 4250 Koval Lane; singles & doubles from $53), just outside the budget category, has 288 guestrooms. The decor in the cheerful rooms varies, but most have blue carpet and white walls. Safes are available in some of the rooms as well as a free movie channel. There's also a pool and a Jacuzzi on the premises. Access to The Strip is easy enough. If you don't have a vehicle and don't want to walk (it's about half a mile), you can take a taxi or walk to nearby Flamingo Rd and catch any westbound CAT No 202 bus. Super 8 offers a free airport shuttle.

Las Vegas Hilton (☎ 702-732-5111, 888-732-7111, fax 702-732-5790; W www .lvhilton.com; 3000 Paradise Rd; standard rooms from $69) has 3479 guestrooms with decor consisting of earth tones, mostly greens and tan. The furnishings may be described as upscale-contemporary American hotel – there is nothing particularly memorable about it, but it isn't cheap. You can expect to pay three times the standard room rate for a suite. The standard rooms are spacious and include a number of pleasant amenities such as automated drapes (push a button and a machine opens and closes them for you), marble-topped dressing tables, deeper-than-usual bathtubs and deep closets with an ironing board and iron. If the rooms at the Las Vegas Hilton have a drawback, it is that none of the views are special. High rollers are offered luxurious Sky Villas, which range in size from 12,600 to 15,400 sq ft, and occupy the space where Elvis Presley lived during the time he performed at the Hilton.

Notable Numbers

The Las Vegas Hilton
- has 5290 telephones and 603 computers
- uses 153,000 decks of cards and 8357 dice annually
- has 101,562 lightbulbs and 4552 parking spaces
- cleans 29.8 million pieces of laundry annually
- has 224,936 sq ft of windows

No Ordinary Cactus

On the grounds of the San Remo is a very statuesque 60-year-old Saguaro *(Carnegiea gigantea)* cactus. The Hakusui Chemical Company of Japan donated the plant to the hotel-casino as a thank-you for the service it provided to Hakusui officials during a stay in 1997. The Saguaro cactus, which is naturally found in Arizona and Mexico, can reach a height of 50ft, a width of 2ft and a weight of many thousands of pounds.

San Remo *(☎ 702-739-9000, 800-522-7366, fax 702-736-1120; W www.sanremolasvegas.com; 115 E Tropicana Ave; standard rooms in garden/tower $39/59)* is a hotel-casino with 711 guestrooms (including Jacuzzi and International suites), most of which are in two towers. Given their price and location near The Strip, the rooms here are a good value, particularly the suites. The standard rooms are nothing special; at 360 sq ft they are on the small side, and their green-blue carpet, green-blue sofa and bold floral-print bedcovers appear cheap and tacky. The walls are off-white and adorned with low-brow pictures of rivers painted in unnatural colors. The decor in the suites is no better. The smallest of the suites is a mere 400 sq ft and costs $20 above the standard room. The International and Jacuzzi suites are a full 800 sq ft and cost a reasonable $60 and $80 above the going rate of a standard room, respectively. Both suites feature a wet bar, a refrigerator, an intimate dining area and a marble entryway. Whereas the Jacuzzi suite features a Jacuzzi, it contains only one bathroom with a separate vanity stall. The International suite features two full bathrooms.

Places to Stay – Top End

Hard Rock Café & Hotel *(☎ 702-693-5000, 800-473-7625, fax 702-693-5010, 800-473-7625; W www.hardrockhotel.com; 4455 Paradise Rd; standard rooms from $75, suites from $250)* has oversize guestrooms which are as smart as the rest of the glorious shrine to rock 'n' roll. Each of the 668 rooms, including 57 suites, is designed and furnished in European style. French doors and tasteful paintings and/or prints of rock stars adorn all rooms. Suites also come with state-of-the-art music systems, large-screen Sony TVs, marble bathrooms and a wet bar. There's a swimming pool with a sandy beach, private poolside cabañas, whirlpools and spas, all in a lush tropical setting. Wondering about the Hard Rock's relative isolation? The hotel provides free transport to and from The Strip.

WEST OF THE STRIP

Further descriptions of the west-of-Strip hotel-casinos can be found in the Things to See & Do chapter.

Places to Stay – Budget

Gold Coast *(☎ 702-367-7111, 888-402-6278, fax 702-365-7505; W www.goldcoastcasino.com; 4000 W Flamingo Rd; standard rooms from $29, suites from $150)* is a hotel-casino with 750 rooms, including 18 suites, in two buildings. The rooms are perfectly fine, but absolutely nothing special; their blue carpeting and furnishings are similar to what you'd find at any quality American motel. At 355 sq ft apiece, the rooms won't leave you feeling cramped, but that's also because the guestrooms don't have a lot of furniture (there's no room for a sofa, for example). A room with a view, or with a floor-to-ceiling window? No, there's not much of a view from any of the rooms at the Gold Coast, and the window doesn't occupy even a third of the narrow wall. The suites are much larger (576 sq ft), and include one king-size bed (as opposed to two queens), a separate sitting and dining area, and a wet bar. You could do better on The Strip. The Gold Coast provides free shuttle service to and from The Strip.

Places to Stay – Mid-Range

The Orleans *(☎ 702-365-7111, 800-675-3267, fax 702-365-7535; W www.orleanscasino.com; 4500 W Tropicana Ave; rooms from $39)* is a hotel-casino with 840 tastefully appointed petite suites in a French provincial style. Each of the good-value suites contains a generous 450 sq ft of living room with sitting and dining areas, a bedroom with either a king-size bed or two queens, and an oversize tub in the bathroom. The guestrooms are in a 22-story structure and face either The Strip or the mountains. The Orleans provides free shuttle service to and from The Strip and airport.

Places to Stay – Top End
The Palms (☎ 702-942-7777, 866-725-6773; Ⓦ www.thepalmslasvegas.com; 4321 W Flamingo Rd; guestrooms from $69) offers 450 guestrooms, among which are 120 suites. The standard rooms are spacious (440 sq ft) and done up in pleasing earth tones. All have a window-side sitting area with reading chair, sofa and coffee table, with a desk nearby in those rooms with a king-size bed (a choice of one king-size bed or two queen-size beds is available). All rooms feature a TV, in-room safe, in-room refreshment center, dual-line telephone, separate modem line, convenient data ports and power outlets for laptop computers, a coffeemaker, hair dryer, iron, on-television Internet access, and a complimentary *USA Today* newspaper. Be sure to request a room on an upper floor and a view of The Strip.

Rio (☎ 702-252-7777, 888-684-3746; Ⓦ www.harrahs.com/our_casinos/rlv/loca tion_home.html; 3700 W Flamingo Rd; guestrooms from $79) offers only suites, and most are a great deal. The Rio has 2563 'standard' rooms, 600 sq ft in size and most boasting a king-size bed or two queen-size beds, floor-to-ceiling window, fridge, drip coffeemaker, iron, safe, hair dryer, cocktail table, TV, separate dressing areas, and a fully detailed bathroom. And who could forget the crescent-shaped couch in every room? Beware that some of the guestrooms are windowless; be sure to specify that you want a room with a view if that's important to you. In addition to the regular suites, there are a number of Masquerade suites for three times the price of a regular suite. These suites are spread out over 1600 sq ft and contain everything you'd find in one of the Rio's standard rooms, plus a Jacuzzi tub and 180-degree views of the mountains and The Strip. The Rio provides free shuttle service to and from The Strip.

DOWNTOWN
See the Things to See & Do chapter for further descriptions of the Downtown hotel-casinos.

Places to Stay – Budget
Unless you're able to receive a discounted rate, you won't find a place on The Strip with rooms for less than $39 a night.

Las Vegas International Hostel (☎ 702-385-9955; Ⓔ lasvegashostel@yahoo.com; Ⓦ www.lasvegashostel.com; 1208 S Las Vegas Blvd; dorm beds $12, singles/doubles $26/28), just four blocks north of The Strip, is a no-frills place that offers space in four-bed dormitories. There's a heater in each of the worn rooms with worn beds, but no air-con. Free access to a nearby pool and tours to the Grand Canyon and other national parks are available. There's a kitchen and a laundry for guests' use, as well as Internet access. Local calls are permitted, and there's a pay phone just around the corner for long-distance calls. There are three markets and two Cuban restaurants within a short walk. Be advised: prostitutes can often be found standing at curbside a short distance from the hostel.

USA Hostels – Las Vegas (☎ 702-385-1150, 800-550-8958, fax 561-258-4691; Ⓔ lasvegas@usahostels.com; Ⓦ www.usa hostels.com; 1322 Fremont St; dorm beds from $12 Sun-Thur, $15 Fri & Sat; singles $38 Sun-Thur, $43 Fri & Sat; doubles $40 Sun-Thur, $45 Fri & Sat), nine city blocks east of the Fremont Street Experience, has excellent facilities, a caring management and 24-hour access. The basic but clean non-smoking rooms have air-con and heating, a private bathroom, and breakfast included in the nightly rate. Facilities include a swimming pool and Jacuzzi (spring and summer months only), laundry facilities, a kitchen for guest use and Internet access ($1 for eight minutes).

Keg parties and barbecues are often held during the summer. Cheap tours to the Grand Canyon and area national parks can be arranged at the hostel. A shuttle from the hostel to Los Angeles leaves three times a week ($35 each way). Safe deposit boxes are available for rent ($5 for the length of your stay). Shuttle trips are provided to/from The Strip daily. There's also free pick up from the Greyhound bus depot ($2 return) and transportation to/from the airport *in a limousine* for a mere $5.50 each way (two person minimum). Also available are three public phones, special car-rental rates and free passes to most of the city's dance clubs. This hostel is so excellent (never mind its location in a crappy part of town) that the management is somewhat strict about who it's willing to let stay there. American guests must have an out-of-state ID and proof of travel. Foreigners need to show only an ID. Guests under 18 years old must be accompanied by a parent.

Budget Inn *(☎ 702-385-5560, 800-959-9062, fax 702-382-9273; 301 S Main St; rooms from $36)* offers 80 pleasant rooms with air-con, heating and satellite TV in a four-story building 75m or so from the Greyhound bus depot. There's no laundry room, nor is there a swimming pool or a slot machine, but if all you're looking for is a quiet place to stay downtown, this may be for you.

California *(☎ 702-385-1222, 800-634-6255, fax 702-388-2610; w www.thecal .com; 12 E Ogden Ave; rooms from $39)* is a hotel-casino with a decor best described as contemporary American hotel. The 781 guestrooms, including 74 suites, are in two towers – one with 11 stories and the newer one with nine stories. There are slightly larger rooms in the West Tower, but those in the East Tower have been recently renovated. The Cal doesn't divulge square-footage figures, but the rooms seemed to be of average size. The towers share a consistent decor, though it's neither particularly Californian nor particularly Hawaiian (the Cal receives many Hawaiian guests and dresses appropriately, as it were). It has handsome mahogany furnishings, attractive marble baths, and color schemes that tend to be either apricot/teal or mauve/burgundy. If views are important to you, stay elsewhere; the views from the rooms here are generally unappealing.

Fremont *(☎ 702-385-3232, 800-634-6182, fax 702-385-6229; w www.fremont casino.com; 200 E Fremont St; rooms from $39)*, a hotel-casino, contains 447 rooms, which are noticeably smaller than most in town (hotel staff won't divulge figures), but they are also attractive and reasonably priced. Most of the rooms have beige carpeting, low-profile wallpaper and gold bedspreads with a mild floral-pattern overlay. There's a choice of bed sizes, but be advised that a guestroom with two double beds is much more cramped than the same room with just one king-size bed. There's little in the way of a view from Fremont rooms. Kids under 12 stay free with parents, but there's a limit of three guests per room – no exceptions. There are suites, but they are reserved for players' club cardholders. If you intend to be doing some serious gambling, you'd be wise to enroll in the players' club (it's free) and ask to be rated. Then, as you gamble, the amount you gamble will be tallied. You don't need to gamble very much before the hotel will upgrade you to a suite or offer you a discounted rate on your standard room.

Jackie Gaughan's Plaza *(☎ 702-386-2110, 800-634-6575, fax 702-382-8281; w www.plazahotelcasino.com; 1 Main St; standard rooms from $39, suites from $79)*, built in 1971, has two towers: one with 21 floors and the other with 25 floors. The guestrooms overlook either downtown Las Vegas or freeway spaghetti; neither sight is lovely, and the rooms facing downtown catch a lot of noise coming up from the Fremont Street Experience (bring a pair of earplugs). At 378 sq ft, the standard rooms are average in size, but they're attractively decorated. All of the 1034 rooms (including the 136 suites) have balconies, which you'll appreciate if you've just got to have fresh air.

Victory Hotel *(☎ 702-384-0260, 307 S Main St; rooms most nights from $29)*, dating from 1908, is Las Vegas' oldest hotel. It offers 32 clean and comfortable rooms with central air-con, heating and private hot-water bathrooms. The Victory features laundry facilities and gated parking, and it makes lockers available to its guests. This is a good budget hotel, a fine option for people considering either of the hostels in this chapter but who want to be closer to the action.

Places to Stay – Mid-Range

Golden Nugget (☎ 702-386-8121, 800-634-3454, fax 702-386-8362; Ⓦ www.golden nugget.com; 129 E Fremont St; standard rooms from $49, suites from $275) has popular guestrooms. This was gaming tycoon Steve Wynn's first major project in Las Vegas (he's now better known for The Mirage and Bellagio). In fact, the 1907 rooms at the Golden Nugget closely resemble those of The Mirage, only the rooms at the Golden Nugget are gold and brown in color (as opposed to beige). All of the standard rooms are a particularly good deal, and are a generous 425 sq ft in size. They include half-canopy beds, marble entryways, vanity tables with magnifying makeup mirrors, and marble bathrooms with hair dryers.

The one- and two-bedroom luxury suites are unlike any others found in Las Vegas megaresorts. Each features a spiral staircase that leads from a spacious living room to the bedroom area. Floor-to-ceiling windows span the length of the room, providing guests with a captivating view of Las Vegas. Each of these suites contains two bathrooms; one designed for men, the other (with potpourri and a Jacuzzi tub) for women. Each bathroom contains a TV, just in case.

The Golden Nugget's casino clings to its Victorian-era theme, just as it has since the hotel-casino opened in 1946, only now it's fairly classy. There's no shortage of brass or cut glass, and the entire casino, once dimly lit and a bit depressing, is bright and cheerful.

Also on the premises are a lavish spa, a salon, five restaurants, a swimming pool and whirlpool, a fitness center and the requisite gift shop.

Main Street Station (☎ 702-387-1896, 800-713-8933, fax 702-386-4466; 200 N Main St; rooms from $39) has 406 guestrooms that are as handsome as the rest of the hotel-casino, in a 17-floor tower featuring marble-tile foyers, Victorian sconces and marble-trimmed hallways. The spacious rooms are elegant, bright and cheerful, with large plantation shutters instead of drapes, soft home-style fabrics and upholstery, rich wood tones, white-embossed wall coverings, wall sconces and tasteful framed art. These are among the loveliest rooms in all of Las Vegas, yet the prices are extremely agreeable. There are suites, but the casino controls them; they are available mostly to members of the players' club (which operates the same way as the Fremont's players' club). However, suites are occasionally available on a walk-in basis; if you've just got to have one, say so when you reach the reception desk, and vow to gamble like there's no tomorrow. They've heard it all before, but it never hurts to try.

Places to Stay – Top End

Standard rooms in the downtown area don't top $70 except on the weekends, and many are available then. However, there are many places charging well over that sum for a standard room during a huge convention or if New Year's Eve lands midweek.

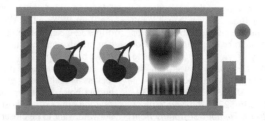

Places to Eat

Excluding the city's 1300 or so fast-food joints, its 50 ice-cream and candy shops and over 120 bakeries and buffets, there are more than 700 restaurants in Las Vegas, serving more than 30 ethnic varieties of cuisine. Las Vegas has, as Sin City's perspicacious spin doctors like to say, a veritable smorgasbord of dining options.

With so many restaurants – and so many really fantastic ones – within only 10 sq miles, deciding where in Las Vegas to don a bib and unsheathe the fork can pose a problem. Trouble is, who can think on an empty stomach?!

If the prospect of making a meal decision becomes so daunting that you feel the need to toss back a few vodka martinis before committing yourself, you might like to know that many of the 400-plus bars and cocktail lounges in Las Vegas offer full dinners – which, of course, only complicates matters.

Decisions, decisions. If you can at least decide on what type of food you want, you've won half the battle. The following restaurant descriptions are arranged geographically and listed alphabetically within price categories. Note that not every restaurant in town is mentioned here, just many of the noteworthy ones. A complete restaurant guide to Las Vegas would be so unwieldy it would pose a hazard to your health.

Speaking of health hazards, there's one more dining option to consider: buffets. For the skinny on these Rabelaisian feasts, see the boxed text 'A Few Words about the Buffets' later in this chapter. But remember, just because Vegas buffets are always 'all you can eat,' don't feel you have to eat all you possibly can. As author Anthelme Brillant-Savarin once wrote, 'Tell me what you eat, and I will tell you what you are.'

Then again, Virginia Woolf once noted in her immortal *A Room of One's Own*, 'One

Killer Vegas Eateries

Best Bakery
Freed's Bakery (East of The Strip)
Best Buffet
Le Village at Paris-Las Vegas (The Strip)
Best Brazilian
Yolie's Brazilian Steak House (East of The Strip)
Best Chinese
Chin Chin at New York-New York (The Strip)
Best Coffee Shop
Café Bellagio at Bellagio (The Strip)
Best Delicatessen
Jason's Deli (East of The Strip)
Best Doughnuts
Krispy Kreme Doughnuts (West of The Strip)
Best German
Café Heidelberg (East of The Strip)
Best Gourmet
Pamplemousse (East of The Strip)
Best Indian
Gandhi India's Cuisine (East of The Strip)
Best Italian
Ristorante Italiano at Riviera (The Strip)

Best Japanese
Hyakumi at Caesars Palace (The Strip)
Best Late-Night Dining
Ruth's Chris Steak House (West of The Strip)
Best Mediterranean
Mediterranean Café & Market (East of The Strip)
Best Mexican
Taqueria Cañonita at The Venetian (The Strip)
Best Rotisserie Chicken
Sonia's Café & Rotisserie (West of The Strip)
Best Salad Bar
Sweet Tomatoes (West of The Strip)
Best Seafood
808 at Caesars Palace (The Strip)
Best Steakhouse
The Steak House at Circus Circus (The Strip)
Best Takeout
Pick Up Stix (West of The Strip)
Best Thai
Prommare's Thai Food (West of The Strip)

'cannot think well, love well, sleep well, if one has not dined well.' Now *that's* more like it. To Hades with Anthelme!

THE STRIP

Most of the restaurants on The Strip are nestled inside the huge hotel-casinos that flank both sides of Las Vegas Blvd from the Stratosphere to Mandalay Bay. These get the lion's share of the restaurant business, but some of the independents (GameWorks Grill and Harley-Davidson Café among them) are crowd-pleasers too and warrant consideration.

One of the neat things about the restaurant options on The Strip is that so many are actual attractions in themselves. It's not simply that they have *ambience*; on the most basic level, so does a Pizza Hut. Rather, many of these places qualify as bona fide entertainment. The Rain Forest Café, for example, creates a dining experience that rivals a mild theme-park ride, with animatronic jungle animals and simulated thunderstorms with lightning and rain.

Not only that, amid all the restaurant attractions are some great culinary choices. Emeril Lagasse's New Orleans Fish House (inside MGM Grand) and Picasso (inside Bellagio) would receive rave reviews in New York. Aureole, one of New York's finest restaurants, now has an identical twin at Mandalay Bay. Another of New York's best, Le Cirque, is also now represented in Las Vegas (at Bellagio).

There's some great dining to be had in Las Vegas. Bon appetit!

Places to Eat – Budget

Café Bellagio (☎ 702-693-7111; *most dishes under $10; open 24hr*), inside the Bellagio, has breakfast, lunch, dinner and late-night supper menus featuring a wide range of dishes and exciting twists on café favorites. We like it best for its delicious coffee and views of the pool and garden areas through turn-of-the-century arched windows.

Coyote Café & Grill Room (☎ 702-891-7777; *entrées under $10; open 8:30am-10:30pm daily*), inside MGM Grand, is two establishments in one, both serving spicy

Southwestern cuisine. The popular café, which opens early and closes late, offers lots of fun food, such as jerk chicken tacos and blue-corn pancakes with toasted pine nuts, in an inviting room featuring colorful terra-cotta walls adorned with Southwestern art. See Places to Eat – Top End for the Grill Room.

GameWorks Grill (☎ 702-597-3122; *3769 S Las Vegas Blvd; entrées $7-9; open 11am-10pm Sun-Thur, 11am-11pm Fri & Sat*) is a very popular and casual restaurant located amid the high-tech video games and virtual-reality experiences of GameWorks. A fair variety of sandwiches, salads, pastas and pizzas are offered.

La Piazza Food Court (☎ 702-731-7110; *entrées under $10; open 7:30am-11pm daily*), in the casino at Caesars Palace, offers lunch and dinner selections that spotlight a variety of the world's most popular cuisines, including Chinese stir-fry, Italian pasta and pizza, Mexican favorites, American deli fixtures and Japanese ramen soups and teriyaki.

Liberty Café (☎ 702-383-0101; *1700 S Las Vegas Blvd; dishes around $6; open 24hr, 365 days a year*), inside White Cross Drugs, features an old-fashioned drugstore with red-leather booths and counter seats. Generous breakfasts, fatty-but-delicious burgers, hotcakes, New York steaks and even awesome malts are served around the clock. This place is a great budget find.

Taqueria Cañonita (☎ 702-414-1000; *entrées around $10; open 11am-11pm Sun-Thur, 11am-midnight Fri & Sat*) is situated alongside The Venetian's Grand Canal, but don't let the Italian ambience fool you – the food is pure Mexican, and it is good. Along with the usual standbys are some delicious dishes from the Yucatan peninsula, including pork roasted in banana leaves.

Places to Eat – Mid-Range

Chin Chin (☎ 702-740-6969; *entrées $5-12; open 8am-11pm Sun-Thur, 8am-midnight Fri & Sat*), inside New York-New York, serves wonderful traditional Chinese food in a cheerful café setting. Among the wide range of sumptuous dishes prepared in the open

A Few Words about the Buffets

The age-old axiom 'you get what you pay for' applies to Las Vegas hotel buffets. Circus Circus boasts one of the cheapest buffets in town, but it's certainly not the best. For the really good stuff you usually have to pay twice as much, but the difference in quality is as apparent as the difference between a filet mignon and an overcooked meatball.

Generally, you can predict which hotel-casinos will have killer buffets. Circus Circus and Excalibur, for example, are geared for families and thus charge prices that are family-friendly. Their buffet food tends to be cheap as well: heavy on spaghetti, low-grade meats and starches. Paris-Las Vegas, Bellagio, Luxor and other elegant hotel-casinos are competing for top honors in the Class Act category; you won't find a lot of spaghetti and other typical 'food for the masses' at their buffet cooking stations.

What you will tend to find at the buffets in the better hotel-casinos are various food stations specializing in sushi, seafood, pasta, stir-fry, carved meats and so on. Among the standard entrées at the upscale megaresorts: mounds of fresh shrimp, lobster claws, red snapper, pasta and antipasti, beef tenderloin, roast meats carved to order, bowls of fresh fruits, various soups and lots of salads.

Buffet prices, like hotel rates, fluctuate in Las Vegas. When there's a big convention in town, they're set a little higher than usual. Generally, at the memorable buffet restaurants you can expect to pay $6 to $10 for breakfast, $10 to $15 for lunch, and $15 to $25 or more for dinner. Breakfast prices usually are in effect from 7am till 11am, lunch prices from 11am till 4pm and dinner prices from 4pm till closing (10pm, generally).

The best daily buffets can be found at Bellagio, Paris-Las Vegas and Luxor. The Garden Court buffet at Main Street Station, until recently one of the best buffet spreads in town, had taken a turn for the worse when we visited, and we can't recommend it.

The Rio has two buffet restaurants. Its Carnival World Buffet features dishes from China, Brazil, Mexico, Italy and around the US. Many people view Carnival World as the best buffet in town, and it's hard to dispute that – unless you're a seafood fiend. Then, the choice is simple: Rio's Village Seafood Buffet. It features lots of fresh seafood flown in daily, and although some may find it expensive (generally $20 for lunch, $25 for dinner), it's worth it.

Other excellent buffets can be found at Mandalay Bay, Bally's, Caesars Palace, Mirage, Golden Nugget, Fremont and the Las Vegas Hilton.

In addition to the buffets at Circus Circus and Excalibur, other relatively low-quality (and less expensive) buffets can be found at Sahara, Stardust, Stratosphere and Lady Luck.

If you had tremendous luck at the gaming tables on Saturday night and want to spend Sunday morning celebrating, head to Bally's, home of the best Sunday brunch in town. Bally's Sterling Sunday Brunch will set you back $40, and it's very impressive. Ice sculptures and lavish flower arrangements abound, as do food stations laying out roast duckling, steak Diane, seared salmon with beet butter sauce – you get the idea. There's even a sushi and salmon bar. Reservations (☎ 702-739-4111) are recommended.

kitchen is Chin Chin's signature classic shredded-chicken salad. Also available are an assortment of dim sum items.

Dragon Noodle Company (☎ 702-730-7965; entrées $6-18; open 11am-11pm Sun-Thur, 11am-midnight Fri & Sat), in the casino area of the Monte Carlo, feels like an authentic Hong Kong eatery dropped into Las Vegas. Many of the meals are displayed for diners' inspection, the food is cooked on grills in plain sight, and there's a tea bar where many brands can be sampled. Try the air-dried roast duck (all the flavor, half the fat).

Harley-Davidson Café (☎ 702-740-4555; 3725 S Las Vegas Blvd; entrées $7-17; open 11am-midnight daily) is more a tourist attraction than a biker joint, with a dozen shiny hogs, lots of celebrity-autographed gas tanks and plenty of Harley racing photos on display. American roadside cuisine (mostly burgers and barbecued meats) is the specialty here.

Montana's Café & Grill (☎ 702-380-7711, 800-998-6937; entrées $10-15; open 6pm-11pm Sun-Thur, 6pm-midnight Fri & Sat), in the casino area of the Stratosphere, is a casual, Old West–themed restaurant specializing in prime rib and a variety of barbecued meats. Typical side dishes include coleslaw, corn on the cob and baked beans.

Rainforest Café (☎ 702-891-1111; entrées $9-20; open 10:30am-1am Mon-Thur, 10:30am-2am Fri & Sat, 7:30am-11:30pm Sun), in the casino area of the MGM Grand, is a jungle-themed restaurant where the selection of pasta, burgers, sandwiches and salads is secondary to the lush faux-forest setting, a host of mechanized exotic animals and simulated tropical downpours. The fruit smoothies are divine.

Ristorante Italiano (☎ 702-794-9363; entrées around $14; open 5:30pm-11pm Fri-Tues), located in the casino area of the Riviera, is a quiet, elegant restaurant with superb service and great food (the lasagna is especially delicious). It's easy to overlook the restaurant's door inside the casino, and if you have trouble finding it, keep looking; one bite into your meal and you'll be glad you did.

Stage Deli of Las Vegas (☎ 702-893-4045; entrées $6-14; open 8:30am-10:30pm Mon-Thur, 7:30am-11:30pm Fri & Sat, 7:30am-10:30pm Sun), inside The Forum Shops at Caesars Palace, is the twin of the legendary Stage Deli of New York, and has more than 300 items on its terrific menu. Typical items include oven-roasted prime brisket of beef, stuffed cabbage, and an assortment of sky-high sandwiches.

Tony Roma's: A Place for Ribs (☎ 702-732-6111; entrées $7-27; open 5pm-midnight daily), in the casino area of the Stardust, is an informal, very popular restaurant specializing in barbecued baby back ribs served with a variety of sauces, barbecued shrimp and broiled chicken. Entrées range in price, with most around $11.

Places to Eat – Top End

Aqua (☎ 702-693-7111, 888-987-6667; 1st courses $15-18, entrées $30-$35; open 5:30pm-11:30pm daily), in the Bellagio, features the acclaimed seafood preparations of chef Mark Lo Russo, former sous chef of San Francisco's famous Aqua. House specialties include Hawaiian swordfish and medallions of ahi tuna.

Aureole (☎ 702-632-7777; à la carte entrées from $22, prix-fixe menu $65; open 6pm-11:30pm daily), inside Mandalay Bay, is a sibling of the famous New York Aureole. The menu features seasonal American dishes, which could include a sea-scallop sandwich, smoked capon ravioli and pan-seared veal T-bone. At the heart of the elegant restaurant is a four-story wine tower.

Buffet at Bellagio (☎ 702-693-7111; breakfast $12, brunch $15, dinner Sun-Thur $25, Fri & Sat $35; open breakfast 8am-10:30am Mon-Fri; brunch 8am-4pm Sat & Sun; lunch 11am-3:30pm Mon-Fri; dinner 4pm-10pm Sun-Thur, 4pm-11pm Fri & Sat), inside Bellagio, frequently takes top honors as the best buffet in town in an annual local independent survey, and for good reason. The Bellagio's sumptuous spread includes crowd pleasers such as smoked salmon, roast turkey, and many wonderful Chinese, Japanese and Italian dishes.

Coyote Café & Grill Room (☎ 702-891-7777; entrées $15-35; open 8:30am-10:30pm daily), inside MGM Grand, serves spicy Southwestern cuisine. The Grill Room features more substantial dishes than the café (see Places to Eat – Budget earlier), such as grilled rack of lamb, wild venison and a garlicky black bean soup. Casual attire is fine.

808 (☎ 702-731-2222; entrées $15-25; open 5:30pm-10:30pm Thur, Sun & Mon, 5:30pm-11pm Fri & Sat), inside Caesars Palace, takes its name from Hawaii's area code (you knew that?). Expect a divine mingling of French, Mediterranean, Indian and Pacific Rim elements in what many Las Vegans regard as their city's No 1 seafood restaurant (Aqua at Bellagio being a close second).

Emeril Lagasse's New Orleans Fish House (☎ 702-891-7374; entrées $20-40; open

11am-2:30pm & 5:30pm-10:30pm daily), inside MGM Grand, features the famous Crescent City chef's creative Creole and Cajun dishes, including lobster cheesecake, barbecued shrimp and oysters on the half-shell with a tangy sauce. Not to be missed is the banana cream pie with banana crust and caramel.

Hyakumi (☎ 702-731-7731; entrées $30-65; open 5:30pm-10:30pm Sun-Thur, 5:30pm-11pm Fri & Sat), inside Caesars Palace, is the top Japanese restaurant in Las Vegas, and offers visitors a choice of seating at the sushi bar or a *teppan* table. Hyakumi's chef, Hiroji Obayashi, has won many awards. Reservations are required at this dinner-only eatery decorated to resemble an old Japanese village.

Jasmine (☎ 702-693-7111; entrées $16-45; open 5:30pm-11pm daily), inside Bellagio, is a contemporary gourmet Chinese restaurant flanked by lovely garden and lake views. Chef Philip Lo specializes in modern interpretations of Cantonese, Szechuan and Hunan styles, in an elegant dining room featuring authentic and exquisitely replicated Chinese art.

Le Cirque (☎ 702-693-7111; entrées $32-42; open 5:30pm-10:30pm daily), at Bellagio, features haute cuisine and world-class wines in an intimate and opulent setting. The chef is Marc Poidevin, formerly the chef de cuisine at New York's legendary Le Cirque 2000. The restaurant is known for its varieties of foie gras and its signature black-tie scallops.

Le Village (☎ 702-946-7000; buffets $15-25; open 7:30am-10:30pm daily), inside Paris-Las Vegas, is arguably the best buffet in Las Vegas (no surprise there, considering France is the culinary capital of our world). Selections from France's various regions are represented at numerous cooking stations, allowing the sampling of many French delicacies at reasonable prices.

Mizuno's (☎ 702-739-2713; standard dinners $15-20, superior dinners $30-40; open 5:30pm-10:45pm daily), at the Tropicana, has chefs preparing tempura, shrimp, lobster, chicken and steak with swordsmen-like moves on a grill in front of you. The restaurant itself is a work of art, with gorgeous marble floors and Japanese antiques.

Morton's of Chicago (☎ 702-893-0703; entrées $18-30; open 5:30pm-10pm Mon-Thur, 5pm-11pm Fri & Sat, 5pm-10pm Sun), inside Fashion Show Mall, is one of America's great steak and lobster chains. Succulent Midwestern steak, whole baked Maine lobster, Sicilian veal, and prime rib are served in a room lined with mahogany and adorned with LeRoy Neiman prints.

The Palm (☎ 702-732-7256; entrées $16-150; open 11:30am-11pm daily), inside The Forum Shops at Caesars Palace, is one of the best restaurants in town for lobster. Among the entrées is a 7lb lobster ($140). The shrimp cocktails and prime steaks are also fantastic.

Picasso (☎ 702-693-7111, 888-987-6667; 4-course meals $70, 5-course meals $80; open 6pm-9pm Thur-Tues), inside Bellagio, features the memorable Mediterranean cooking of chef Julian Serrano. Serrano's cuisine is inspired by the regional cuisine of France and Spain where Pablo Picasso spent much of his life. Guests have a choice of a four-course meal or a five-course meal, with two or three selections for each. Among Serrano's signature dishes are lobster salad served with a saffron sauce and fried leeks, and seared foie gras served with a balsamic vinaigrette and sliced cucumber. Several original Picasso masterpieces and a large collection of his charming ceramic pieces further delight the senses.

Prime (☎ 702-693-7111; entrées $18-54; open 5:30pm-10:30pm daily), inside the Bellagio, is another excellent steakhouse. Prime's signature dishes include garlic soup with frog legs, rib-eye steak for two with wild mushrooms and roasted garlic, and fresh Maine lobster.

The Range (☎ 702-369-5000; entrées $20-29; open 5:30pm-10:30pm daily), inside Harrah's, is as notable for its spectacular view of The Strip as it is for its steak. The short menu in this semiformal restaurant features various cuts of beef, a few chicken dishes and salads. The prices are a bit on the high side, but the beef is of a superior grade. All entrées come with sides, and the elevated view is stunning.

The Steak House (☎ 702-734-0410; entrées $15-25; open 5pm-10pm Sun-Fri, 5pm-11pm Sat), inside Circus Circus, leaves all clowning aside. In a city filled with steakhouses, the one under the big top is, well, tops. Unlike the rest of Circus Circus, which *looks* like a circus, The Steak House takes itself very seriously, resembling a British hunting lodge, with lots of dark wood and a stained-glass ceiling over an elegant bar.

Spago (☎ 702-369-6300; entrées $15-30; open 11am-11pm Sun-Thur, 11am-midnight Fri & Sat), inside The Forum Shops at Caesars Palace, features Californian-style cuisine made famous by chef Wolfgang Puck's landmark Los Angeles restaurant of the same name. Specialties include Puck's signature Chinois chicken salad, and pizza topped with salmon. Spago is well known for its rich desserts.

Top of the World (☎ 702-380-7711, 800-998-6937; entrées $21-33; open 11am-11pm Sun-Thur, 11am-midnight Fri & Sat) is a dressy, revolving restaurant perched high atop the Stratosphere Tower. While taking in cloud-level views of Las Vegas Valley, patrons enjoy impeccable service and delicious though overpriced entrées such as veal, lobster, and almond-crusted salmon.

EAST OF THE STRIP
Places to Eat – Budget

Einstein Bros Bagels (☎ 702-795-7800; 4624 Maryland Parkway; all items under $6; open 6am-6pm Mon-Fri, 6am-5pm Sat, 6am-4pm Sun) produces 17 varieties of fresh bagels every morning and offers 10 flavors of cream cheese to accompany them (even jalapeño!). Wash your bagel down with a quality blended coffee.

Freed's Bakery (☎ 702-456-7762; 4780 S Eastern Ave; open 7am-6pm daily) has been a Las Vegas favorite since it opened in 1959. Despite a recent explosion in bakeries with great buns, time and again local surveys pick Freed's as tops among the yeast-driven businesses. You've just got to like a place that advertises same-day made-to-order wedding and birthday cakes.

Jason's Deli (☎ 702-893-9799; Ⓦ www .jasonsdeli.com; 3910 S Maryland Parkway; items under $6.50; open 8am-10pm daily) is part of a rapidly growing chain like Krispy Kreme and Starbucks, and like the other two this chain is thriving due to the superior quality of offerings. Here you'll find a super colossal selection of sandwiches, killer salads and wickedly sinful desserts. The full menu can be downloaded from JD's website.

La Barca Mexican Seafood Restaurant (☎ 702-657-9700; 953 E Sahara Ave; entrées $5-20; open 10am-10pm Fri-Sun) offers a full menu of excellent, authentic Mexican seafood dishes. Among the restaurant's popular specialties are a 45oz shrimp cocktail and a chopped clam tostada that's to die for. Film buffs might like to know that the restaurant scene in *Leaving Las Vegas* was shot here. Many menu items are under $10.

Mediterranean Café & Market (☎ 702-731-6030; 4147 S Maryland Parkway; entrées $4-13; open 11am-9pm Mon-Sat, 11am-4pm Sun) is a great find for vegetarian items such as baked eggplant with fresh garlic, baba ganoush, tabouli and hummus. Carnivores may prefer the kabob sandwich, the gyros salad or rotisserie lamb. Most sandwiches are under $5.

Toto's (☎ 702-895-7923; 2055 E Tropicana Ave; entrées $7-15; open 11am-10pm daily) is where locals go when they want enormous quantities of Mexican food at reasonable prices. Toto's burritos are just a tad smaller than a zeppelin. A shark could live comfortably in a Toto's margarita. The chips are grease-free and there is plenty of seafood to choose from. Many entrées are under $10.

Places to Eat – Mid-Range

Café Heidelberg (☎ 702-731-5310; 610 E Sahara Ave, behind Marie Callenders; lunch $7-10, dinner $16-20; open lunch 11am-4pm; dinner 4pm-8:30pm daily) is nothing fancy, but it's a fine place to sink your teeth into some traditional German fare. Among the tastier items: the rouladen (beef rolls), goulash, and Bavarian plate (a sampling of sausages).

Cozymel's (☎ 702-732-4833; 355 Hughes Center Dr; lunch under $7, entrées $9-16; open 11am-10pm Sun-Thur, 11am-11pm Fri & Sat) features Mexican coastal fare in a delightful setting. Lunch specials, served weekdays till 4pm, include fresh fish of the day, chicken or beef fajitas and the Cozy Combo (a pork tamale, chicken enchilada, soft beef taco, rice and beans). Dinner items include grilled salmon topped with a delicious cream sauce, and plump shrimp sautéed in garlic lime butter and julienne ancho chilies.

Gordon-Biersch Brewing Company (☎ 702-312-5247; 3987 Paradise Rd; open 11am-11pm Sun-Thur, 11am-midnight Fri & Sat) is both a brewpub and a popular restaurant featuring good Californian cuisine. Among the tasty dishes on its extensive menu are peppered ahi tuna, spit-roasted porkloin chops with Creole bread pudding, and Moroccan spiced grilled lamb sirloin. The food is as delicious as it sounds. Also available are exotic pizzas cooked in a wood-burning oven.

Hard Rock Café (☎ 702-733-8400; 4475 Paradise Rd; entrées $6-16; open 11am-11pm daily) is, like the adjacent Hard Rock Hotel, dripping with rock memorabilia. The piped-in music ain't classical, unless it's classic Zeppelin, Clapton or Hendrix. The cuisine is predictable (burger, sandwiches, ribs etc) with a few surprises – among the better ones is the lime barbecued chicken. There's a kids' menu to boot. Rock on!

P.F. Chang's (☎ 702-792-2207; 4165 Paradise Rd; entrées $8-13; open 11am-11pm Sun-Thur, 11am-midnight Fri & Sat) is a classy, modern Chinese bistro with lots of artistic touches, from an enormous mural that recreates a mid-12th-century narrative screen painting, to the inviting menu items. Among Chang's top sellers are lemon pepper shrimp, Cantonese duck and orange-peel beef (Szechuan-style beef tossed with red chilies and fresh orange peel).

Shalimar (☎ 702-796-0302; 3900 S Paradise Rd; entrées $11-16; open 11:30am-2:30pm & 5:30pm-10:30pm Mon-Sat,5:30pm-9:30pm Sun) is known throughout Las Vegas for its terrific North Indian cuisine. Lunch is served buffet-style and is a bargain at $8. The same dishes appear à la carte for dinner. The marinated tandoori chicken is particularly good, and the spicy vindaloo chicken curry is likewise exceptional.

Z'Tejas Grill (☎ 702-732-1660; 3824 S Paradise Rd; entrées $8-18; open 11am-11pm daily) is a Texan-based chain restaurant with a real friendly atmosphere and imaginative Southwestern cuisine. Typical entrées include blackened catfish tacos, king salmon brushed with miso glaze, and blackened tuna served with a spicy soy sauce. The red-tufted leather and cowhide bar is a good place to be during happy hour (4pm to 7pm weeknights).

Places to Eat – Top End

Gandhi India's Cuisine (☎ 702-734-0094; 4080 Paradise Rd; entrées $13-19; open 11am-2:30pm & 5pm-10:30pm daily) features excellent Indian food in a colorful and charming atmosphere. Specialties include tandoori chicken, lamb and chicken curries and a host of vegetarian dishes. Big eaters should consider Gandhi's superb lunch buffet. A children's menu is available.

Hamada of Japan (☎ 702-733-3005; 365 Hughes Center Dr; entrées $12-42; open 11am-3:30am Mon-Fri, 4pm-3:30am Sat), on the corner of Flamingo and Paradise Rds, features a Teppan grill, a sushi bar and a sukiyaki dining room that has the feel of an authentic Japanese home. Specialties include tenzura, donburi and beef sukiyaki. Dress is informal and reservations are not needed.

Lawry's The Prime Rib (☎ 702-893-2223; 4043 Howard Hughes Parkway; steaks $20-28; open 5pm-9:30pm Sun-Thur, 5pm-10:30pm Fri & Sat) is the king of the Vegas prime-rib scene. Although Lawry's also offers fresh fish and lobster, it's the prime rib and accompanying spinning-bowl salad, Yorkshire pudding, mashed potatoes and whipped-cream horseradish that has made Lawry's a meat-lover's magnet since the original opened in Los Angeles in 1938. Diners have the option of four cuts.

McCormick & Schmick's (☎ 702-836-9000; 335 Hughes Center Dr; entrées $14-20; open 11am-10pm daily) is an excellent seafood house, perhaps the best in Las Vegas, dollar for dollar. McCormick's long list of specialities includes grilled Hawaiian mahi mahi served with a spicy tomato sauce,

Oregon dungeness crab cakes served with red pepper aioli, and sautéed seafood with Asian vegetables.

Pamplemousse (☎ 702-733-2066; 400 E Sahara Ave; entrées $18-30; open 6pm-9:45pm Tues-Sun) is one of Las Vegas' landmark restaurants, featuring a French Riviera–style salad (a basket of fresh veggies and vinaigrette house dip), appetizers such as escargots and soft-shell clams, and entrées such as Wisconsin duckling with orange curry sauce. Semiformal to formal attire is required at this romantic hideaway.

The Tillerman (☎ 702-731-4036; 2245 E Flamingo Rd; entrées $20-40; open 5pm-10pm Mon-Fri, 5pm-10:30pm Sat & Sun) is among the best seafood restaurants in Las Vegas, with prices to match. Specialities include farm-raised salmon from Norway, Florida red snapper, Australian whole lobster, and blackened yellowfin tuna served almost rare in a tangy mustard sauce. Entrées include a Lazy Susan salad bar.

Yolie's Brazilian Steak House (☎ 702-794-0700; 3900 Paradise Rd; lunch specials $5-13, entrées $25; open 11am-11pm Mon-Fri, 5pm-11pm Sat & Sun) is a Brazilian-style steakhouse. It features daily lunch specials and fixed-price dinners, which include your choice of soup or salad, followed by a procession of waiters carrying trays of New York sirloin, sausage Ipanema, turkey breast wrapped in bacon, and on and on. This is a meat-lover's paradise.

WEST OF THE STRIP
Places to Eat – Budget

Buckingham Smokehouse (☎ 702-638-7799; 2341 N Rainbow Blvd; entrées $8-14; 11am-9:30pm Sun-Thur, 11am-10:30pm Fri & Sat) is as good as barbecue gets in Las Vegas. Yes, salads, chili and soups *are* available, but the specialties of the house are hickory smoked barbecue chicken, sliced beef brisket and hickory smoked pulled pork, and these items we highly recommend.

Coffee Pub (☎ 702-367-1913; 2800 W Sahara Ave; dishes $3-8; open 7am-4pm Mon-Fri, 7am-3pm Sat & Sun), nestled within a small shopping plaza, is a casual delight. A variety of coffee drinks and smoothies,

pastas, quiches, salads, sandwiches, soups and loads of breakfast options are served inside or on a patio. Salad lovers will be especially satisfied, and The Big Scramble (chicken apple sausage, tomato and cheddar cheese scrambled together with three eggs) is an excellent choice for a hearty breakfast. Breakfast is served till 2pm daily.

Krispy Kreme (☎ 702-222-2320; 7015 W Spring Mountain Rd; open 24hr) is a doughnut chain – a *really good* doughnut chain. At the heart of Krispy Kreme's operation are melt-in-your-mouth glazed doughnuts. Also heavenly are KK's raspberry- and blueberry-filled doughnuts. Seating is available early till late every day, and there's 24-hour drive-thru service. A box of 12 glazed doughnuts costs $4.50.

Pick Up Stix (☎ 702-636-6600; 2101 N Rainbow Blvd; entrées about $5; open 11am-9pm daily) is a great place to keep in mind if you're on a budget and want to pick up a meal or two to go. Chinese wok food is prepared to order – for what you'd pay for one meal anywhere else, you can take home two from Pick Up Stix.

Sonia's Café & Rotisserie (☎ 702-870-5090; 3900 W Charleston Blvd; entrées under $10; open 11am-7:30pm Mon-Fri, 11am-4pm Sat) is one of those places that's just plain habit forming. Not only is Sonia's rotisserie chicken the best in town, but her pasta salad and roasted potatoes are fine. And Sonia offers some excellent Mexican specialties to boot.

Sweet Tomatoes (☎ 702-648-1957; 2080 N Rainbow Blvd; open 11am-9pm daily) is a salad and soup establishment thriving in a city filled with salad bars. Its dressings go well beyond the regular ranch/Italian/thousand-island selection and the produce is always crispy fresh. The cream of broccoli soup and the chili are delicious as well. The all-you-can-eat salad bar costs $7.

Places to Eat – Mid-Range

All American Bar & Grill (☎ 702-252-7767; lunch entrées $5-8, dinner entrées $12-26; open 11am-11pm daily), inside the Rio, specializes in steaks, seafood and pork ribs, which are cooked to order on a mesquite grill at the entrance to the handsome dining room. All entrées come with salad, sourdough bread and vegetables. Burgers and sandwiches are also available.

Café Nicolle (☎ 702-870-7675, 4760 W Sahara Ave, in front of the Sahara Pavillion shopping complex; entrées $11-26; open 11am-11pm Mon-Sat, noon-8pm Sun) offers a yummy variety of beautifully prepared entrées, including seared ahi tuna in a port wine sauce, orange roughy stuffed with crab meat, herb-crusted chicken, and pork tenderloin smothered in a nectarine plum sauce. Seating is available inside at black-and-gray Lucite tables accented with brass fixtures, or outside amid swaying palm trees and lovely flower boxes on a variously mist-cooled or heated patio. Very nice indeed.

Fiore (☎ 702-252-7777; entrées $26-50; open 6pm-11pm Thur-Mon), at the Rio, is a semiformal restaurant with superb cuisine. The dining room boasts an exhibition kitchen and dramatic windows overlooking a lush pool area. Though the menu changes seasonally, expect to see creative presentations of beef, veal, pork, ostrich and buffalo. Seafood offerings might include pan-seared striped bass with lobster sauce, or grilled Maine lobster stuffed with wild mushroom risotto.

Joe's Crab Shack (☎ 702-646-3996; 1991 N Rainbow Blvd; entrées $10-20; open 11am-10pm Sun-Thur, 11am-11pm Fri & Sat) is a great find for seafood lovers on a budget. Specialities include coconut shrimp, king crab legs, blue and Alaskan snow crabs, red lobster and even fish and chips. The atmosphere is fun – the setting resembles a fishing shack and the servers are rather entertaining.

Little Buddha Café (☎ 702-942-7777; entrées $10-25; open 5:30pm-11pm Sun-Thur, 5:30pm-12:30am Fri & Sat), inside the Palms, is an offshoot of Paris' terribly popular Buddha Bar restaurant. Both offer a fusion of French and Chinese cuisine. Among the dishes offered are Peking-style duck, tempura, pizza and spicy tuna tartar.

Prommare's Thai Food (☎ 702-221-9644; 6362 W Sahara Ave; entrées from $10; open 11am-10pm Mon & Wed-Sat, 5pm-10pm Sun) serves some of the best Thai food in Nevada, but you do pay handsomely for it.

House specialties include catfish smothered in a tangy sauce, crab, squid and a variety of curries.

Viva Mercados (☎ 702-871-8826; 6182 W Flamingo Rd; entrées $8-18; open 11am-9:30pm daily) serves traditional homemade Mexican food without all the artery-clogging lard used south of the border. Only heart-friendly canola oil is used here, and the chili rellenos, steak asada and enchiladas poblanos taste great all the same. The portions are large, the food is fresh and tasty and the service friendly.

Places to Eat – Top End

Alizé (☎ 702-942-7777; entrées $22-35; open 5:30pm-10:30pm daily), inside Palms, is named after the gentle trade wind along the French Mediterranean. Alizé features gourmet French cuisine and breathtaking views of The Strip. Chef Andre Rochat has won numerous awards, and the wine selection is awesome (indeed, a 5000-bottle tower dominates the middle of the dining room).

Antonio's (☎ 702-252-7737; entrées $18-50; open 5pm-11pm daily), inside the Rio, serves sumptuous Northern Italian cuisine in a stylish Mediterranean atmosphere, replete with inlaid marble floors and pillars and a domed faux sky. Appetizers include a paper-thin carpaccio with shaved parmesan cheese, and a five-onion soup served in a hollowed-out onion. There are plenty of pastas available. Veal lovers will want to sample the fork-tender osso bucco, served on a bed of saffron-infused risotto.

Hungry Hunter (☎ 702-873-0433; 2380 S Rainbow Blvd; entrées $13-33; open 11:30am-10pm Mon-Fri, 4pm-10pm Sat, 4pm-9pm Sun) is the local favorite for steaks, such as the restaurant's signature Whiskey Peppercorn Filet. But Hungry Hunter also offers a fine rack of lamb, grilled swordfish and even pressed duck. There's a children's menu to help keep family costs down, and dress is casual.

Rosemary's Restaurant (☎ 702-869-2251; 8125 W Sahara Ave; lunch entrées $12-16, dinner entrées $23-30; open 11:30am-2:30pm & 5:30pm-10:30pm Mon-Fri, 5:30pm-10:30pm Sat & Sun) is one of the best gourmet restaurants in town. Offerings vary, but typically include such exotics as seared sea scallops in a parsnip potato puree, green-curry-and-shellfish stew with jasmine rice, and a grilled eggplant stack with roasted red bell peppers.

Ruth's Chris Steak House (☎ 702-248-7011; 4561 W Flamingo Rd; entrées $19-34; open 4:30pm-3am daily) is *the* place to go when you're looking for high-quality beef, especially in the wee hours of the night. Served amid elegant brass and etched glass, Ruth's Chris steaks come only from selected Midwestern corn-fed beef. A late-night menu featuring a selection of lighter choices, including pasta, is available after 11pm.

DOWNTOWN
Places to Eat – Budget
Binion's Horseshoe Coffee Shop (☎ 702-382-1600; 128 E Fremont St; meals under $10; open 24hr), inside Binion's Horseshoe, is the Las Vegas coffee shop of yesteryear – a place where it's still possible to get a hearty breakfast for under $5 and a 16oz T-bone steak for under $8. In fact, very little at the coffee shop sells for more than $10, which is one reason it's so popular with locals.

Carson Street Café (☎ 702-385-1111; entreés $8-15; open 24hr), inside the Golden Nugget, is a semi-elegant coffee shop with surprisingly good food. Although a tad pricier than Binion's coffee shop, the café produces superior sandwiches, Mexican fare, filet mignon and prime rib. For dessert, Carson Street features a slew of delectable sundaes. All bar drinks are available (the same can be said for Binion's), and the café never closes.

Center Stage (☎ 702-386-2110; entrées $6-16; open 4:30pm-10pm daily), inside Jackie Gaughan's Plaza, is a particularly good place to be when the crowds are thick. From its second-story position, with semicircular booths overlooking the Fremont Street Experience, it's hard not to feel you're on top of the world. However, the typical coffee-shop food is mediocre and the entrées are overpriced.

Dona Maria Tamales (☎ 702-382-6538; 910 S Las Vegas Blvd; entrées $5.50-8.50; open 8am-10pm daily) specializes in tasty chicken, cheese, beef and pork tamales. A pleasant, family-run cantina, it also has made-to-order enchiladas, burritos, tacos and chimichangas.

Golden Gate (☎ 702-385-1906; 1 Fremont St; dishes from 99¢; open 24hr), inside Golden Gate hotel-casino, is famous for one thing: the best shrimp cocktail in town for a penny under $1. If you love the chewy crustaceans, don't think twice: head to Golden Gate for a goblet full of them at a price you can afford. Nothing else here warrants a special trip, even if that trip is only a block or two long.

Rincon Criollo (☎ 702-388-1906; 1145 S Las Vegas Blvd; open 11am-10pm Tues-Sun) is a no-frills local hangout with some very tasty Cuban offerings; among the better ones are the Cuban sandwich (mostly ham, roast pork and cheese on bread toasted and pressed flat), marinated pork leg and chorizo. Many items are under $5.

Places to Eat – Mid-Range
Tony Roma's: A Place for Ribs (☎ 702-385-3232; entrées $7-14; open 4:30pm-11pm Sun-Thur, 4:30pm-12am Fri & Sat), in the casino area of the Fremont, is an informal, very popular restaurant. Its specialties are barbecued baby back ribs served with a variety of sauces, barbecued shrimp and broiled chicken. Most entrées are around $10. There's a steak-and-lobster special for $11 between 9pm and 11pm daily.

Places to Eat – Top End
Andre's (☎ 702-385-5016; 401 S 6th St; entrées $20-28; open 6pm-11pm Mon-Sat) is yet more proof that you don't have to go to one of the megaresorts on The Strip to taste superb cuisine in Las Vegas. Inside this converted 1930s house you can enjoy excellent Dover sole served *à la facon du chef*, stuffed pork tenderloin with apple and walnuts, marinated salmon tartare, and Maryland blue crab cakes, to name a few of the many French entrées that are offered.

Hugo's Cellar (☎ 702-385-4011; 202 E Fremont St; entrées $25-50; open 5:30pm-11pm daily), inside Four Queens, is an elegant brick-and-brass restaurant where each female diner is presented with a red rose, and the salads, which are included in the price of the entrées, are prepared tableside. Specialities include tournedos Hugo, roast rack of lamb, broiled swordfish and veal. For dessert, say yes to the chocolate-dipped fruits served with whipped cream.

Limerick's (☎ 702-388-2460; 301 E Fremont St; entrées $7-17; open 5pm-11pm Thur-Mon), inside Fitzgerald's, is the product of a renovation that transformed a forgotten diner into a posh steakhouse decked out like a British gentlemen's club. Meat is the mainstay and it comes big and tender. Particularly good is the beef Wellington and the filet mignon. The apricot chicken is likewise memorable. Prices for entrées are quite competitive considering the portions and the quality.

The Pullman Grille (☎ 702-387-1896; meat entrées $14-18, seafood entrées $18-40; open 5pm-10pm Sun, Wed & Thur, 5pm-10:30pm Fri & Sat) at Main Street Station is a well-kept secret. The restaurant features the finest Black Angus beef and seafood specialities in addition to an extensive wine list. The food is excellent, but equally memorable is the setting. Most of the gorgeous carved wood paneling that surrounds patrons was originally from Prestwick Castle in Scotland. The centerpiece of the restaurant is a Pullman train car built in 1926 for Louisa Alcott; it was one of only four car series named after famous women authors.

Second Street Grille (☎ 702-385-3232; entrées $18-35; open 6pm-10pm Sun, Mon & Thur, 6pm-11pm Fri & Sat), inside the Fremont, is a great find. It's an intimate, semi-formal and generally overlooked restaurant serving wonderful international cuisine with a Hawaiian influence. Specialties include wok-charred salmon, lobster, ahi tuna and filet mignon. Veal, chicken and beef dishes are also available.

Entertainment

Las Vegas isn't widely regarded as the entertainment capital of the world for nothing. The city is famous for its showgirls, lounge acts, illusionists, championship fights, headliner performances by some of today's biggest stars and, of course, for its standard-setting gaming houses.

During the past decade, Las Vegas has also become a major venue for music concerts, amusement rides, nightclubs, acrobatic performances, virtual-reality arcades, circus acts and impressive outdoor attractions, such as the regularly erupting volcano at The Mirage, the light shows over Fremont Street and the pirate battles at Treasure Island.

A person can go broke seeing and doing all there is to see and do in Las Vegas, but a person can also see and do a lot in Sin City at little or no cost. The choices seem almost infinite, with new shows, new venues and new sights opening all the time.

In the Things to See & Do chapter, you'll find information on casinos, museums, arcades and rides, outdoor attractions and other sights. Here you'll find information on the more typical forms of evening entertainment – dance clubs, bars, music venues, production shows, performances and cinema – as well as all of the spectator sports available in Las Vegas.

Most of Las Vegas' bars are open around-the-clock. The hours of the dance clubs vary, with most closed Sunday and Monday. It's best to call ahead, not only for times but for music news as well. A club that was featuring rock 'n' roll when this was written may have turned to hip-hop or something else by the time these words reach you. Nothing remains the same for very long in Las Vegas.

Unfortunately, there's not much to report regarding the gay and lesbian club scene in Las Vegas. For up-to-date information on Las Vegas' gay scene, visit the Gay Vegas website (w www.gayvegas.com), the best website of its kind serving Sin City.

THE STRIP
Dance Clubs

The dance clubs found inside the mega-resorts along the spectacular Las Vegas Blvd are a Hollywood set designer's dream. Seemingly no expense has been spared to bring Las Vegas on par with New York and Los Angeles in the area of wildly extravagant and exceedingly hot dance clubs.

The most popular of the city's many dance clubs are described here. Other popular dance clubs to be considered are Light (Bellagio), Drai's (Barbary Coast), La Playa (Harrah's), Club Rio (Rio), C2K (The Venetian).

Cleopatra's Barge Nightclub (☎ 702-731-7110; 3570 S Las Vegas Blvd; admission free with 2-drink minimum; open 10:30pm-4am nightly), inside Caesars Palace, is one of the most unusual dance clubs in Las Vegas. This imposing floating cocktail lounge is a replica of one of the majestic ships that sailed the Nile in ancient Egypt. A hydraulics system constantly raises and lowers the boat to mimic sailing. Due to the relatively small size of the vessel, there are few places to sit aboard the swaying nightclub, although there are a few more tables set around the boat on terra firma. The music is mostly live.

Insomnia (☎ 702-699-9196; 3663 S Las Vegas Blvd; admission out-of-state visitors/Nevada residents $20/10; open 11pm-3am Fri & Sat), at the corner of Harmon Ave, opened in 2001 and continues to enjoy enormous popularity due to its appealing ambience and pleasing selection of rock bands.

Monte Carlo Pub & Brewery (☎ 702-730-7777; 3770 S Las Vegas Blvd; admission free, no drink minimum; open 10:30pm-3am nightly) is an industrial-size place inside the Monte Carlo, popular mostly with twenty- and thirtysomething locals after sundown. As its name suggests, this place is mostly a pub and brewery. The warehouse-like establishment is, by day, a restaurant serving pizzas, salads, sandwiches, steaks and its own beers, brewed in huge copper barrels; at night, the creature transforms into a heaving, pulsating dance club. The blaring music is variously live or spun, but there's always something to dance to. More of a couch potato than a John Travolta? There are three dozen TV monitors and a big-screen TV on the premises, tuned to sports during the day and rock videos after dark. No ripped clothing, T-shirts or gangsta pants allowed.

Ra *(☎ 702-262-4000; 3900 S Las Vegas Blvd; admission varies with entertainment $10-20; open 10pm-3am Wed-Sat)*, inside Luxor, is the most spectacular dance club in Las Vegas. Ra takes its name from the ancient Egyptian god of the sun, who was said to travel through the heavens by day and rage in the underworld at night. Today, a possible likeness of this winged, radiating god towers over the nightclub's primary bar: Ra sits upon a golden throne, has a 30ft wingspan and lights up the club with a dozen fire-green lasers that beam from its sunken eye sockets.

The Old Egypt theme is heavily applied throughout the club, beginning with the entryway – a stunning marble-and-sandstone corridor lined with statues of Egyptian gods and guards. The interior is rectangular, with the main bar at one end, a bandstand built into one of the long walls, and the dance floor in front of the stage. Flanking the bandstand are cages containing go-go girls in red-velvet bikinis. Scattered about the club are VIP booths and cigar lounges. Although the music at Ra is mostly furnished by disc jockeys, it occasionally hosts big-name bands. Blue jeans, ripped trousers and collarless shirts aren't allowed.

Seven *(☎ 702-739-7744; Ⓦ www.seven lasvegas.com; 3724 S Las Vegas Blvd; no cover, no drink minimum; open 10:30pm-4am Fri & Sat)* is a new, one-level, pseudo–Art Deco dance club with numerous bars, a fine dance floor and saddle-up-to-a-stool sushi bar. Music at this hip, spacious club is usually DJ driven, although there's occasional live entertainment in the Strip-side patio during summer months.

Studio 54 *(☎ 702-895-1111; 3799 S Las Vegas Blvd; admission men/women $10/free;*

Biggest Bangs for the Buck	
Bars	• The Bar at Times Square
	• Double Down Saloon
	• Fireside Lounge
Bars with Views	• Top of the World Lounge
	• VooDoo Lounge
Blues Venues	• House of Blues
	• Sand Dollar Blues Lounge
Cinemas	• Century Orleans
	• IMAX Theater at Luxor
Dance Clubs	• The Beach
	• Seven
	• Studio 54
Illusionists	• Lance Burton
	• Rick Springfield
	• Siegfried & Roy
Jazz Venues	• Blue Note Las Vegas rumjungle
Production Shows	• Cirque du Soleil's Mystère
	• Cirque du Soleil's O
	• Folies Bergère
Rock Venues	• House of Blues
	• The Joint
	• Le Theatre de Arts

open 10pm-3am Tues-Sat) is inside MGM Grand. Like a poor remake of a great film, it doesn't exactly capture the magic that once existed at New York's legendary Studio 54. For one thing, the original nightclub attracted a classy clientele – or at least a well-dressed one. No matter how the people inside behaved, they weren't kicking around in blue jeans and looking like they'd spent the day slumped over slot machines. This version of Studio 54 does have a dress code – no T-shirts, no gangsta pants, no tank tops, no work boots and no sandals – but in reality it rarely denies admission to anyone. What you find when you get inside is mostly casually dressed tourists wondering where the glamorous people went. The club, by the way, is

ENTERTAINMENT

huge – three stories, with four dance floors, four bars, semiprivate lounges and a gallery of celebrity photos taken at the original Studio 54. The decor is black, silver and industrial; the music always DJ-driven chart toppers.

Utopia *(☎ 702-740-4646; 3765 S Las Vegas Blvd; admission $5-10; open 11pm-4am Tues-Sat)* better be good with a name like that. Utopia features something different every night, and most nights it's *very* good. On Tuesday, it's usually canned rhythm & blues or hip-hop; Wednesday night is ladies night, with free entry and drinks for women; progressive house music plays on Thursday; and Friday and Saturday feature live music (usually of the hip-hop, hard rock or funk variety).

Bars

Every megaresort on The Strip has several bars in addition to numerous restaurants that offer a full palette of alcoholic beverages. Drinks are available in casinos to persons aged 21 years and older at all hours. Most of the bars boast two-for-one happy hours,

which generally run from 4pm to 6pm or 5pm to 7pm, with times varying from one establishment to another.

The vast majority of Sin City's bars are smoke filled; the antismoking laws in neighboring California banning cigarette, pipe and cigar smoking in all public facilities are viewed with heartfelt disgust, disdain and indignation in Las Vegas. If you can cope with the smoke, you'll likely enjoy your time in the bars mentioned here.

Bar at Times Square *(☎ 702-740-6969; 3790 S Las Vegas Blvd; admission Fri & Sat after 8pm $10; dueling pianos 8pm-2am nightly)*, inside New York-New York, is possibly the liveliest bar in Las Vegas. Every night the pub fills to overflowing as not one but two singing pianists lead a raucous crowd through old favorites. This is the kind of place where young and old alike raise their steins and their voices in camaraderie, where they dance between the tables, and where latecomers press their faces against the windows to catch a glimpse of the festivities taking place inside. Arrive early if you want to get in;

Drinking Las Vegas

If, like Nicolas Cage's character in *Leaving Las Vegas*, you've come to Sin City to drink yourself to death, we encourage you to sample the following beverages.

The Atlantis Served at the Hard Rock Hotel, this drink is made of equal parts Blue Curacao, Montecristo Rum and sour mix sweetened with Sweet 'N Low, with a line of sugar and cinnamon added to the rim. Named after the fabled lost city, a few of these and you'll forget the name of *your* home town.

Ghostini Served at the Palms' rooftop Ghost Bar, this concoction consists of 1oz of Midori, 3oz of Absolut Vodka and 1oz of sour mix. Many people gradually reconnect with their inner spirit while sipping Ghostinis 42 floors above the gaming areas at the Palms hotel-casino.

Jell-O Shot Served at Coyote Ugly in New York-New York, the cultural boob of the drink world consists of strawberry Jell-O and vodka, mixed 2 parts water to 1 part vino de Russia. At Coyote Ugly, expect to receive it in a shooter from an anything-but-ugly bar chick in hipster jeans and a snug top.

Monte Melon Berry Smash Served at Mandalay Bay's Rum Jungle, the MMBS is a melding of Montecristo Rum, a 4oz scoop of watermelon, seven raspberries and ¾oz of sour mix. The drink arrives in a martini glass rimmed with red sugar and a split strawberry, and beautified with floating blueberries.

Petrossian Served at Bellagio, this award-winning cocktail, named for the traditional start of happy hour (4:30pm), contains 1½oz of Bacardi rum, ½oz of Bacardi Tropico, a dash of Campari, 2oz of guava nectar, 2oz of fresh sour mix and several thin slices of lime and orange.

arrive late and you'll have to wait for someone to leave before you can enter – at this fun place, that could be a while.

Fireside Lounge at the Peppermill (☎ 702-735-7635; 2985 S Las Vegas Blvd; admission free; open 24hr) is a romantic and cosy place for couples. The plush, dimly lit red-velvet booths are perfect for intimate conversations. Most of the dozen or so booths are separated by plants, which increase privacy in a subtle and soothing way. The carpet is jet black. The Fireside Lounge is also known for its circular fire-on-water fireplace; gas rising from the depths of a Jacuzzi-like tub ignite at the water's surface, creating a scene that's particularly spellbinding after a couple of piña coladas and several fistfuls of honey-sweetened peanuts (they're free and generously provided). The lounge serves lots of tropical concoctions, such as blue Hawaiians, tequila sunrises and mai tais – all are reasonably priced and arrive in bowl-glasses large enough for goldfish. The background music is unintrusive and easy listening. Tasty appetizers such as nachos and deep-fried potato skins are also available.

The Polo Lounge (☎ 702-261-1000; 3745 S Las Vegas Blvd; admission after 9:30pm $10; open 7am-3am daily), atop the Polo Towers, offers captivating views of Las Vegas Blvd even though it's only 19 floors up – or a full 88 floors lower than the sky-high bar inside the Stratosphere Tower. Its decorator went way overboard with the black paint; the entire place is jet black, which perhaps makes it look thinner?! Music varies nightly, but the club's best nights – Friday and Saturday – usually feature live hip hop and a twentysomething crowd. The Polo Lounge can get very smoky due to lousy ventilation. You've been warned.

Top of the World Lounge (☎ 702-380-7711; 2000 S Las Vegas Blvd; free admission most nights; open 10am-1am Sun-Thur, 10am-2am Fri & Sat) is on the 107th floor of Stratosphere. Like to listen to music and get high? There's no place in Las Vegas where you can get higher without the approval of an air traffic controller. Every night, beginning about 9pm, a trio or pianist plays popular tunes in the 220-seat cocktail lounge that overlooks the revolving restaurant on the 106th floor. Beyond the restaurant is an eagle's perspective of Las Vegas. There's rarely a cover charge (with the exception of New Year's Eve), but there is a $7 fee to take the elevator to the lounge from Sunday through Thursday; it costs $8 on Friday and Saturday. There's also a small dance floor, so bring your blue suede shoes.

Coyote Ugly (☎ 702-740-6969; 3790 S Las Vegas Blvd; admission from 8pm $10; open noon-4am daily), inside the New York-New York hotel-casino, is a twentysomethings' bar featuring steaming-hot female bartenders who take the expression 'pouring drinks' to another level. Bar-top dancing by staffers and drunken tourists attracts lots of encouragement from all angles to release inhibitions and, for women, to release suspension apparatus on the Bra Wall of Fame. Made famous by a silly movie of the same name, this is definitely a good place to come very late at night if you *love* to tie on a major hangover and enjoy the company of hundreds of people just like you.

Production Shows

Las Vegas offers the visitor more production shows – which typically include a variety of song, dance and magic numbers that don't follow a story line – than any other city in the world. Leaving Sin City without seeing one is like leaving Paris without seeing Notre Dame; it's surely some kind of crime. But don't just see any show. Las Vegas has some great ones, some terrible ones and many that fall somewhere in between.

American Superstars (☎ 702-380-7707, 800-998-6937; 2000 S Las Vegas Blvd; tickets $30; shows 7pm & 10pm Wed, Fri & Sat, 7pm Sun, Mon & Tues), at Stratosphere, is one of the many Vegas shows featuring celebrity impersonators. All in all, the performers are quite entertaining, and resemble the top pop vocalists today in appearance and voice, such as Madonna, Gloria Estefan and Michael Jackson. The impersonators come and go, so exactly who you'll see will depend on when you see the show. For those of you with poor eyesight or distant seats, there's an enormous video screen on each side of the stage

ENTERTAINMENT

Ain't Nothing to Gettin' Free Drinks

'A gin and tonic, please.'

If you're 21 years or older and can say those words, or words like them, while shoving coins into a slot machine or otherwise distributing wealth in a Vegas casino, you've mastered the fine art of obtaining complimentary beverages. It's that simple. Really.

Simply saddle up to a one-eyed Jack, get the attention of a cocktail waitress and order a drink. Unless you're asking for a fine Merlot at Cheapo Casino, nine times out of 10 the cocktail waitress will vanish and return with your drink.

The key to endless bar service in Vegas casinos resides in the answer to this question: 'Are you playing?' If you're putting your child's college fund into dollar slots, or wowing a poker dealer with your deadpan face, you are playing and have met the not-so-rigid requirements for free booze.

If you're just walking through a casino and ask a cocktail waitress for a drink, expect her to ask you where you're sitting. Replying that you're just wandering aimlessly around and would prefer to do it with a drink in each hand isn't going to get you fistfuls of hootch.

If you've holed yourself up with a slot machine that doesn't appear on the radar screen of a cocktail waitress, feel free to hunt one down, tell her where you're sitting and ask her to bring you a drink. In fact, feel free to order two drinks. Unless you're falling-down drunk or being obnoxious, the casino couldn't care less how much swill you swallow.

Remember, the gears of Las Vegas are greased by tips. The smiling, fresh-faced cocktail waitress who descended on you like an angel and brought you a Cuba libre in record time might vanish forever if you don't favor her with a tip. The drink is free, but the cocktail waitress lives on tips. One George Washington per order will keep her coming.

---

displaying the performances. In general, the impersonators are well received, but seem a degree or two less convincing than the impersonators appearing in the show Legends in Concert (see later).

Blue Man Group (☎ 702-262-4400, 800-557-7428; 3900 S Las Vegas Blvd; early/late shows $70/80; shows 7pm & 10pm nightly), at Luxor, consists of three blue-headed, non-speaking comedic percussionists who mix some mindbending audio-visual displays with some juvenile but fun behavior in what is an extraordinarily odd but amusing show. Among their bizarre behavior: The men perform a laryngoscopy on an audience member, whose close-up views of her tonsils (among other parts) are displayed on a giant screen; they play tribal-sounding music on instruments made of large plastic pipes; and they make paintings by spitting spray paint on several large canvasses. At various times, the first six rows of the audience find themselves the recipients of catapulted Jell-O tubs, hurdled marshmallows, and paint splattered off the

tops of snare drums. The show is a real crowd pleaser, but the talents of the individuals involved actually leave a lot to be desired.

Bottoms Up (☎ 702-733-3333, 888-308-8899; 3555 S Las Vegas Blvd; tickets $13; shows 2pm & 4pm Mon-Sat), at the Flamingo, is the only afternoon variety show in Las Vegas featuring topless women. This blur of vaudeville acts, plump-chested showgirls and one-liners from veteran funnyman Breck Wall is enthusiastically recommended. It's a small show – just 10 performers in all – but gets big laughs and hearty applause show after show. For the money, Bottoms Up is one of the best entertainment deals on offer.

Crazy Girls (☎ 702-794-9433, 800-634-3420; 2901 S Las Vegas Blvd; tickets $24; shows 8:30pm & 10:30pm Wed-Mon), at the Riviera, could be called nothing but a titty show gussied up with costumes, props and sets to pass as something of value, but this would be wrong; after all, between the lip-synched tits-and-ass numbers there *is* a stand-up comedian who comes out and tells funny jokes.

An Evening at La Cage (☎ 702-794-9433, 800-634-3420; 2901 S Las Vegas Blvd; tickets $23; shows 7:30pm & 9:30pm, Wed-Mon), at the Riviera, will be a very pleasant surprise if you haven't yet seen a female-impersonator revue. The show features the extremely likeable Frank Marino as a catty Joan Rivers, who dispenses naughty jokes and remarks between mostly lip-synched impersonations of Madonna, Diana Ross, Cher, Judy Garland and others. The show has the potential to flop big-time, but instead it rides to a much-deserved standing ovation on the basis of rock-solid choreography, very believable performances by the drag queens and some top-notch work by supporting female dancers (at times it's difficult differentiating the men from the women). A Las Vegas revue featuring drag queens may not appeal to everyone, but few people leave An Evening at La Cage without a smile on their face.

Folies Bergère (☎ 702-739-2411, 888-826-8767; 3801 S Las Vegas Blvd; table/booth seating $45/55; covered/topless shows 7:30pm/10pm Fri-Wed), at the Tropicana, is Las Vegas' longest-running production show, and a tribute to the Parisian Music Hall. Appropriately, Folies Bergère contains the most beautiful showgirls in town. The show's theme consists of presenting 'France through the years,' from the end of the 19th century to 2000; among the mostly song-and-dance numbers are a French fashion show, a royal ballroom number and the inevitable can-can routine. After a surprisingly weak opening, the show is very entertaining, with the ladies displaying considerable talent as well as knockout good looks. In the midst of a long string of superior acts is one, in particular, that's quite lovely; a fine snowy ballet number that's at once playful, dreamy and divine. The covered show is the more enticing of the two.

Danny Gans: The Man of Many Voices (☎ 702-791-7777, 800-929-1111; 3400 S Las Vegas Blvd; tickets $80; shows 8pm Sat, Sun & Tues-Thur), at The Mirage, puts on a super show. As the title suggests, Gans is an impressionist, and perhaps the best one alive. Of course, you have to be fluent in Americanisms to enjoy him; if you're unfamiliar with the voices of such American celebrities as Clint Eastwood, Peter Falk, Stevie Wonder, Frank Sinatra and Bill Clinton (among many others), much of the show won't translate. The rest of you will likely join the house in rising to an enthusiastic standing ovation when Gans bows out.

Jubilee! (☎ 702-739-4567, 800-237-7469; 3645 S Las Vegas Blvd; early/late shows $50/66; shows 7:30pm & 10:30pm Sat-Thur), at Bally's, is a show that Vegas wouldn't be Vegas without. The long-running show opens with a huge topless routine performed by showgirls in classic showgirl attire (huge, feathered headdresses and sequined bikini bottoms) and men, first in tuxedos, later in G-strings. Each number is very visually appealing, with tremendously colorful outfits and marvelous sets. The voices, by and large, are so-so, and the dancers aren't always in step. Clearly the audience is supposed to be so dazzled by the spectacular costumes and sets, and the sheer number of people on stage that it's not supposed to notice the mediocre singing or dancing. Instead, we're supposed to look on in total awe as a *Titanic* sinks and other impressive props come and go. And as it started, so does it end: with lots of nipples and twinkling rhinestones on display. If you're of the opinion that big is always beautiful, you'll love this show, since every number's a big one. But a little less quantity and a little more quality in the talent department wouldn't hurt.

King Arthur's Tournament (☎ 702-597-7777, 877-750-5464; 3850 S Las Vegas Blvd; tickets $40; shows 6pm & 8:30pm daily), at Excalibur, is a show that you've got to be wired a certain kind of way to fully appreciate. Firstly, it's not a cocktail show but a dinner show where guests are expected to eat the medieval way – with their fingers. Secondly, the show demands audience participation. Armor-clad knights joust and battle with swords in the arena before you, and you're encouraged time and again

And Now, Our Very Special Guest ...

To many people in Las Vegas, Frank Sinatra and his Rat Pack pals built this town. For years, they weren't merely legendary headliners; they were the darlings of gossip columnists from LA to New York, and their all-night partying and tumultuous lives entertained millions of readers daily. Their antics in Vegas brought adoring fans by the planeload.

Today, there's only one surviving member of the Rat Pack (Joey Bishop), and most of the other legendary headliners who 'built Las Vegas' – Elvis among them – are no longer entertaining crowds here on Earth. But Las Vegas continues to book top entertainers such as The Rolling Stones, U2 and Tori Amos for two- and three-night engagements. These brief engagements are often overlooked by visitors, due to the fact that the performances are fleeting and information about them can't be found in any guidebook.

The easiest way to get the lowdown on upcoming headliners is to access the Las Vegas Online Entertainment Guide (W www.lvol.com) and enter the dates you're intending to visit Vegas.

HD

Ol' Blue Eyes

to pound on the table and shout words of support to your designated knight. The constant encouragement to shout aloud and pound on the table is popular with kids, but it gets stale quickly for everyone else. There are magic acts and singing as well, but for the money you can do better.

Lance Burton: Master Magician (☎ 702-730-7160, 877-386-8224; 3770 S Las Vegas Blvd; balcony/mezzanine $55/60; shows 7pm & 10pm Tues-Sat) performs his magic at the Monte Carlo. There are lots of illusionists in Las Vegas, but few are as engaging and talented as Lance. He has several grand illusions, including his signature 'flying' white Corvette. But Burton differs from Siegfried, Roy and others by emphasizing sleight-of-hand tricks and other close-up magic tricks involving disappearing birds and whatnot. Instead of moving about the stage in a heightened state of alert like most magicians, Kentucky-raised Burton is attractively low-key in his delivery. The juxtaposition of his mellow manner with his mind-boggling feats makes what he's doing all the more enjoyable. Adding excitement and laughs to Burton's show is Michael

Goudeau, who juggles the most unusual objects. Burton's show offers great value, and the $27-million theater built for him doesn't contain a bad seat.

Legends in Concert (☎ 702-794-3261, 877-777-7664; 3535 S Las Vegas Blvd; adult/child 12 years and under $35/20; shows 7:30pm & 10:30pm Mon-Sat), at Imperial Palace, is the best of the impersonator shows. It's been around since 1983 and will likely be around for years to come. The award-winning cocktail show features performers who must not only look like famous vocalists such as Elton John, Neil Diamond, Prince and Dolly Parton, but they must sound like them as well; no lip-synching is allowed. The acts frequently change, but the quality doesn't. Adding to the show's appeal are well-choreographed male and female dancers, who appear in most of the acts. On one particular night, the evening started with several hits from a convincing Gloria Estefan impersonator to get the crowd in the mood, then segued into a very likeable Rod Stewart, who upped the heat with a scalding rendition of 'Hot Legs.' The show progressed to Diana Ross, Garth Brooks, Tina

ENTERTAINMENT

Turner and the Four Tops. While the impersonators sing former chart toppers and do it amazingly well, large video screens on both sides of the stage show not only the live action but also clips of the real performers in concert; the screens add a lot to the entertainment value of Legends, which is already one of the biggest crowd pleasers in town.

Melinda: The First Lady of Magic (☎ 702-414-1000, 877-881-4225; 3355 S Las Vegas Blvd; tickets $38-88; shows 6:30pm & 8:30pm Mon, Tues, Thur & Sun, 6:30pm Fri & Sat), at The Venetian, features a series of acts that gracefully combine sexy dancing and amusing but not amazing illusions. What makes this show a joy to watch is Melinda, who is clearly having a good time on stage going through her routines. Her enjoyment is contagious, she's very cheeky and cute, and the hour-long show seems to be just the right length. Melinda performs few dazzling numbers, but the show is good overall and worth the money (especially if you get a cheaper seat).

Midnight Fantasy (☎ 702-262-4000, 800-557-7428; 3900 S Las Vegas Blvd; tickets $30; shows 8:30pm & 10:30pm, Tues, Thur & Sat, 10:30pm Wed & Fri), inside Luxor, is a tasteful topless revue set along the Nile a long, long time ago and features gorgeous women moving to Egyptian and English music. Most of the music is lip-synched, and there seems to be more emphasis on speed than sex appeal, with more than a few of the numbers having the feel of cheerleading routines; though the audience is clearly appreciative. A comedian and a James Brown impersonator appear at times, adding pleasant touches of humor between the sexy scenes. Although not nearly as well done as La Femme, which is the best of the topless revues, Midnight Fantasy is a good show.

Mystère (☎ 702-894-7722, 800-392-1999; 3300 S Las Vegas Blvd; tickets $90; shows 7:30pm & 10:30pm Wed-Sun), at Treasure Island, is described by Franco Dragone, director of this Cirque du Soleil production, as a celebration of life. It begins with a pair of babies making their way in a world filled with strange creatures and brilliant colors. It also features a mis-

guided clown, who can bring this smooth-running production to a halt with his humorous antics, as well as acrobats, dancers and musicians who display remarkable and at times nearly unbelievable talent. Mystère features one spectacular feat of human strength and agility after another, often suspended over the audience and performed by people in fantastic costumes. The show is entertainment at its finest. Tickets are pricey, but they're worth every penny.

Wayne Newton (☎ 702-732-6325, 800-824-6033; 3000 S Las Vegas Blvd; tickets $45; shows 7pm & 10pm Wed-Sat, 7pm Sun & Mon), at the Stardust, has taken a lot of criticism in recent years because he doesn't repeatedly reinvent himself like an old, male rendition of Madonna. Instead, he continues to perform in the manner to which he's grown accustomed and in the manner his fans have always appreciated. He's old-school Las Vegas, one of the last of a dying breed, like the Stardust itself. Indeed, the Stardust enjoys his style so much that it has named a theater after him and signed him to a long contract. Wayne Newton isn't widely regarded as 'Mr Las Vegas' for nothing. For a taste of traditional Vegas in the style of Frank, Dean, Sammy and other Vegas legends, catch him before he retires. He's already taking 12 weeks off each year – vacation time he well deserves.

O (☎ 702-796-9999, 888-488-7111; 3600 S Las Vegas Blvd; early/late shows $100/121; shows 7:30pm & 10:30pm Fri-Tues), at Bellagio, phonetically speaking, is the French word for water (spelled 'eau'). Steve Wynn, former chairman of the company that initially owned Bellagio, is quoted in a media guide about the resort as saying, 'We had to produce an entertainment experience that people would talk about in Singapore, Rome, Hong Kong, London, New York and Buenos Aires.' After searching the globe, Steve Wynn and company approached Montreal-based Cirque du Soleil about producing a show worthy of the most expensive hotel on Earth. This is the result. With an international cast of 74, performing in, on and above water, *O* tells the tale of theater through the

ENTERTAINMENT

ages. The show features daring displays of aerial acrobatics and synchronized swimming. Cirque du Soleil's first venture into aquatic theater is a spectacular feat of imagination and engineering. It is indeed the kind of entertainment that has people talking about it in cities around the planet.

Rita Rudner (☎ 702-740-6815; 3790 S Las Vegas Blvd; tickets $40-50; shows 8pm Mon, 9pm Thur & Fri, 4pm & 8pm Sat), at New York-New York, is a kick in the pants. The comedian, whose trademark is telling stories and delivering one-liners with soft-spoken naivete, packs a powerful whallop into every joke. Her shrewd observations cover everything, from life within her marriage to the joys of grocery shopping. Typical of her style of humor is this reference to the importance she gives to owning many shoes: 'My husband asked me, "You have two feet, why do you need so many shoes?" I asked him, "You have two eyes, why do you need so many channels?".' Rudner is a joy to listen to, and the intimate theater in which she performs (only 425 seats) lends itself well to her shtick; you feel like she's sharing her most personal thoughts with you. And as she likes to say, 'I'm a woman. I have to tell you everything.'

Siegfried & Roy (☎ 702-791-7777, 800-963-9634; 3400 S Las Vegas Blvd; tickets $101; shows 7:30pm Sun & Mon, 7:30pm & 11pm Tues, Fri & Sat), the legendary illusionists at The Mirage, have been performing sold-out shows in Las Vegas and elsewhere for more than three decades, and remain the hottest ticket in town. The Germans made a name for themselves with their charm, illusions and white tigers, and despite more than 5000 performances, today's Siegfried & Roy show is as good as ever. The pair mix illusions and dance with fairytale, fueling a series of spectacles with so many special effects, showgirls and wonderful props that the show can at times be a bit overwhelming. And that, of course, is how it should be. Perhaps cognizant of the fact that they could appear somewhat mechanical, as if simply 'going through the motions,' they do an excellent job of reaching the audience by communicating with viewers at times and, at others, appearing and disappearing from the viewing booths. These two are an absolute treat, arguably the best illusionists alive.

Skintight (☎ 702-369-5111, 800-392-9002; 3475 S Las Vegas Blvd; tickets $40; shows 10:30pm Mon-Wed, 10pm & midnight Fri, 10:30pm Sat), at Harrah's, is a sexy medley of near-naked showgirls singing, dancing and slithering around. It's rounded out by an appearance by Miss Nude World.

Splash (☎ 702-794-9433, 800-634-6753; 2901 S Las Vegas Blvd; early/late shows $50/60; shows 7:30pm & 10:30pm nightly), at the Riviera, has a variety of unrelated production numbers – some better than others. Most of the acts are excellent. There's a contortionist whose feats of strength and balance are scarcely believable, and a magician whose close-up illusions are good plain fun. The showstopper features four daredevil motorcyclists who enter a round cage and execute 360° upside-down moves that require split-second timing to avoid a horrific accident. In the show's current incarnation, the hope is that good taste will move the

Siegfried & Roy Aren't All Show

Though world famous for their grand illusions, Siegfried & Roy take great pride in their efforts to protect white lions. On April 1, 2001, for example, one of the illusionists' white lions, Prosperity, gave birth to four cubs at the Cincinnati Zoo. The cubs have the distinction of being the first litter of white lions born in the United States. With their birth, the cubs bring the number of white lions in Siegfried & Roy's breeding program to save the endangered cats from extinction to 23. At the time of writing, Prosperity and her suitors Sunshine and Future were on loan to the zoo as part of that program. You knew that? Well, here's something you probably don't know: Prosperity is the official mascot of the United States Senate.

Even if you're made of wax, the show must go on!

Liberace sparkles in spangles at Madame Tussaud's

Hang out with the Rat Pack at Madame Tussaud's, in the Venetian

RICHARD CUMMINS

King Arthur would feel right at home at Excalibur

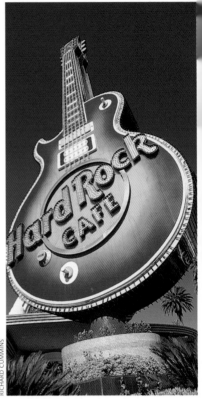
Now all we need is a giant guitarist

Siegfried, Roy and friend at the Mirage

Another 'Dive' on The Strip

producers to pull the plug on the truly stupid number featuring a topless singing biker chick on a motorcycle. Also entirely forgettable is a weak John Travolta impersonator who performs two hits from *Saturday Night Fever*. All things considered, Splash is a very entertaining show.

Rick Springfield in EFX Alive (☎ 702-891-7777, 800-929-1111; 3799 S Las Vegas Blvd; early/late shows $55/75; 7:30pm & 10:30pm Tues-Sat), at MGM Grand, revolves around the many talents of Rick Springfield as an actor-singer-dancer. Supporting him is a talented and superbly choreographed cast, as well as $40 million in truly spectacular props, sets and special effects. EFX takes the audience on a musical journey through space and time during which Springfield, who plays a regular Joe who's lost his imagination, is able to assume the personas of Harry Houdini, HG Wells and King Arthur in order to rediscover his powers of imagination. The story line allows the seamless inclusion of wonderful special effects, while introducing well-delivered song, dance, acrobatic and magical numbers one after another. This is a show everyone enjoys.

Viva Las Vegas (☎ 702-380-7711, 800-998-6937; 2000 S Las Vegas Blvd; tickets $12; shows 2pm & 4pm Mon-Sat), at the Stratosphere, is the longest-running daytime production show in Las Vegas. Viva Las Vegas offers tremendous value. It's a variety show with beautiful showgirls, an entertaining magician, a comedian-emcee and two other very funny men. It's fun for the whole family (yes, the women keep their tops on), but beware: the jokes are intended for adults. If you're wondering what a Vegas production show is like but are traveling on a tight budget, Viva Las Vegas will entertain and educate at low cost and won't cut into your nocturnal activities.

Live Music
Rock Inside MGM Grand, **Grand Garden Arena** (☎ 702-891-7777, 800-929-1111; 3799 S Las Vegas Blvd) is a 17,157-seat special events center that's home to rock concerts as well as championship boxing

and other forms of entertainment. Barbra Streisand, during her first concert in more than 20 years, opened the Grand Garden Arena on December 31, 1993, in conjunction with the grand opening of MGM Grand.

House of Blues (☎ 702-736-7607; W www.hob.com; 3950 S Las Vegas Blvd), at Mandalay Bay, is one of the top Vegas venues for live rock 'n' roll and rhythm & blues. The House, which opened in March 1999 with a performance by Blues Brothers Dan Ackroyd, Jim Belushi and John Goodman, features live music in a venue that can accommodate 2000 people, along with a 600-seat restaurant just off Mandalay Bay's casino floor. The decor is Mississippi Delta juke joint, and the deep purple lighting casts an ethereal glow on everything and everyone, which is all the more striking against the bright, brassy backdrop of the resort's elegant casino.

Despite its name, the House of Blues provides a wide variety of quality live music that includes blues, soul, pop and rock (mostly the latter). Acts range from living legends such as Tom Jones, Chuck Berry and BB King to the Crash Test Dummies, Chris Isaak and Sheryl Crow. Ticket prices vary with performers. Be advised that the number of tickets sold usually exceeds the number of available seats; if seating is important to you, arrive early or you'll end up standing during the show. For current information about the House of Blues' entertainment schedule, call or visit the website. There's music most nights in a corner of the House of Blues restaurant, in a courtyard off the main arena. The music is usually performed by talented local bands, who generally get going around 9pm. A DJ takes over after midnight.

Le Theatre de Arts (☎ 702-967-4567, 800-237-7469; 3645 S Las Vegas Blvd), at Paris-Las Vegas, is a 1200-seat theater presenting some of the top headliners. Among the artists who have performed at Le Theatre are Natalie Cole, The Moody Blues, Pati LaBelle, Howie Mandrel and Tony Bennett.

Jazz A sister jazz club of the original Blue Note found in New York City's West Village is **Blue Note Las Vegas** (☎ 702-862-8307; Ⓦ www.bluenotejazz.com; 3667 S Las Vegas Blvd, cnr Harmon Ave; admission $20, minimum drinks and/or food $10; sessions 8pm & 10:30pm Mon-Sat). Most of the huge names in contemporary jazz have played here, and the setting is intimate and stylish. Doors open at 6pm for dinner (excellent but expensive, with entrées from $20 to $30), with the first show two hours later. Sunday night is local jam-session night (no 'shows,' per se), with talented musicians dropping in from around 8pm to make beautiful music together. The sessions, which often last until 3am, do not carry a cover charge or minimum food/drink tab. The rest of the week management honors a two-for-one discount on the admission charge to couples who produce a Lonely Planet Las Vegas guide.

rumjungle (☎ 702-632-7000; 3950 S Las Vegas Blvd), at Mandalay Bay, is a tropical-themed bar/restaurant/dance club that actually spells its name rumjungle (one word and lowercase) to the annoyance of writers and editors alike, and it is often the place in Las Vegas to hear Latin jazz (sadly for some, techno is getting increasingly popular here). rumjungle is notable for the wall of fire at its entrance, the tumbling ceiling-to-floor cascades inside the bar, and its dance floor, which really heats up on weekend nights. Also remarkable about rumjungle is its selection of rums – more than 100 at last count. If you're wondering which brands are offered, just read the labels on the tower of rum bottles behind the bar. Yes, an actual tower of rum bottles. There's a restaurant attached to the bar and it has its own attraction: a window into the kitchen. Indeed, rumjungle's chefs are a fairly animated group. Admission is free unless there's live music (usually Tuesday through Saturday, starting about 11pm), which attracts a $10 cover charge. No athletic wear, baggy pants, bell bottoms, hats or T-shirts are allowed. Also, be advised the bathrooms are unisex. If you've got a bashful bladder or otherwise prefer the relative privacy of a Gentlemens or Ladies room, use the bathrooms between rumjungle and the gaming area.

Cinemas

The best movie theater in town is the **IMAX Theater** at Luxor (☎ 702-262-4555; 2-D/3-D movies $8/9). See the Things to See & Do chapter for more details.

First-run films can be seen at the **United Artists Showcase** (☎ 702-740-4911; 3785 S Las Vegas Blvd). Admission is $8 for adults and $4.50 for children.

EAST OF THE STRIP
Dance Clubs

Baby's (☎ 702-693-5000; 4455 Paradise Rd; men/women $15/free; open 11pm-4am Thur-Sat), at the Hard Rock Hotel, is difficult to find but a joy to discover most nights. At the end of a dark flight of stairs which lead from an unmarked door (ask a Hard Rock employee to lead you to it), is a very hip dance club with luminescent walls, floating bars and private booths overlooking the dancefloor. The music is mostly hip-hop and top-40 tunes, and the crowd is in the 20- to 30-year-old range. A very fine find.

The Beach (☎ 702-731-1925; 365 Convention Center Dr; cover charge $10; open 24hr) will undoubtedly be the first or second place mentioned when you ask any Vegas hipster to name the hottest straight dance clubs in town. The Beach is the only dance club in Las Vegas open around-the-clock, although sparks don't usually start flying much before midnight. When the clock strikes 12, this roomy, rectangular, two-story club with heavy Southern Californian surfer-bar overtones hangs ten. Throngs of mostly twenty-somethings burn up the dance floor under lots of black light and a suspended Corvette, bumping the night away to hip-hop, R&B and rock from the 1950s. Booze is poured at all five of the club's lengthy bars, and hard-bodied, bikini-clad women roam the club with shot belts, trying to keep up with the demand for their breathtaking libations.

The Nightclub (☎ 702-732-5755; 300 Paradise Rd; admission free; open 3pm-3am most days), inside the Las Vegas Hilton, is for those of us closer in age to 50 than 20. Its classy Art Deco interior has tremendous sound and light systems, and the club features a variety of lounge acts. Most of the acts are led by male vocalists who belt out soul, funk or soft rock, or by female vocalists who put on 'adult dance shows' featuring 'hot girls, hot music, hot dancing and much more,' to borrow a few words from the club's announcer. There's a one-drink minimum, but never a cover charge at The Nightclub, which opens at 3pm and remains quiet until 9pm or 10pm.

Bars

Double Down Saloon (☎ 702-791-5775; 4640 Paradise Rd; admission free; noon-3am daily) isn't your typical Vegas bar. You just gotta love a gin joint that shows midget porn flicks on its TV monitors and whose tangy, blood-red house drink is named 'Ass Juice.' For one thing, it has a behavior code: 'You puke, you clean.' For another, the club mostly appeals to the well-heeled lunatic fringe. Here, the decor is dark and psychedelic, and the jukebox vibrates with New Orleans jazz, British punk, Chicago blues and surf-guitar king Dick Dale. On Wednesday nights, the music is usually provided by a local blues band. Regardless, there's never a cover charge at this club, which doesn't accept any credit cards, and claims to be 'the happiest place on Earth.'

Favorites (☎ 702-796-1776; 4110 S Maryland Parkway) is the place to head for if your idea of a good time involves being surrounded by rowdy college students in a club where the music's cranked to an ear-damaging level and the dance floor's so small that you're never dancing with one person but actually three or four. Yes, Favorites is a favorite with the UNLV crowd; the establishment's variety of live music runs from blues to jazz to swing to rock. There's also bar-top video poker, two pool tables, darts, shuffleboard, a basketball machine and video games. A traditional bar menu is available 24 hours. Cover fees are rarely charged.

Gold Mine Bar & Grill (☎ 702-696-9722; 252 Convention Center Dr) is a place you could never set foot in and still live a full and rewarding life, but if you just love places with a gold-mine theme, you won't want to miss it. Rock walls, mighty beams,

a gold cart and a trestle loom above the bar. There's also a jukebox, a sports ticker, keno machines and video poker. Occasionally there's even live entertainment. Burgers, sandwiches, salads and some more substantial items are always available; there are usually a few food specials.

Hard Rock Café (☎ 702-733-8400; 4475 Paradise Rd; open 11am-midnight daily) is one of 80 worldwide on a growing list and is just like all the others: walls plastered with memorabilia from rock stars, recorded rock music coming at you from every direction, the usual burgers-sandwiches-salads menu and the requisite Hard Rock sportswear counter. Unlike the Hard Rock Hotel, about 100 yards away, the café is no big deal. But if you absolutely, positively must have a T-shirt that reads 'Hard Rock Café Las Vegas,' this is where to come for it.

Lone Star Steakhouse & Saloon (☎ 702-893-0348; 1290 E Flamingo Rd; 11am-10pm Sun-Thur, 11am-11pm Fri & Sat) is a country bar – if the tables have large buckets of peanuts on them and the patrons are tossing the shells on the floor, you can bet your silver belt buckle you've stumbled into it. That's exactly what you'll find at the Lone Star. The waiters and waitresses sing along and dance when their favorite country songs are played, and the walls are decorated with cattle heads and paintings of cowboys bringing home the herd. The Lone Star is a little slice of Texas for all the homesick cowpokes in Vegas.

PT's Pub (☎ 702-792-4121; 532 E Sahara Ave; open 24hr) has cheap beer and a happy hour that never quits. Can do without the cow heads? Really don't care much for rock stars, gold mines or other gimmicky themes? If all you really want in Sin City is a regular bar, this is your kind of place. You won't find any psychedelic paint jobs here, no Ass Juice, no wet T-shirt contests, no one-man band. PT's Pub has pool tables that have been around since the time of Moses, and dartboards that have seen better days. You'll be sharing the bar with local college kids, drunks and off-duty cops.

T.G.I. Friday's (☎ 702-732-9905; 1800 E Flamingo Rd; open 11am-1am Sun-Thur,

11am-2am Fri & Sat) stands for Thank God It's, which means that the inclusion of the apostrophe 's' at the end of 'Friday' is all wrong. It's a quibble, but that's what the T.G.I. stands for. But what's really important is that if you're single and cruising for Mr or Ms Right – especially if it's Mr or Ms Right Just for One Night – this is a good place to come. It's a veritable meat market most evenings, attended primarily by white-collar singles who can really relate to the name of the place – even when it isn't Friday. Easing their pain are two daily happy hours (from 4pm till 7pm, and from 10pm till midnight) and six TV monitors. A chicken wing's toss from the bar is a full-on restaurant with a long menu of fun food. Warning: There are no gambling devices in this establishment.

Production Shows

Showgirls of Magic *(☎ 702-739-9000, 800-522-7366; 115 E Tropicana Ave; tickets $27; covered/topless shows 8pm/10:30pm Tues-Sun)*, at the Hotel San Remo, is a variety show that features sexy women singing, dancing and performing many entertaining illusions. Joining the ladies on stage is the very funny comedian Joe Trammel. This show does not rival the full-blown heart-racing antics of Siegfried & Roy or a few of the other really big shows in the neighborhood, but at a quarter of the price it offers excellent value. Be advised that to attend the 10:30pm session of Showgirls of Magic you must be at least 21 years of age.

Rock

Las Vegas occasionally attracted big-name rock bands prior to the mid-1990s, but until then it didn't have a regular venue for such groups.

The Joint *(☎ 702-226-4650; W www.hardrockhotel.com; 4455 Paradise Rd)*, inside the Hard Rock Hotel, opened in 1995 and became a beacon for rock bands. The Joint not only attracts megabands like The Rolling Stones and U2, but it's so small (a mere 1400 seats, *when* seats are available) that concerts here feel more like private shows. It's a great place to see hugely popular groups in an intimate setting. Unfortunately for nonsmokers, smoking *is* permitted at The Joint, even when the chairs are brought out (some shows are 'general admission,' which in Joint parlance means standing room only; other shows are assigned seating). Ticket prices typically start at $25 and can be purchased no more than 30 days in advance. The Eagles were the first group to perform at The Joint, and since then the venue has presented lots of big-name talent, including Stephen Stills, Iggy Pop, Duran Duran, Sheryl Crow, Hootie and the Blowfish, Ziggy Marley, Johnny Cash and Bob Dylan.

Cinemas

Dollar Cinema *(☎ 702-434-8101; 3330 E Tropicana Ave)* is the one movie theater within striking distance of Las Vegas Blvd and east of The Strip. Good for its name, the Dollar Cinema charges only $1 for its second-run English-language films. This is

One for the Money, Two for the Show

The Joint at the Hard Rock Café & Hotel often loses money on big-name groups, charging less for tickets than the performers demand. But don't mistake the losses for charity; in Vegas, the house always wins.

About 10 steps from the door of The Joint is the Hard Rock's dish-shaped gambling area. For the casino, the concert hall is a way to draw thousands of affluent baby boomers and Generation-X music fans within arm's reach of its slot machines and gaming tables.

'The business boost we get from shows like that is quite significant,' the Hard Rock's Gary Selesner once said after a sold-out Sheryl Crow concert. 'There's the potential for one player to pay for the show's box-office loss. Seriously. It's like hosting a Tyson fight, only safer.'

the least expensive cinema in town and an excellent value.

WEST OF THE STRIP
Dance Clubs

Club Rio (☎ 702-252-7777; 3700 Flamingo Rd; admission $20; open 10:30pm-3am Wed-Sat), at the Rio, has one of the largest dance floors in Las Vegas – a huge circular floor on which are focused 10 cameras that allow you to watch yourself dance on a dozen screens. Club Rio is enormously popular despite an unforgiving dress code, a steep admission fee and the fact that you must be at least 21 years old to enter. The club has tall ceilings, lots of seating and many intimate booths. However, the lines to get in are often enormous and slow moving, and no allowances are made to the dress code – no uncollared shirts, tennis shoes, gangsta pants or ripped clothing – even if you've waited in line an hour. The music is generally top-40 hits (Thursday night features Latin sounds), and the crowd ranges in age from twentysomething to fortysomething. On Friday and Saturday, be sure to arrive at least an hour early to avoid a near-motionless line and to stand a chance of obtaining a booth.

Bars

Today, following the enormous success of the Rio, west of The Strip, lots of tourist-oriented businesses are opening in this part of town. Others have been around a long time and are just now feeling the effects of tourism.

Andy Capz Pub (☎ 702-647-1178; 1631 N Decatur Blvd; open 24hr) is a friendly neighborhood bar that serves food and liquor 24 hours, and is the Las Vegas rallying point of Denver Broncos fans. If you're a Broncos fan and there's a Broncos game on when you're in town, this is where you want to be. Andy Capz has a big-screen TV, pool tables and British draft beer; the pub takes its name from the British comic-strip character who spends his days slumped over a beer, opining on subjects of common interest. Unlike the bar the comic-strip character frequents, Andy Capz has video poker. Way to go, Andy!

Big Dog's Bar & Grill (☎ 702-876-3647; 6390 W Sahara Ave; open 24hr) is filled with photos and memorabilia of – yes – big dogs. Hey, in a town where practically every business owner assumes that you must have a theme to survive, why not big dogs? Big Dog's is a fun establishment that, in addition to all things canine, has 35 video poker machines, a restaurant serving steaks, ribs, chicken, burgers, fajitas and so on, and a daily midnight special of steak and eggs for a mere $3.

Ghost Bar (☎ 702-938-2666; 4321 W Flamingo Rd), located atop the Palms hotel-casino, is an upscale and trendy place with a killer view back onto The Strip.

Pink E's (☎ 702-252-4666; 3695 W Flamingo Rd; admission Thur-Sat nights $5) is a place you'll probably like if Big Dog's made you howl. Everything – including the pool tables (all 57 of them!), the faux-leather booths and the bar's lava lamp – is as pink as that mischievous panther of cartoon fame. Beware: there are no pink elephants on the premises; if you see one, switch to coffee! For you athletes, there's shuffleboard, a dartboard and three pink Ping-Pong tables. There's a dance floor, occasional live music (usually late-eighties rock 'n' roll on Friday and Saturday), food (burgers, Philly cheesesteaks, chicken wings and so on) and an excellent daiquiri bar. There's no charge to shoot pool at Pink E's on Sunday and Wednesday. Seasonal wet T-shirt contests occur during the summer (usually on Monday). Also, 16oz draft beers are available for only $1.50 on weekdays from 11am till 7pm. Not so important is the fact that the bar top stretches 250ft.

Tommy Rocker's Cantina & Grill (☎ 702-261-6688; 4275 S Industrial Rd) is the place to steer yourself into for something completely fun and different on a weekend night. Tommy Rocker's features live, sing-along rock 'n' roll and dancing every Friday and Saturday night with the one-and-only, truly incomparable Tommy Rocker, and disco dancing before and after the show. Tommy Rocker's also has pool tables, video poker gaming, eight TV monitors and a crystal-clear big screen receiving all major satellite

ENTERTAINMENT

sports. Tommy's menu features burgers, barbecued baby back ribs, Southwest and Mexican favorites, salads, sandwiches and appetizers 24 hours a day. The whole place has a surfer/beach theme going on, an atmosphere that feels thoroughly frat house, and a clientele that's mostly thirtysomething Jimmy Buffet parrothead types. There's never a cover charge or drink minimum.

Production Shows

The Scintas (☎ 702-777-7776, 888-746-7784; 3700 W Flamingo Rd; ⓦ www.playrio .com; tickets $45; shows 8pm Fri-Mon, 8pm & 10:30pm Tues), at the Rio, is a musical-comedy act consisting of three Italian family members (brothers Frank and Joe Scinta, and sister Chrissi) and 'adopted' Scinta Peter O'Donnell (there's a good Irish name for you). Together, they put on a terrific, family-friendly show. Indeed, the Scintas are so funny and so gifted (Chrissi sounds like Barbra Streisand, and her brothers are top-notch impersonators) that most people leave their show awestruck. This is truly a family affair, one that warms up to the audience splendidly, and if you have the slightest chance to see them, you'd be wise to do so. This writer can't say enough about The Scintas.

Blues

Sand Dollar Blues Lounge (☎ 702-871-6651; 3355 Spring Mountain Rd) is the preeminent blues venue in Las Vegas. Every major US city has one. Sure, there's the House of Blues

at Mandalay Bay, but most nights it doesn't feature blues music. The Sand Dollar is a blues club all of the time, and it books captivating but generally unknown blues musicians, most of whom you haven't heard of unless you really follow the blues scene. There's nothing pretentious about the Sand Dollar: the facade could belong to an accounting office, and the club's 'art' consists mostly of bumper stickers like 'Work is the curse of the drinking class' and posters distributed by beer company reps. Same goes for the clientele, who would look equally at home fixing bikes at the Harley-Davidson repair shop five doors down. It's a friendly place, and there's definitely no dress code; if you want to hear some good blues in a club that's made for it, put on your jeans, a T-shirt and sneakers, and come on down. There's live blues almost every night (call ahead), and only a cover charge when the status of the band warrants a larger fee. Also on the premises are video poker machines and pool tables.

Rock

VooDoo Lounge (☎ 702-252-7777, 800-752-9746; 3700 W Flamingo Rd; admission $10; open 5pm-2:30am Wed-Sat), at the Rio, is an ultra-hip rock 'n' roll lounge with a small dance floor and a breathtaking view of The Strip. Situated at the top of an exhilarating glass-elevator ride, 51 floors above ground, the VooDoo Lounge combines forces late at night with the equally impressive VooDoo Café (entrées $27-35), one

---

Talk about Making an Impression

When The Scintas arrived in Las Vegas, few people knew who they were. Within months, they were the talk of the town. Here's what a few of their fans have said about them.

'I want you to remember you heard it here first… these people are going to be big, big stars!'
Wayne Newton, legendary Vegas singer

'One of the best entertainment groups I have ever, ever seen… I lost count of the standing ovations.'
Breck Wall, legendary Vegas comedian

'Dynamite family affair… where you laugh, you cry and you sing along. I definitely recommend it.'
Lance Bass, N'Sync

ENTERTAINMENT

flight below it, to produce a killer nightclub. The walls and ceilings of both sites, painted by artists brought in from New Orleans, depict objects often found in Haitian voodoo ceremonial flags – snakes, crosses, fanciful hearts. The major colors are purple, yellow and red; the furniture is black and modern. You can sit inside or on a patio with sweeping views of Las Vegas. The drinks are as exotic and potent as their names suggest – Witchy Woman, Jamaican Hellfire, Sexual Trance – and often contain Midori, rum and tropical juices. The live music (around 9pm nightly) is usually rock but occasionally contemporary jazz, Cajun or hip-hop. Admission costs substantially more on special occasions such as Halloween and New Year's Eve, or the night of a big boxing match. Its dress code – banning tank tops, T-shirts, athletic shoes, blue jeans and ripped trousers – is strictly enforced.

Cinemas

There are three sets of movie theaters west of The Strip. The best of the three is located at the Palms hotel-casino (☎ 702-942-7777, 866-725-6773; Ⓦ www.thepalmslasvegas .com; 4321 W Flamingo Rd; tickets $8.25) and consists of a complex containing 14 standard movie theaters.

The next-best cluster of theaters is **Century Orleans 12** (☎ 702-227-3456; 4500 W Tropicana Ave; tickets before/after 6pm $5/8), at The Orleans hotel-casino, features the only stadium-style staggered seating in town. The advantage of this is that your line of sight is never obscured by someone's oversize head.

For Music and Dancing, Call ...

Ninety-nine pages. That's the length of the Entertainment/Entertainers section in the Las Vegas Yellow Pages. The businesses that advertise here are not fronts for prostitution, run by a handful of rich people, as Las Vegas police officers have testified on numerous occasions. They can't be; prostitution is illegal in Sin City and the rest of Clark County. Has been for years.

In fact, prostitution has been banned from Las Vegas since the 1940s – when the US Air Force built a base nearby and forced the closure of the city's brothels. Since then an interesting (and surely unrelated) development transpired: the number of the city's entertainment services soared. These services offer, in their own words, entertainment for adults only in your hotel room. But do these off-duty 'full-service Barbie girls,' 'barely legal Asian playmates' and 'exotic student nurses looking for fun' do more than dance, sing, take their clothes off and leave?

Absolutely not, they testify. But no one would blame you if you got the wrong idea. Before 1997, the Yellow Pages ads contained photographs of scantily clad women who suggested they would indeed be offering sex. That year, however, the police proposed a bill to outlaw escort services; the bill failed, but the services voluntarily toned down their advertisements as a result. Now they only show exploding skyrockets, strawberries with whipped cream, cheerleading uniforms and so on, but no actual women – you know, because they aren't offering sex. No doubt their singing and dancing justify their $300-an-hour rates.

Not everyone is against the idea of prostitutes in Las Vegas. Mayor Oscar Goodman has gone on record with his 'pro-prostitution' stance, calling prostitution 'great,' though he's said he won't try to legalize it. And there's George Flint, an ordained minister who is Nevada's only paid lobbyist for the state's legal bordellos. His job is to see that attempts to end legal prostitution in Nevada, where it is permitted in 10 of the state's 17 counties, don't get too far. The good minister has been working for the Nevada Brothel Association since 1985, and he seems to like his work: when people ask George to reconcile his theology degree with his job, he says, 'I just remind them that Jesus' best friend, outside his family, was a working girl named Mary from a little town called Magdalen.'

It's true. You can look it up in that other large book found in many Vegas hotel rooms.

Gold Coast Twin (☎ 702-367-7111; 4000 W Flamingo Rd; tickets before/after 6pm $5/8), at the Gold Coast, features a mix of little-known but high-quality films and first-run Hollywood blockbusters. This intimate cinema is popular with locals who recall the time when it was the closest thing the city had to an art house. Amazingly, the prices at the snack bar haven't changed much over the years.

DOWNTOWN
Bars
Of course, every hotel-casino in the downtown area has a bar or two or three inside its main gaming area. Generally, there isn't much more to them than a beverage counter, lots of libations and a bartender named Mac or Barb.

East of the Fremont Street Experience are quite a few down-and-out bars offering cheap booze, cheap company and little or nothing else.

Bunkhouse Saloon (☎ 702-384-4536; 124 S 11th St) is an exception to the down-and-out places. The Bunkhouse Saloon is owned by a judge and is popular with the downtown legal community. As you might have guessed by the name, it's got a cowboy theme and even free barbecues on occasion. Gamewise, there's video poker, pool tables and darts, and occasional live music. If you're looking for a decent bar downtown, give this place a try – unless you've got a problem with saddles, Old West art, or lawyers. It's a good find.

SPECTATOR SPORTS
Las Vegas offers the fan a plethora of spectator sports, from baseball and basketball to rodeos, rugby and volleyball. In between there's boxing, football, golf, ice hockey, ice skating, marathon running, motor sports and tournament poker.

Baseball
The Las Vegas Stars, the AAA franchise of the San Diego Padres, play a 70-game home schedule at **Cashman Field** (☎ 702-386-7200; 850 N Las Vegas Blvd). Triple-A ball is just one step down from Major League Baseball, so the level of play is extremely

high quality. Tickets generally range from $5 to $8, which is an excellent value. The season runs from early April through August. Call for game dates.

Basketball
The Runnin' Rebels of the University of Nevada, Las Vegas, won the national collegiate basketball title in 1990. Since the Rebels played their first game in 1958, UNLV has sent many players to the pros. The quality of play is outstanding. The Rebels hold their home games at **Thomas and Mack Center** (☎ 702-895-3900; cnr Tropicana Ave & Swenson St). The season runs from November till March. Tickets cost $12 to $50.

Boxing
Las Vegas has hosted more championship fights than any other city in the world. These bouts are variously held at **Caesars Palace** (☎ 702-731-2222, 800-634-6661), **MGM Grand** (☎ 702-891-1111, 800-929-1111) and **The Mirage** (☎ 702-791-7111, 800-627-6667). Call these megaresorts for schedules and ticket prices. Tickets for major bouts typically sell for between $200 and $1500.

Football
The UNLV Runnin' Rebels have never been ranked No 1 in the country, and in fact the team has had a losing record in recent years. As a result, it's easy to obtain good seats to their six annual home games. Ticket prices start at $12. The team opens its season in September and plays until December. The Rebels play their home games at the 32,000-seat **Sam Boyd Stadium** (☎ 702-895-3900), at the end of E Russell Rd, past Boulder Hwy.

Golf
There is one major professional competition in Las Vegas every year. The **Las Vegas Senior Classic** is held every April at the Tournament Players Club at **The Canyons** (☎ 702-242-3000; 1951 Canyon Run Dr), which is in the western foothills of the city, off Summerlin Parkway. Top players from the senior tour compete for $1 million at this

HD

event. Ticket prices start at $20 per day for the four-day event.

Ice Hockey

You've probably never heard of the Las Vegas Thunder of the International Hockey League, but some of its players have gone on to the National Hockey League in years past. The Thunder play 41 regular-season home games from October through April at **Thomas and Mack Center** (☎ 702-895-3900; cnr Tropicana Ave & Swenson St). Tickets run $5 to $8.

Ice Skating

Olympic medalists and national champions always compete in the **Tour of World Figure Skating Champions**, sponsored by Campbell Soups and held at the **Thomas and Mack Center** (☎ 702-895-3900; cnr Tropicana Ave & Swenson St) every July. Tickets generally run from $20 to $45. Be advised that the event is often held on Independence Day (July 4), which means you'll want to reserve a hotel room and purchase your ticket as far in advance as possible.

Marathon Running

The **Las Vegas International Marathon** (☎ 702-876-3870), held in early February, attracts long-distance runners from all corners of the globe. The 26.2-mile race begins in the Nevada town of Sloan and ends at the southern end of The Strip. The event usually draws in excess of 6000 competitors from more than 40 countries. It's quite an event to be a part of as a competitor or a spectator. The entry fee is $40. There's no fee for viewing.

Motor Sports

The **Las Vegas Motor Speedway** (☎ 702-644-4444, 800-644-4444; 7000 N Las Vegas Blvd) is a 1500-acre complex featuring a 1.5-mile superspeedway, a 2.5-mile road track, a drag strip, a half-mile dirt track, go-cart tracks and a racing school. Events are held nearly every day. Call for information.

The **Richard Petty Driving Experience** (☎ 702-643-4343, 800-237-3889) features one-on-one training and, of course, high-speed trips around the superspeedway. Packages start at $350.

Rodeos

There are three main rodeo events in Las Vegas each year, all held at the **Thomas and Mack Center** (☎ 702-895-3900; cnr Tropicana Ave & Swenson St). The most spectacular of the three is the **National Finals Rodeo**, which ropes in the top 126 money winners in the Professional Rodeo Cowboys Association, who compete for $3 million in prize money. The event spans 10 days and is held in December. Tickets, which are difficult to come by, start at $25 per competition.

The **Wrangler Bull Riders Only World Championships** is a three-day event in April that attracts the world's best bull riders. The action is fast, furious and frightening as these men compete for $1 million in title money. Daily tickets start at $35.

Helldorado Days is the name of a four-day hoedown held in early June that features three nights of professionally sanctioned rodeo activity and one night of bull riding. Tickets for bull-riding night generally go for $15, while admission on other nights is usually $12.

Rugby

More than 70 teams from around the world compete for prize money and trophies during

December at the **Las Vegas Rugby Challenge** held in **Freedom Park** (*☎ 702-656-7401; cnr E Washington Ave & Mojave Rd*). Entry fees go to local charities. There is no charge to view the two days of fast-paced action.

Volleyball

The **Hard Rock Hotel** (*☎ 702-693-5000, 800-693-7625; ⓦ www.hardrockhotel.com;* *4455 Paradise Rd*) hosts the **Miller Lite King of the Beach Invitational** each March. This three-day volleyball event features two-person teams playing in round-robin style and competing for $250,000 in prize money. Tickets range from $10 to $30 per day. The competition takes place on 350 tons of sand in the hotel's parking lot. It seems that Las Vegas still doesn't have an ocean – yet.

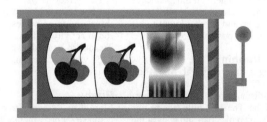

Shopping

Las Vegas is a shopper's paradise, and not just for one socioeconomic group. Sin City will please you if you're seeking everyday bargains, including designer clothes at greatly reduced prices. It'll delight you if you're looking for a special gift, such as an excellent bottle of wine or a basketball signed by Michael Jordan. And if you're looking for something truly spectacular, such as a piece of jewelry with history, Las Vegas has plenty to offer. Among the pieces for sale – and not likely to be sold any time soon – are the 17th-century, 430-carat carved Moghul Indian Emerald (the world's largest carved emerald) and Ginger Rogers' engagement ring with a marquis diamond of 7.02 carats (see Fred Leighton: Rare Collectible Jewels under Jewelry, later).

WHAT TO BUY

Las Vegas isn't a city like, for example, Istanbul, where a full 80% of foreign visitors purchase at least one handmade carpet before they head home. Las Vegas is famous for many things, but it isn't known for any particular souvenir. Rather, it's a place where you can buy almost anything if you have the money. And because so much merchandise in Las Vegas is sold to visitors, most merchants can arrange to have your purchase shipped home if you don't want to take it with you.

Clothing

Belz Factory Outlet World (☎ 702-896-5599; W www.belz.com; 7400 S Las Vegas Blvd, cnr Warm Springs Rd; open 10am-9pm Mon-Sat, 10am-6pm Sun), America's largest factory-outlet mall, is a short drive south of Mandalay Bay. At Belz, you can buy direct from the manufacturer at 155 outlets. At some stores it's possible to get up to 75% off regular prices. Among the clothing manufacturers with outlets at Belz are Adolfo II, Bugle Boy, Burlington Brands, Danskin, Esprit, Geoffrey Beene, Jockey, Levi's, Nautica, Reebok and Van Heusen.

The Boulevard Mall (☎ 702-732-8949; W www.blvd.com; 3529 Maryland Parkway; open 10am-9pm Mon-Fri, 10am-8pm Sat, 11am-6pm Sun), at the corner of E Desert Inn Rd, is Nevada's largest mall. Like Belz, this 140-store mall is only minutes by car or bus from The Strip. Among the dozens of stores at The Boulevard Mall are The Gap, Sports Logo, Lane Bryant, and Victoria's Secret. There are also five department stores: Dillard's, JC Penney, Macy's, Marshall's and Sears.

The Forum Shops (☎ 702-893-4800; W www.shopsimon.com; 3570 S Las Vegas Blvd; open 10am-11pm Sun-Thur, 10am-midnight Fri & Sat), at Caesars Palace, is the most successful shopping center in the US, with average annual sales of more than $1200 per sq ft (the industry average is $300) at stores such as Bvlgari, Gucci, DKNY, Emporio Armani, Escada, Fendi, Gianni Versace, Judith Leiber, MaxMara and NikeTown. One stroll through this mall and you'll understand why it's so successful; not only does it contain upscale restaurants, shops, services and a motion-simulator ride, but it also contains two groups of robots that perform throughout the day. There are other attractions as well, and the location can't be beat.

Fashion Show Mall (☎ 702-369-8382; W www.thefashionshow.com; 3200 S Las Vegas Blvd; open 10am-9pm Mon-Fri, 10am-7pm Sat, noon-6pm Sun), located mid-Strip, is home to more than 120 specialized shops and stores, as well as Nordstrom, Bloomingdale's, Macy's, Dillard's, Saks Fifth Avenue, Robinsons-May and Neiman Marcus department stores. The mall was extensively renovated in 2002; if you liked it before, you'll love it now.

Meadows Mall (☎ 702-878-4849; W www.themeadowsmall.com; 4300 Meadows Lane; open 10am-9pm Mon-Fri, 10am-7pm Sat, 10am-6pm Sun) received a much-needed remodelling in 2001. The two-level mall is home to 144 shops and restaurants. Among the mall's many clothing stores are Coda, Casual Corner, Charlotte Russe, Frederick's of Hollywood, Lane Bryant, The Limited, Motherhood Maternity, Petite Sophisticate and Victoria's Secret. There are also four department stores: Macy's, JC Penney, Dillard's and Sears.

Leather Jackets An item many visitors leave Sin City with is a leather jacket, with 'Las Vegas' boldly emblazoned on the back. These pricey souvenirs usually sell for $200 to $300. The ones found at the three sites mentioned here are high quality and good looking. They won't fall apart on you, and they *will* turn some heads.

Hard Rock Hotel Store (☎ 702-693-5000, 800-473-7625; W www.hardrockhotel.com; 4455 Paradise Rd; open 8am-1am Sun-Thur, 8am-2am Fri & Sat), inside the Hard Rock Hotel, has lots of spiffy leather jackets with the hotel's logo stitched on the back and a tastefully muted 'Las Vegas' appearing underneath it.

World of Coca-Cola (☎ 702-597-3122, 800-720-2653; 3769 S Las Vegas Blvd; open 10am-midnight Sun-Thur, 10am-1am Fri & Sat) has several bomber-style leather jackets with 'Coca-Cola' and 'Las Vegas' displayed in an attractive design on the backs.

There are three **Harley-Davidson merchandise stores** in town (☎ 702-795-7073; MGM Grand ● ☎ 702-383-1010; cnr 4th & Fremont Sts ● ☎ 702-736-9493; Concourse B, McCarran International Airport), and all carry a large selection of motorcycle and bomber jackets, some bearing 'Las Vegas' and some *sans* Sin City markings. Call for store hours.

Stripper Apparel In a town that has as many strip clubs as it does McDonald's, it should come as little surprise that the stripper-apparel business is ba-booming. All those beefy guys and sultry women don't make their own G-strings, tasseled undies or dominatrix wear. They buy it at stores which differ little from regular apparel stores, except they feature dancer, fetish and theme wear. So if you were hoping to find a little sexy something you can't find at home – or you want to surprise a loved one with a truly memorable Vegas souvenir – head for one of the following comprehensive stores.

Bare Essentials (☎ 702-247-4711; 4029 W Sahara Ave; open 10am-7pm Mon-Sat, noon-5pm Sun) is the shop that many professional dancers turn to for their business attire. It's got everything you could possibly want and a lot of things you don't need. The store features merchandise for both men and women, with many items in plus sizes. This place is heavily into theme wear – lots of cheerleader, nurse and schoolgirl outfits, though possibly not as much zookeeper attire as we'd like to see!

A Slightly Sinful Adventure (☎ 702-387-1006; 1232 S Las Vegas Blvd; open 10am-10pm Sun-Thur, 10am-midnight Fri & Sat), on the same stage as Bare Essentials, sells some really mischievous outfits. Many are layered, with tiny outer garments and much tinier undergarments.

Jewelry

There is a jewelry store inside each of the megaresorts. Most, such as the Cartier boutique inside Caesars Palace, sell lovely adornments.

Fred Leighton: Rare Collectible Jewels (☎ 702-693-7050; 3600 S Las Vegas Blvd) inside the Bellagio, is one store that's definitely worth a look even if you aren't in the market. Fred's been a busy man since he entered the jewelry business 25 years ago, building the world's largest and most prestigious collection of estate and antique jewelry. Many of the necklaces and earrings worn by stars on Academy Awards night are on loan from Fred. Among the celebrities who've worn his jewelry to the Oscars are Sharon Stone, Melanie Griffith, Madonna, Cameron Diaz and even Antonio Banderas (a ruby and diamond stud). At Fred Leighton you can find jewelry that once belonged to royalty. Prices run from about $100 for a tiny but exquisite pin to well over $1 million for jewelry that's simply incredible.

The Jewelers (☎ 702-893-9979; Las Vegas Hilton; open 24hr ● ☎ 702-796-6000; The Boulevard Mall; open 10am-9pm Mon-Fri, 10am-8pm Sat, 11am-6pm Sun ● ☎ 702-731-3700; Flamingo; open 9am-1am daily) is Nevada's largest chain of discount-jewelry stores. There's a wide selection of rings and necklaces at affordable prices. The store at the Las Vegas Hilton is open around-the-clock to accommodate any middle-of-the-night urge to buy a solid gold rope chain.

Memorabilia

Field of Dreams (☎ 702-221-9144; 3700 W Flamingo Rd; open 11am-midnight Tues-Fri, 10am-midnight Sat-Mon) is inside Masquerade Village at the Rio. There's really only one name in sports and celebrity memorabilia in Las Vegas, and this is it. Like the Fred Leighton store at the Bellagio, this store deserves a look whether you're buying or not. Among the items that have been sold here are a thank-you note signed by John F Kennedy, a poster of The Beatles signed by all four band members, a football jersey with Dan Marino's autograph, and a basketball signed by Michael Jordan. If you've been meaning to buy a framed electric guitar with Carlos Santana's signature on it, there's a good chance Field of Dreams has got one or can locate one for you. How about an autographed photo of Jack Nicholson? Usually not a problem. The John Hancock of John Travolta? No big deal. But a blue dress with a past president's personal mark of approval? That could be more difficult.

Wine

With all the money that enters Las Vegas on any given day, it's no surprise that many of the city's premier restaurants possess some very impressive wine lists. What *is* surprising is that Las Vegas is home to the largest public collection of fine wines in the world.

The Wine Cellar (☎ 702-252-7718, 800-752-9746; 3700 W Flamingo Rd; open 3pm-midnight daily), inside Masquerade Village at the Rio, has a tasting room and retail shop that has in excess of 45,000 bottles of wine worth more than $6 million. The wines have been collected from the world's top wine-producing regions. There's no shortage of superb grape juices from the Bordeaux area of France, and California's Napa Valley.

The cellar contains scores of wines that are extremely difficult to find. Some of the

bottles are sold 'as a set,' as it were; such is the case with the cellar's $1-million Chateau d'Yequem collection, with bottles from every vintage produced between 1855 and 1990. Assisting customers with their purchases and/or sampling of wines are a dozen stewards (every one of whom has at least one wine-related qualification – some with as many as 20) who can make informed recommendations. Directing the entire operation, and continuing the education of its staff, is the Rio's master sommelier Barrie Larvin, former president of the International Court of Master Sommeliers.

There are always specials on selected wines, and custom glass etching is available. Shipping is not a problem. This is a great place to pick up a special gift for a wine lover, and every bottle here is available for sale. It's also a super place to sample wines; the price of three 1oz tastings generally runs from $7 to $25, depending on the quality of the wines selected for sampling. Tasting is available during shop hours.

Antiques

Antiques in Las Vegas? Yes, indeed, and lots of them, including many objects that must have been regarded as junk when they were created and haven't appreciated with age. You'll also find fancy crystal and china, and lovely grandfather clocks. There's a dizzying array of older, unusual furniture, as well as a seemingly infinite number of items that could easily fit in a suitcase. If you've got a hankering to get something for someone who's 'impossible to shop for,' you might want to give the following sites the once-over twice.

Scores of antiques dealers sell their goods in a mall-like setting at **The Sampler Shops** (☎ 702-966-7580; 6115 W Tropicana Ave; open 10am-6pm Mon-Sat, noon-6pm Sun). The shops feature lots of clothing, shoes, lamps and silver from the 19th century, as well as many quirky items that most people would view as unnecessary, to put it diplomatically.

Toys of Yesteryear (☎ 702-598-4030; 2028 E Charleston Blvd; open 11am-4:30pm Mon-Sat), downtown, is a fun little place specializing in toys of the not-so-distant past.

The store's inventory is constantly changing, but generally it includes several lovely old train sets, carnival dolls and wind-up toys.

Thrift Stores

The resurging popularity of retro styles has made thrift stores the place to head to for authentic 1960s and '70s clothing. As the saying goes, one person's trash is another person's treasure. Here, then, are a few of the larger thrift stores in the Las Vegas area.

Value Center (☎ 702-399-0552; 1304 E Lake Mead Blvd, North Las Vegas; open 9am-7pm Mon-Sat, 10am-5pm Sun) boasts that it's 'a thrift store with department store atmosphere.' We suppose that's substantially better than a thrift store with thrift store atmosphere, but we're not sure. Regardless, Value Center receives on average 5000 'new' items daily. For selection, Value Center is tough to top.

Retro Vintage Clothing (☎ 702-877-8989; 906 S Valley View Blvd, between Charleston Blvd & Alta Dr; open 12pm-6pm Tues-Sat) specializes in men's and women's clothing from the 1920s through the 1980s. How serious is this store? It even rents vintage clothing for special occasions.

C & O Thrift Store (☎ 702-631-9917; 1164-1176 W Lake Mead Blvd; open 1pm-6pm Tues-Sat) has a vast selection of clothing, and also sells shoes, cookware, costume jewelry, silverware, antiques and books. If you're serious about thrifty shopping, check out C & O.

Art

The art bearing price tags in Las Vegas is typically of low quality. But if you're determined to buy artwork in Sin City, start your search at **Galerie Lassen** (☎ 702-731-6900) or **Galleria di Sorrento** (☎ 702-369-8000), both of which are in The Forum Shops at Caesars Palace. They are two of the best galleries in town. Still, once when a sales rep at Galerie Lassen was asked if she had any Robert Batemans or Carl Brenders, she replied: 'Who are they?' Answer: Only the top wildlife painters in the country. When it comes to art-world sophistication, Las Vegas can't compare to Los Angeles or New York.

Gambling Merchandise

If you fancy shoving coins into a slot machine, consider buying one. There are many places in Las Vegas selling new and reconditioned electronic slot and video poker machines (they generally cost between $600 and $1000, although some prices climb much higher); putting coins in a machine that you own will ultimately cost you less than putting money into a casino-owned machine.

Gamblers General Store (☎ 702-382-9903; 800 S Main St; open 9am-5pm daily) is a great place to check out even if you're only a tiny bit tempted to buy a gambling device. It has one of the largest inventories of slot machines in Nevada, with new models and beautiful vintage machines. Also available are roulette, craps and blackjack tables identical to those in casinos around town. Gamblers General Store stocks just about every book ever written on gambling, and loads of paraphernalia such as coin changers, dice, customized poker chips, dealer aprons and even dice-inlaid toilet seats. Yes, even something for grandpa.

Souvenirs

If all you really want is a T-shirt, a snow dome or a coffee mug announcing that you've been to Las Vegas or know someone who has, you'll find such things everywhere you turn in Sin City. Every megaresort on The Strip has gift shops chockful of mementos and souvenirs, and some of these places carry their own product lines.

For instance, the Flamingo sells lots of toys with 'Flamingo' on them, and there's even a Flamingo Apparel store brimming with 'Flamingo' clothing. O'Shea's Casino put thousands of hours of thought into their product line and came up with a design that – are you seated? – features a green four-leaf clover. If you want to announce to the world that O'Shea's is your kind of place, you can buy shirts and caps with its 'unique' design at the casino. Excalibur features wizard sculptures, pewter axes and an assortment of other disturbing things. At Luxor you'll find lots of Egyptian handicrafts, some of which are actually quite lovely. And so on, and so on....

Books

If you came to Las Vegas intending to shop for books, the city won't likely disappoint you. There's at least one bookstore in all five malls (see the Malls section), and there are many others scattered about. All of the big chains – B Dalton Bookseller, Barnes & Noble Booksellers, Bookstar, Book Warehouse, Borders Book Shop and Waldenbooks – have stores here; most have more than one. Of course, Las Vegas would not be complete without a slew of stores selling books on gambling.

Gambler's Book Club *(☎ 702-382-7555, 800-522-1777; 630 S 11th St; open 9am-5pm Mon-Sat)*, the best of the bunch, is where owner Edna Luckman (great name, huh?) carries more than 4000 gambling-related titles, including lots of out-of-print titles.

Also see Gamblers General Store under Gambling Merchandise.

WHERE TO SHOP

The metropolitan Las Vegas area has more than 30 million sq ft of retail space, and that staggering number is growing all the time. It's almost reached the point where one can say that if it isn't available in Las Vegas, it simply isn't available. The malls are the places to look, although many of the hotel-casinos such as MGM Grand, Bellagio, the Rio and Luxor also contain specialty stores offering good value.

Malls

There are no fewer than five major malls in the city. For more details on clothes shopping, see the Clothing section, earlier. For information on what you can find at these malls in addition to clothing (for one thing, lots of ATMs), read on.

The Forum Shops *(☎ 702-893-4800; W www.shopsimon.com; 3570 S Las Vegas Blvd; open 10am-11pm Sun-Thur, 10am-midnight Fri & Sat)*, adjacent to the casino at Caesars Palace, are a visual as well as a retailing attraction. Storefront facades and common areas resemble an ancient Roman streetscape, with Corinthian columns and triumphal arches, grandiose fountains, delightful piazzas and classic statuary.

Overhead, on a barrel-vaulted ceiling, a painted sky emulates a changing Mediterranean day; as the day progresses, the sky magically transforms from rosy-tinted dawn to cloud-laced picture blue to twinkling evening stars. Elsewhere, visitors are treated to two sensational shows performed by faux-marble animatronic statues of Roman gods that come to life every hour, on the hour, amid dancing waters and laser-light effects. There's also a giant Roman Hall, at the center of which is a 50,000-gallon circular aquarium and a fountain that shoots fire instead of water. Amid all of the free entertainment it's easy to overlook the more than a hundred prestigious emporia, which carry not only clothing and accessories produced by the world's top designers, but also highly unusual objects, such as big-name sports memorabilia, 16th-century hand-painted Turkish boxes and high-quality Native American jewelry. There's even a half-court basketball arena and treadmill machines in an athletic-shoe store where prospective customers can test-run potential purchases. The Forum Shops is much more than simply a grouping of retail stores under one roof; it's an excursion.

Fashion Show Mall *(☎ 702-369-8382; W www.thefashionshow.com; 3200 S Las Vegas Blvd; open 10am-9pm Mon-Fri, 10am-7pm Sat, noon-6pm Sun)*, conveniently located on The Strip, has lots of tenants that aren't particularly fashion conscious. There are, for example, seven art galleries and four full-service restaurants, including the excellent Morton's of Chicago. There are dozens of specialty stores, which sell sunglasses, skin and health products, electronic devices, coffee beans, compact discs, watches, cookies and chocolates, jewelry, fast food, and shoes, shoes, shoes. Among some of the clothing stores not previously mentioned are Abercrombie & Fitch, Banana Republic, Diane's Swimwear, North Beach Leather, Private Collections, Schwartz Big & Tall and Victoria's Secret.

The Boulevard Mall *(☎ 702-732-8949; W www.blvd.com; 3529 Maryland Parkway; open 10am-9pm Mon-Fri, 10am-8pm Sat, 11am-6pm Sun)*, at the corner of E Desert

Inn Rd, is a 1.25-million-sq-ft mall with 140 tenants. Natural lighting and lush landscaping add to the pleasure of shopping here. In addition to a tremendous variety of stores featuring men's, women's and children's apparel, there are many specialist stores. Card and gift stores include African & World Imports, Bath & Body Works, The Disney Store and The Nature Company, to name a few. For hobbies and electronics, try The Good Guys, Nordic Trak, Ritz Camera, Software Etc and others. There are also 11 jewelry stores and 12 shoe stores, though for bargains in footwear you're better off shopping at Belz. Satiate your appetite at Ethel M Chocolates, General Nutrition Center, Mrs Fields Cookies and Pretzel Time, among others.

Belz Factory Outlet World (☎ 702-896-5599; Ⓦ www.belz.com; 7400 S Las Vegas Blvd, cnr Warm Springs Rd; open 10am-9pm Mon-Sat, 10am-6pm Sun) is the largest factory-outlet mall in the US. At Belz, you can buy direct from the manufacturer at 155 outlets. In addition to nearly 100 factory apparel outlets, Belz is home to dozens of others specializing in accessories (luggage, hats, bags, sunglasses etc), cameras and electronics (power tools, watches, video cameras etc), health and beauty products (with an emphasis on perfumes), housewares and linens (including Corning-Revere), jewelry (seven discount jewelers in all), lingerie (Jockey, Leggs, Haines, Bali, Playtex, Maidenform, Olga and Warner), sportswear (Nike, Reebok, Nautica and Danskin, among others), toys and gifts.

Meadows Mall (☎ 702-878-4849; Ⓦ www .themeadowsmall.com; 4300 Meadows Lane; open 10am-9pm Mon-Fri, 10am-7pm Sat, 10am-6pm Sun) is the next best bet if you have been to all of the places listed and still haven't found what you're looking for, or you just really love to shop. It's got many of the same stores as the other malls, plus a few different ones. The mall is home to no fewer than 12 shoe stores, 15 hobby and leisure stores, eight stores specializing in home furnishings and exactly 20 stores that do business in jewelry and gifts.

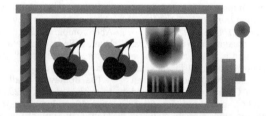

The awe-inspiring Grand Canyon

Sleek walls and Art Deco details of Hoover Dam

The overpowering and magnificent scenery of Zion National Park

Snaking towards Valley of Fire State Park, Nevada

Tunnel Arch in Utah's Red Rock Canyon

Heading north out of Las Vegas

Breathtaking vistas overlooking the 'Amphitheater' at Bryce Canyon National Park

Excursions

Las Vegas is the antithesis of a naturalist's vision of America. It is, however, surprisingly near some of the Southwest's most spectacular attractions. Beautiful Red Rock Canyon is just outside town, while the forests and snowfields of Charleston Peak are less than an hour's drive away. Also within easy striking distance of Sin City are the imposing Hoover Dam, Lake Mead National Recreation Area and the popular gambling gulch of Laughlin.

The brilliant Valley of Fire State Park northeast of town is just a short, scenic drive away, and for those with more than an afternoon to spare, the most incredible natural wonders await. Longer drives bring you to the Grand Canyon in Arizona and to Zion and Bryce Canyon National Parks in Utah. One option is to view these lovely sights by air, which can be easily done from Las Vegas.

The following sections provide basic information for getting away from the neon and into this indescribable country. For further information on the areas surrounding Las Vegas, see Lonely Planet's *Arizona*, and also *Hiking in the USA*.

RED ROCK CANYON

The contrast between the artificial brightness of Las Vegas and the natural splendor of Red Rock Canyon, a mere 20-mile drive west of The Strip, couldn't be greater. The canyon is actually more like a valley, with the steep, rugged red rock escarpment rising 3000ft on its western edge. It was created about 65 million years ago when tectonic plates collided along the Keystone Thrust fault line, pushing a plate of gray limestone up and over another plate of younger red sandstone.

In 1994 President Clinton doubled the Red Rock Canyon Conservation Area to almost 200,000 acres. It should be on the must-see list of every visitor to Las Vegas, but – perhaps fortunately – it usually isn't.

Orientation & Information

To get to Red Rock Canyon from Las Vegas, drive west along Charleston Blvd, which turns into SR 159, for about 30 minutes. A 13-mile, one-way **scenic loop** *(open from 6am-8pm summer months, 8am-6pm the rest of the year)* allows visitors to drive past some of the area's most striking features and to gain access to the hiking trails.

The excellent **Visitor Center** (☎ *702-363-1921; open 8:30am-4:30pm daily)* has maps and information about several short hikes in the area. The park's day-use fee is $5 per car. First-come, first-served camping at the Oak Creek site is available year-round.

Lake Mead & Around

LAKE MEAD NATIONAL RECREATION AREA

It's less than an hour's drive along Hwy 95/93 from Las Vegas to Lake Mead and Hoover Dam, which are the most visited sites within the 2337-sq-mile Lake Mead National Recreation Area. Encompassed within this area are the 110-mile-long Lake Mead, the 67-mile-long Lake Mohave and many miles of desert around the lakes. The Colorado River and the two lakes form a natural border with Arizona to the east. There are very few facilities of any kind in this area.

Built between 1931 and 1935 to back up the Colorado River to form Lake Mead, Boulder Dam (later renamed Hoover Dam) was the largest dam in the world. In 1953 the smaller Davis Dam was completed, forming Lake Mohave.

Admission to Lake Mead National Recreation Area costs $5 per car, and is valid for five days.

Highway 93, which connects Kingman in Arizona with Las Vegas, crosses the dam, passing the main visitor center. Hwy 68 runs between Kingman and Laughlin, at the southern tip of the recreation area.

EXCURSIONS

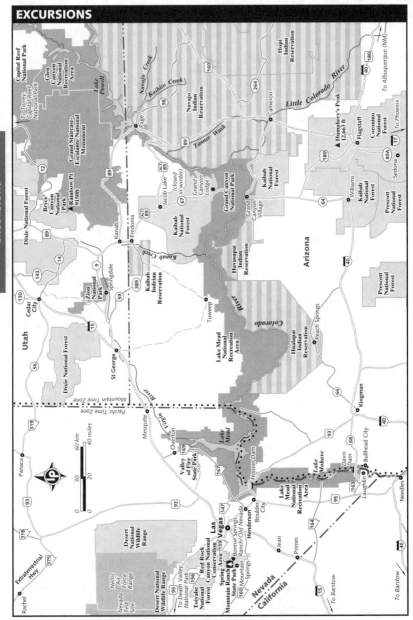

Lake Mead

Lake Mead has 500 miles of shoreline and a capacity of 9.2 trillion gallons, equal to two years of the normal flow of the Colorado River. Popular activities include swimming, fishing, boating, waterskiing and even scuba diving. The lake is set in scenic surrounds, most of which is undeveloped and protected as part of the recreation area.

The **Alan Bible Visitor Center** (☎ 702-293-8990; Hwy 93; open 8:30am-4:30pm daily), about 26 miles east of Las Vegas, is a wellspring of information on recreational options, camping and natural history. Don't miss the free documentary on the history and construction of Hoover Dam.

The most popular scenic drive is along N Shore Rd, which starts near the visitor center and leads up to Valley of Fire State Park and Overton. **Lake Mead Cruises** (☎ 702-293-6180) operates 90-minute sightseeing trips on Lake Mead ($19 per person), from the Lake Mead Resort Marina. Boats depart at 10am, noon, 2pm and 4pm daily.

Shoreside campgrounds are at Boulder Beach, Las Vegas Wash, Callville Bay, Echo Bay and Temple Bar (in Arizona). Accommodations are available at **Echo Bay Resort** (☎ 702-394-4000; rooms $85-115) near Overton, **Lake Mead Resort & Marina** (☎ 702-293-2074; rooms $70-80, apartments $150) near Boulder Beach, and **Temple Bar** (☎ 928-767-3211; rooms $55-105), a hotel in Arizona 40 miles from Hoover Dam. The toll-free booking number for these lodgings is ☎ 800-752-9669.

Hoover Dam

The 726ft-high, concrete Hoover Dam is one of the tallest dams in the world. It has a striking beauty, with its imposing, graceful curve filling a dramatic red rock canyon, backed by the brilliant blue waters of Lake Mead. Its simple form and Art Deco embellishments and design sit beautifully within the stark landscape. Its construction in the 1930s provided much-needed employment as the country struggled through the Great Depression. When the dam opened in 1936, it was possibly the only public works project completed ahead of schedule: by two years and under budget by $14 million. The total cost of construction was $165 million.

Flood control, irrigation, electricity and a regulated water supply were the main purposes for Hoover Dam's construction, and they remain the dam's primary functions today. The waters of the lower Colorado irrigate some one million acres of land in the US and half a million in Mexico; provide water to 25 million people primarily in Las Vegas, Los Angeles, San Diego, Phoenix and Tucson; and generate 4 billion kilowatt hours a year for Southern California, Arizona and Nevada.

There's a snazzy **Visitor Center** (☎ 702-294-3524; open 9am-5pm daily) atop the dam that, prior to the terrorist attacks against the United States in September 2001, used to be the departure points for guided and self-guided tours of the dam. Today, only dam personnel are allowed to enter the structure. Everyone else is limited to seeing a movie (adult/child aged seven to 17 years $10/4) on the history of the dam, shown in the visitor center. This film is also shown at the Alan Bible Visitor Center. Incidentally, the visitor center at Hoover Dam cost US taxpayers $125 million to build – only $40 million less than the dam itself.

If you come by car, park it in the multi-level parking lot *before* you reach the dam. Bus tours from Vegas are a good deal (about $20) and guarantee tickets to the basic tour. The **Snacketeria** at the Nevada spillway on the northern side of the dam wall sells food, film and books.

VALLEY OF FIRE STATE PARK

Near the northern end of Lake Mead National Recreation Area, this park is a masterpiece of desert scenery, a fantasyland of wonderful shapes carved in psychedelic sandstone. It's similar in appearance and geology to the desert landscapes of Utah, Arizona and New Mexico, but it's easily accessible from Las Vegas, and not crowded with tourists.

Early residents included a tribe called the Basketmakers and Anasazi Indians. Several petroglyphs survive throughout the park as a reminder of these early native peoples.

EXCURSIONS

National Parks' Potent Pass

If you intend to visit several national parks, it might be worth your while to consider purchasing an annual national-parks pass. It's available at any official visitor center and provides admission to any national park that charges an entrance fee. The pass costs $50 and is good for one full year from the date of purchase.

The **Visitor Center** (☎ 702-397-2088; open 8:30am-4:30pm daily) is just off SR169, which runs through the park. It has excellent exhibits, general information and hiking suggestions.

Some of the most interesting formations are **Elephant Rock**, the **Seven Sisters** and **Rainbow Vista**. Especially scenic is the winding side road to **White Domes**, and **Atlatl Rock** has some very distinct and artistic petroglyphs. There's a $5 day-use fee per vehicle.

The valley is most vibrant at dawn and dusk, so staying in one of the **campgrounds** (tent sites $13, including day-use fee) is a good move. Further accommodation is in nearby Overton, but Las Vegas is only 55 miles away. The quickest route is via I-15 and SR169, though the drive on Lake Mead's Northshore Rd and SR169 is more scenic and hooks up with Hwy 95 near Henderson, south of Vegas.

Grand Canyon National Park

The Grand Canyon is Arizona's most famous sight – indeed, it is arguably the best-known natural attraction in the entire United States. At 277 miles long, roughly 10 miles wide and a mile deep, the canyon is an incredible spectacle of differently colored rock strata. Its meandering rims and the many buttes and peaks within the canyon itself give access to fantastic views. Descending into the canyon on a short hike or a multiday backpacking trip offers an even better sense of the breathtaking variety in the landscape, wildlife and climate.

Although the rims are only 10 miles apart, as the crow flies, it is a 215-mile, five-hour drive on narrow roads from the visitor center on the South Rim to the visitor center on the North Rim. Thus, the Grand Canyon National Park is essentially two separate areas, and is treated as such here.

In addition, though the South Rim has more facilities and is the most visited side of the canyon, the North Rim is actually a little closer to Las Vegas, and it's a lot closer to Utah's Zion and Bryce Canyon National Parks. Vegas travelers hoping to see more than just the Grand Canyon should consider skipping the South Rim.

GEOLOGY

The oldest rocks, near the bottom of the inner canyon, are 1.7 billion years old, but most of the canyon-wall layers were laid during the Paleozoic Era, about 250 to 570 million years ago. These strata were in place well before the Americas began drifting away from the Old World, roughly 200 million years ago.

Some 60 to 70 million years ago, the massive Colorado Plateau emerged. For millions of years after this uplift, rivers flowed north from the northern side of the plateau and south from the southern side. The Grand Canyon began to form about 5.5 million years ago when a shifting of the San Andreas Fault created the Gulf of California. South-flowing rivers combined to form the lower Colorado River and emptied into this new sea.

Over time, the headwaters of the lower Colorado eroded through the Grand Wash Cliffs (northeast of Lake Mead) and connected with the upper Colorado system. This altered the river's course from a northward flow into Utah to a southward flow into the Gulf of California, and the erosion of the combined rivers created the Grand Canyon.

WHEN TO GO

The peak season ranges from about April to November, and the park is busiest from

Memorial Day to Labor Day – avoid that period if possible. On average, temperatures are 20°F cooler on the South Rim than at the bottom of the canyon. In summer, expect rim highs above 80°F and lows around 50°F.

June is the driest month, and summer thunderstorms make July and August the wettest. Weather is cooler in fall; snow and freezing overnight temperatures are likely by November. Winter weather can be beautifully clear, but be prepared for fierce storms and extreme cold.

GRAND CANYON – SOUTH RIM

The elevation of the South Rim ranges from 7000ft to more than 7400ft and is lower and much more accessible than the North Rim. About 90% of park visitors go to the South Rim. The foremost attraction is the rim itself, paralleled by a 33-mile scenic drive with numerous parking areas, scenic views and trailheads.

Another attraction is Grand Canyon Village, which has both early-20th-century hotels and modern amenities. The canyon is accessed via hiking trails (see Hiking & Backpacking, later). If you'd rather get away from the topside traffic, hike down to the canyon bottom and stay at Phantom Ranch or at one of several campgrounds; reservations are a must. Other activities, including mule rides, river running and backcountry backpacking also generally require advanced planning.

Orientation

It's about a five-hour straight drive to get from Las Vegas to the Grand Canyon's South Rim. From Hoover Dam, which is less than an hour from Vegas, it's 71 miles along Hwy 93 to Kingman, Arizona. Kingman has plenty of places to stay and eat, especially on Route 66, which runs through the center of the town as Andy Devine Ave. From Kingman, pick up I-40 and head east 110 miles to Williams; it's a further 60 miles north on Hwys 64 and 180 to Grand Canyon National Park. At Grand Canyon Village, Hwy 64 turns east and becomesRim Dr. As it exits the park, Hwy 64 continues east through the Kaibab National Forest and the Navajo

Indian Reservation to Cameron. It's 53 miles from Grand Canyon Village to Cameron, and an additional 51 miles south on Hwy 89 to Flagstaff.

Information

Visitor Centers The main visitor center is in Grand Canyon Village, about 6 miles north of the South Entrance Station. A bulletin board provides information on lodgings, weather, tours, talks and a host of other things. If you can't find the information you need, rangers are available to assist you between 8am and 5pm daily, with extended hours from April to November. Park maps and *The Guide* newspaper contain up-to-date park information, and are available for free.

A smaller visitor center at Desert View, near the eastern entrance of the park, is open daily in summer but is usually closed in winter. Ranger stations can provide assistance also. You'll find them near the Grand Canyon Railway depot; at the Indian Garden below the South Rim; the River ranger station and Phantom Ranch at the canyon's bottom; and Cottonwood Campground below the North Rim.

The **main park number** (☎ 928-638-7888) has recorded information on everything from weather conditions to applying for a river-running permit. You can leave your address to receive written information, or you can speak to a ranger during business hours. There's also the park's website (**W** www .nps.gov/grca/index.htm), which contains tons of useful information.

Fees & Permits Entrance to the park is $20 per private vehicle and $10 for bicyclists and pedestrians. Tickets are valid for seven days and can be used at any entrance point, including the North Rim. Golden Access, Age and Eagle passes are honored.

For backcountry camping, permits are required from the Backcountry Office (see the Grand Canyon – North Rim section for details).

Visitor Services Most of the visitor services in the park are at Grand Canyon Village, but prices here are substantially higher

EXCURSIONS

and lines longer than in Flagstaff: plan ahead. Services available include hotels, restaurants, campgrounds, a coin-operated laundry, showers and transportation services. There's also a **gas station** *(open daily)* and a **medical clinic** *(☎ 928-638-2551; open 9am-7pm Mon-Fri, 10am-4pm Sat)*.

Organized Activities

For information about free ranger-led activities, call the park (☎ 928-638-7888) or visit its website (**w** www.nps.gov/grca; click on 'Trip Planner', followed by 'Ranger Programs') or ask at a visitor center. Programs include various talks and slide shows, as well as guided walks ranging from a few hundred flat yards (40 minutes) to 3 miles below the rim (three to four hours). Many of the walks are wheelchair accessible, with wheelchairs available on loan from the visitor center. In summer there are Junior Ranger activities for four to 12 year olds.

Rim Trail

The paved Rim Trail skirts the rim for about 3 miles from **Yavapai Point** to **Maricopa Point**. It extends unpaved almost 7 miles further west past several viewpoints to **Hermits Rest** (see the following section). The Rim Trail is the park's most popular walk and has many interpretive signs, and visitors can hike as far as they feel comfortable. The reward is in the beautiful views. Only foot and wheelchair traffic are allowed – no bicycles. During winter, snow or ice may temporarily cover the trail.

East & West Rim Drives

The West Rim is accessible by road for 8 miles west of Grand Canyon Village (and by the Rim Trail described earlier). At the end of the drive and trail is **Hermits Rest**, with a snack bar and the Hermit Trailhead leading into the canyon; if you don't descend, you must return the way you came.

Cycling along the road is permitted year round, though cars are banned from about mid-March to mid-October; free shuttle buses operate every 15 minutes. In winter you can make this drive in your own car, although planned shuttle-bus services may

change this. Narrated bus tours are also available (see Organized Tours, later).

The East Rim is longer and a little less crowded than the West Rim, but offers equally spectacular views. There are presently no free shuttle buses or walking trails, but you can drive, cycle or take a narrated bus tour.

Tusayan, the most accessible of the park's approximately 2000 Ancestral Puebloan ruins, is along this road. The East Rim Drive ends at **Desert View**, which is about 25 miles east of Grand Canyon Village, and is the highest point on the South Rim. The road then leaves the national park through the Navajo Indian Reservation to Cameron.

Hiking & Backpacking

The **Backcountry Office** *(☎ 928-638-7875; open 8am-noon & 1pm-5pm daily)*, in Grand Canyon Village, has all relevant information on hiking and overnight backpacking, though staff only answer the phone after 1pm. See Backcountry Permits for information on how to obtain a permit for overnight camping.

The easiest walks are on the Rim Trail; hikes below the rim are arduous and some people prefer to use mules (see Organized Tours in the North Rim section). Mule riders have the right of way, so hikers meeting a mule train should stand on the upper side of the trail until the mules have passed.

Keep the following points in mind when hiking into the canyon: First, it's easy to stride down the trail for a few hours, but the steep uphill return during the heat of the day when you are tired is much more demanding. Allow at least two hours to return uphill for every hour of hiking downhill. Second, it's a lot hotter inside the gorge than at the rim, and water is scarce. Carry plenty of water and sun protection. In summer, temperatures can exceed 110°F in the inner gorge.

The most popular below-the-rim trails are Bright Angel Trail and South Kaibab Trail. Both are well maintained and suitable for either day hikes or, with a permit and advance reservation, overnight backpacking trips. No permit is needed for a day trip. Though steep, they are the easiest rim-to-river trails in the canyon. Day hikers should not expect to reach the river and return in one day.

Bright Angel Trail The trail leaves from the Rim Trail, a few yards west of Bright Angel Lodge in Grand Canyon Village. From the trailhead at about 6900ft, the trail drops to **Indian Garden** 4.6 miles away at about 3800ft, where there's a ranger station, campground, restrooms and water. From Indian Garden, an almost flat trail takes you 1½ miles to **Plateau Point**, which has exceptional views into the inner gorge. The 12.2-mile roundtrip from the rim to Plateau Point is a strenuous all-day hike. There are resthouses after 1½ miles (1130ft elevation drop) and 3 miles (2110ft elevation drop). The 1½-mile resthouse has restrooms; both have water in summer only.

From Indian Garden, Bright Angel Trail continues down to the Colorado River (2450ft elevation), which is crossed by a suspension bridge – the only bridge within the park. The **Bright Angel Campground** is a short jaunt north of the bridge and 9½ miles from the South Rim. Just beyond is **Phantom Ranch** with its welcoming water, food, accommodations and ranger station.

South Kaibab Trail This trail leaves the South Rim from near Yaki Point, about 4½ miles east of Grand Canyon Village. From the trailhead at 7262ft there's a 4800ft descent to the river and Bright Angel Campground, but the distance is only 6.7 miles. Clearly, this makes South Kaibab a much steeper trail than Bright Angel, but it follows a ridge with glorious views. The first 1½ miles drop 1300ft to Cedar Ridge, which makes a good short half-day hike.

North Kaibab Trail From the Bright Angel Campground on the northern side of the river, the North Kaibab Trail climbs to the North Rim at 8200ft in 14 miles – allowing a rim-to-rim crossing of the canyon. Descending from the South Rim to the river and returning, or making a rim-to-rim crossing in one long day is discouraged, especially for inexperienced hikers.

Backcountry Permits Permits are necessary for any overnight camping trip. Written applications must be made to obtain a permit. Applications can either be submitted to the Backcountry Office in Grand Canyon Village in person, or mailed or faxed to the **Backcountry Office** *(fax 928-638-2125; PO Box 129, Grand Canyon, AZ 86023).* Space is limited, so apply as far in advance as possible (reservations are accepted up to five months ahead; reservation forms can be downloaded from the park's website, w www.nps.gov/grca). If you arrive without a permit, put yourself on a waiting list for cancellations – sometimes you'll get lucky, especially if you can wait several days.

The three most popular backcountry campgrounds are **Indian Garden** (46 sites), **Bright Angel** (104 sites) and **Cottonwood** (33 sites).These are basic, off-the-beaten-path campsites with little more than clearings for campers, a source of fresh water and a ranger station (yes, there's a ranger station at each of the three campgrounds).

Indian Garden campground is a beautiful riparian area filled with cottonwood trees. A small creek passes through on its way to the Colorado River. The area is home to a small deer herd and offers a wonderful place to rest out of sun. Indian Garden is 4.5 miles below the South Rim and takes about 2 hours of hiking time. The return trip from Indian Garden to the South Rim via the Bright Angel Trail takes about 4 hours.

Bright Angel campground is at the bottom of the Grand Canyon. The campground is half a mile north of the Colorado River, and sits along Bright Angel Creek. The campground is less than half a mile from Phantom Ranch. The area is characterized by the river delta where Bright Angel Creek meets the Colorado River. Cottonwood trees shade Bright Angel campground and the creek offers a great place to cool off. Deer, ringtail cats, gray foxes, and squirrels are often seen. Metal food containers are provided to store food.

Cottonwood campground is a small campground 7 miles below the North Rim of the Grand Canyon on the North Kaibab Trail. It is a great place to rest. Bright Angel

Creek nearby offers a cool refreshing place to get wet. Seasonally (mid-May to mid-Oct) potable drinking water is available at the campground. During other times of the year hikers should be prepared to filter/treat water obtained from the creek. Metal 'ammo' boxes are provided to store food.

Numerous other smaller, less-developed campsites are available on unmaintained trails below the rim. Call or write for a complete listing.

River Running

Well over 20,000 visitors a year run the Colorado River, almost all of them with commercial operators. These aren't cheap; expect to pay up to $400 per person per day. Companies authorized to run the river through the national park include **Arizona Raft Adventures** (☎ *928-526-8200, 800-786-7238)*, **Diamond River Adventures** (☎ *928-645-8866, 800-343-3121)*, and **Grand Canyon Expeditions Co** (☎ *435-644-2691, 800-544-2691)*. Have a look at the national park's website (W www.nps.gov /grca/river) for links to other government approved river operators. Be aware that trips can fill up as much as a year in advance.

Organized Tours

Within the park, most tours are run by a company called **Xantera Parks & Resorts** *(formerly Amfac Grand Canyon National Park Lodges;* ☎ *303-297-2757, 888-297-2757, fax 303-338-2045;* W *www.xantera .com)*, which has a transportation desk (☎ 928-638-2631) at the Bright Angel Lodge and information desks at the visitor centers. Narrated bus tours leave from lodges in Grand Canyon Village. Two-hour West Rim tours ($16) depart at 9am and 4pm daily, and the 4-hour East Rim tour ($28) departs at 9am and 12:30pm. Sunset tours ($13) are offered in summer, when reservations are advised.

Most air tours over the Grand Canyon – as well as other sites – operate out of Las Vegas and are heavily promoted. The main options are a flight over Hoover Dam, Lake Mead and the western portion of the Grand Canyon

(around $95), or an air and ground tour, which involves a similar flight but also lands at Grand Canyon Airport and includes sightseeing at the South Rim (from $150). Overnight trips, some with hiking or rafting options, cost $200 to $300. Operators include **Air Vegas** (☎ *702-736-3599, 800-255-7474;* W *www.airvegas.com)*, **Grand Canyon Tour Company***(*☎ *702-655-6060;* W *www .lasvegasleisureguide.com)* an **Scenic Airlines** (☎ *702-638-3300, 800-634-6801;* W *www .scenic.com)*.

One-day bus tours from Las Vegas are available to the Grand Canyon, Bryce Canyon, Zion or Death Valley; they usually take around 10 hours and prices start at $100. One of the most reputable large bus operators is **Gray Line** (☎ *702-384-1234, 800-634-6579)*.

Places to Stay

Reservations are essential in summer and are a good idea in winter. Cancellations provide a lucky few with last-minute rooms. Call to check. If you can't find accommodation in the national park, try Tusayan (4 miles south of the South Entrance Station), Valle (31 miles south), Cameron (53 miles east), Williams (60 miles south) and Flagstaff (about 80 miles south).

Camping Campers should be prepared for freezing winter nights. Backcountry camping is available by reservation and permit (see Backcountry Permits, earlier). In Grand Canyon Village, **Mather Campground** (☎ *301-722-1257, 800-365-2267; sites without hookup $15; open all year)* has 320 sites, which take a maximum of two vehicles and six people. Make reservations up to five months in advance. Otherwise it's first-come, first-served.

Desert View Campground (☎ *301-722-1257, 800-365-2267; sites $10)*, near the eastern entrance, has 75 campsites on a first-come, first-served basis from mid-May to mid-October, though they're often full by early morning. There is water but no showers or RV hookups.

Trailer Village (☎ *301-722-1257, 800-365-2267; sites for 2 people $26, children* *over 16 $2)*, next to Mather Campground, offers 80 RV sites with hookups.

Lodges About 1000 rooms are available on the South Rim, in several lodges run by **Xantera** (☎ *303-297-2757, 888-297-2757, fax 303-338-2045;* ⓦ *www.xantera.com)*. Grand Canyon Village has six lodges.

Phantom Ranch *(dorm beds $27, basic twin cabins per person $74)* is at the bottom of the canyon. Rates in the (segregated) 10-bed dorms include bedding, soap and towels. Meals are available by advance reservation only. If you lack a reservation, try showing up at the Bright Angel Lodge transportation desk at 7am to snag a canceled bunk. Snacks, limited supplies, beer and wine can be purchased here.

Other places to stay include the **El Tovar Hotel** *(lodge rooms $120-180)* and **Bright Angel Lodge** *(simple lodge rooms $50-90)*, which dates from 1935.

Places to Eat

The American menu at **Bright Angel Restaurant** is available all day; the prices are moderate. The **Arizona Steakhouse** *(open 6:30pm- 10pm Mar-Dec)*, next door to Bright Angel Lodge, serves steaks and seafood.

By far the best place for quality food in an elegant and historic setting is the **El Tovar Dining Room** *(mains $15-25)*; dinner reservations are recommended.

Bright Angel Fountain *(open 8am-4pm Mar-Oct)*, near the Bright Angel trailhead, sells canyonside snacks and sandwiches.

Self-service dining is available at the **Maswik Cafeteria** and at the **Yavapai Cafeteria & Grill** from March through December.

Hermits Rest Snack Bar, at the end of the West Rim Drive, and **Desert View Fountain** near the eastern entrance, are open daily for snacks and fast food; hours vary by season.

Getting Around

Free shuttles (☎ 928-638-0591) operate along three routes from mid-May to mid-October. One goes around Grand Canyon Village, west along Hermits Rest Route and east along Kaibab Trail Route. Buses run every 15 minutes during the day and half-hourly from one

hour before sunrise till daylight, and from dusk till one hour after sunset. Bus stops are well signed and free maps are available. Park your car and ride – it's easier.

Trans-Canyon Shuttle (☎ 928-638-2820) transfers hikers from the South Rim to the North Rim and vice versa from mid-May to mid-October (when the North Rim is open). Shuttles (one way/return $65/110) depart at 1:30pm, take five hours and cover 215 miles. The main purpose of these shuttles is to transport serious hikers; by no means should they be viewed as tour buses and, in fact, it's not possible to see the canyon from the route these shuttles take. Reservations are required.

GRAND CANYON – NORTH RIM

The differences between the North and South Rims of the Grand Canyon are elevation and accessibility. The North Rim is more than 8000ft above sea level. There is only one road in, so visitors must backtrack more than 60 miles after their visit. It's colder and wetter, and the spruce and fir forest above the rim is thicker than the forests of the South Rim. Snows close the roads to car traffic from December until mid-May.

For visitors from Las Vegas, the North Rim is slightly more accessible than the South Rim, though it's a much longer drive from all of the other major cities and airports, and so only 10% of Grand Canyon visitors come to the North Rim. However, the views here are spectacular and the lack of huge crowds makes visiting the North Rim a more peaceful, if more spartan, experience of the canyon's majesty.

Orientation

From Las Vegas, it's 263 miles to the North Rim. Take I-15 north out of the city to Hwy 9, just past St George, Utah; this takes about two hours and passes through some breathtaking artificial canyons chiseled deep into red-rock slopes. From Hwy 9, pick up Hwy 59 south, and then Alt Hwy 89 south at Fredonia, where you can visit Kanab Canyon. Alt Hwy 89 brings you to Hwy 67, which winds another 44 miles south to the Grand

Canyon Lodge; another 30 miles of paved roads lead to overlooks to the east. Alternatively, from St George, you can continue on Hwy 9 and pass through Zion National Park before continuing south on Alt Hwy 89 to the Grand Canyon.

From the junction of Alt Hwy 89 and Hwy 67, you can continue on Alt Hwy 89 to the Navajo Indian Reservation. A few miles after crossing the Colorado River, Alt Hwy 89 becomes Hwy 89 and leads south to Cameron.

Information

The **Visitor Center** (☎ 928-638-7864; open 8am-6pm mid-May to mid-Oct), a two-minute walk from Grand Canyon Lodge (the North Rim's only hotel), has the usual Park Service information and activities.

The North Rim's **Backcountry Office** (☎ 928-638-7868; open 8am-noon & 1pm-5pm daily year-round) is in the ranger station near the campground, 1½ miles north of the visitor center. No phone calls are answered before 1pm at this office. Other services available at the North Rim (in season) are a restaurant, gas station, post office, bookstore, general store, coin-operated laundry and showers, medical clinic and tours. After October 15, all services are closed except the campground, which remains open, weather permitting, until December 1.

During winter, you can ski in and, with a backcountry camping permit, camp. It takes about three days to ski in from where the road closes, so this journey is reserved for adventurous and highly experienced winter campers/skiers.

Park headquarters are at the South Rim. See that section earlier in the chapter for details on fees and permits. Call ☎ 928-638-7888 for information on the South and North Rim.

Climate & When to Go

North Rim overnight temperatures drop below freezing as late as May and as early as October. The hottest month, July, sees average highs in the upper 70°s F and lows in the mid 40°s F. The North Rim is wetter than the South Rim, although the rain pattern

is similar. Snowfall is heaviest from late December to early March, when overnight temperatures usually fall into the teens.

North Rim Drives

The drive through the Kaibab Plateau to Bright Angel Point on Hwy 67 takes you through thick forest. There are excellent canyon views from the point, but to reach other overlooks you need to drive north for almost 3 miles and take the signed turnoff east to **Point Imperial** and **Cape Royal**. It's 9 miles to Point Imperial, the park's highest overlook, at 8803ft.

One of the most spectacular of these remote overlooks is the **Toroweap Overlook** at **Tuweep**, far to the west of the main park facilities. A dirt road leaves Hwy 389 about 9 miles west of Fredonia and heads 55 miles to the Tuweep Ranger Station, which is staffed year-round. It's 5 miles further to the overlook, which has spartan camping (no water).

Hiking & Backpacking

The most popular quick hike is the paved half-mile trail from the Grand Canyon Lodge south to the extreme tip of **Bright Angel Point**, which offers great views at sunset. The 1½-mile **Transept Trail** goes north from the lodge through forest to the North Rim Campground.

Two trailheads start from the parking lot 2 miles north of the lodge. The **Ken Patrick Trail** travels through rolling forested country northeast to Point Imperial, about 10 miles away. This trail may be overgrown and can require route-finding skills. About a mile into it, a fork to the right (east) becomes the **Uncle Jim Trail**, a fairly rugged 5-mile loop offering fine views.

The **North Kaibab Trail** descends sharply from the parking lot down to Phantom Ranch at the Colorado River, 5750ft below and 14 miles away. This is the only maintained rim-to-river trail accessed from the North Rim, and it connects with trails to the South Rim. The first 4.7 miles are the steepest, dropping well over 3000ft to **Roaring Springs** – a popular all-day hike and mule-ride destination. Water is available at Roaring Springs from May to September only. If you prefer a shorter day hike below the rim, you can walk just three-quarters of a mile down to **Coconino Overlook**, or 1 mile to the **Supai Tunnel**, 1400ft below the rim, to get a flavor of steep, inner-canyon hiking.

Cottonwood Campground is 7 miles and 4200ft below the rim and is the only campground between the North Rim and the river. Phantom Ranch and the Bright Angel Campground are 7 miles and 7½ miles, respectively, below Cottonwood (see the South Rim section, earlier).

Backcountry Permits In winter, the trails of the North Rim are backcountry use areas, as snow can be 5ft deep. The North Rim Campground (see Places to Stay & Eat) is still open for backcountry use, though there are only two ways to get to the campground in winter – either by hiking from the South Rim up to the North Rim via the North Kaibab Trail (only for the truly Nordic), or cross-country skiing 52 miles from Jacob Lake, a route that takes three days.

Permits for Cottonwood Campground and any other backcountry campgrounds must be applied for in writing as early as possible with the Backcountry Office on the South Rim (see the previous South Rim section for full details). If you don't have an advance permit, get on the waiting list at the **Backcountry Office** (☎ 928-638-7868; open 8am-noon & 1pm-5pm daily year-round) in the North Rim ranger station near the campground as soon as you arrive. Your chances of getting a Cottonwood or Bright Angel Campground permit for the next day are slim; however, if you can wait two to four days, you're likely to get one. The ranger station can advise you of more remote backcountry campgrounds along the North Rim, most of which require a long drive on dirt roads followed by a hike.

Organized Tours
In season, daily three-hour narrated tours to Point Imperial and Cape Royal (adult/child $20/10) leave from the lodge; a schedule is posted in the lobby.

Trail Rides (☎ 928-638-9875; open 7am-7pm) offer mule rides for an hour ($20) or

half day ($45). An all-day tour into the Grand Canyon, including lunch, costs $95. All tours have minimum-age requirements. Advance reservations are recommended, or you can check availability at the company's desk in the Grand Canyon Lodge.

Places to Stay & Eat
North Rim Campground (☎ 301-722-1257, 800-365-2267; sites $15), 1½ miles north of the Grand Canyon Lodge, has 82 sites. There's water, a store, snack bar and coin-operated showers and laundry, but there's no hookups. Make reservations up to five months in advance. Without a reservation, show up before 10am and hope for the best. All other campgrounds require a backcountry permit.

Grand Canyon Lodge (☎ 888-297-2757, 928-638-2611 from mid-May through mid-October, 303-297-2757 other times; doubles $88-100), is a historic spot which is usually full; reservations should be made as far in advance as possible. Its 200 motel rooms and cabins have private bathrooms and each sleeps up to five people. There's a snack bar, restaurant and bar at the lodge.

Utah's Canyon Country

ZION NATIONAL PARK
From St George, Utah, it's about 43 miles northeast along I-15 and Hwy 9 to Zion National Park (admission per car/person $20/10, valid for 7 days), the first national park established in Utah. The white, pink and red rocks here are so overpowering and magnificent that they are at once a photographer's dream and despair. Few photos can do justice to the magnificent scenery.

The highlight is Zion Canyon, a half-mile-deep slash formed by the Virgin River cutting through the sandstone. Everyone wants to follow the narrow paved road at the bottom, straining their neck at vistas of looming cliffs, domes and mountains. So popular is this route that it became over-crowded with cars and the Park Service began implementing a shuttle-bus service in 1999 to mitigate the problem. Other scenic drives are less crowded and just as magnificent. For those with the time and energy, day and overnight hikes can take you into spectacularly wild country.

The nearby Mormon city of St George has plenty of accommodation options and makes a good base for exploring Zion and other nearby national parks. The tiny town of Springdale, just outside the entrance to Zion, also has a number of decent hotels catering to park visitors.

Climate & When to Go

From March to November, campgrounds may fill to capacity, often by late morning in high season. Almost half of the park's annual visitors arrive in the Memorial Day to Labor Day period, while only about 7% visit between December and February.

Summer weather is hot (well over 100°F is common), so bring plenty of water and sun protection. Temperatures drop into the 60°s F at night, even in midsummer. Summers are generally dry, except from late July to early September, when the so-called monsoons – short but heavy rainstorms – occur.

There is snow in winter, but the main roads are plowed, and though it may freeze at night, daytime temperatures usually rise to about 50°F. Hikers climbing up from the roads will find colder and more wintry conditions, with snow and ice.

Spring weather is variable and hard to predict; rainstorms and hot sunny spells are both likely. May is the peak of the wildflower blooming. Spring and early summer are also the peak of bug season – make sure you bring insect repellent.

Fall is magnificent, with beautiful foliage colors at their best in September on the Kolob Plateau, and through October in the Zion Canyon. By then, daytime weather is pleasantly hot and nights are between 40°F and 60°F.

Orientation

Three roads enter the park, and hiking trails depart from all of them, leading you further into the splendor. At the southern end, the paved Zion–Mt Carmel Hwy (Hwy 9 between Mt Carmel Junction and Springdale) is the most popular route, and leads past the entrance of Zion Canyon. This road has fine views, but it is also exceptionally steep, twisting and narrow. The tunnel on the eastern side of Zion Canyon is so narrow that escorts must accompany vehicles over 7ft, 10 inches wide or 11ft, 4 inches tall. Escorts can be arranged in advance by calling ☎ 435-772-3256; a fee is charged. Bicycles are prohibited in the tunnel unless transported on a vehicle.

The main visitor center and campgrounds lie at the mouth of Zion Canyon. The elevation in Zion Canyon is about 4000ft, and at the eastern entrance it's 5700ft.

To reach the middle of the park, take the paved Kolob Terrace Rd, which leaves Hwy 9 at the village of Virgin before climbing north into the Kolob Plateau for about 9 miles. It becomes gravel for a few more miles to Lava Point, with a ranger station and primitive campground, then continues out of the park past Kolob Reservoir, to Hwy 14 and Cedar City. This dirt road becomes impassable after rain, and is closed by snow from about November to May.

The northern end is reached via the paved Kolob Canyons Rd, which leaves I-15 at exit 40 and extends 5 miles into the park. There is a visitor center at the start of the road, but no camping. The road climbs to more than 5000ft, is open all year, and has several lookouts over the **Finger Canyon** formations.

Information

The main **Visitor Center** (*☎ 435-772-3256; Hwy 9; open 8am-5pm daily, later in summer*) is near the park's southern entrance. The smaller **Kolob Canyons Visitor Center** (*☎ 435-586-9548; open 7am-5pm*), is at the beginning of Kolob Canyons Rd.

Entrance tickets are valid for seven days, and Golden Age, Eagle and Access passes are accepted. The south and east entry stations (located at either end of the Zion–Mt Carmel Hwy) and the visitor centers provide park maps and information about guided hikes.

Zion Canyon

From the visitor center, it's a 7-mile drive to the northern end of the canyon. The narrow road follows the Virgin River and the only places to stop are at parking areas, of which there are nine; most are signed trailheads. In order of increasing difficulty, the best trails accessible from the Zion Canyon road are outlined below. All have superb views. The distances listed here are one-way.

You can stroll along the paved **Pairus Trail** (2 miles), which parallels the road from Watchman Campground to the main park junction. Take an easy walk near the canyon's end, along the paved and very popular **Riverside Walk** (about 1 mile), which is fairly flat and partly wheelchair-accessible. You can continue further along into The Narrows – see the Backpacking section. The **Weeping Rock Trail** (440 yards) climbs 100ft to a lovely area of moist hanging gardens. **Emerald Pools** can be reached by a mile-long paved trail or a shorter unpaved one climbing 200ft to the lower pool; a shorter trail scrambles another 200ft to the upper pool. Swimming is not allowed here.

Hidden Canyon Trail (just over 1 mile) has a few long drop-offs, and climbs 750ft to a very narrow and shady canyon. **Angels Landing Trail** (2½ miles) has a 1500ft elevation gain. Allow three to four hours roundtrip. There are steep and exposed drop-offs with chains to hold on to for security. Views are superb, but don't go if you're afraid of heights. **Observation Point Trail** (almost 4 miles long) has a 2150ft elevation gain; it's less exposed than Angels Landing and offers great views too.

Zion–Mt Carmel Hwy

The road east of Zion Canyon is somewhat of an engineering feat, with switchbacks and a long tunnel (see the Orientation section for vehicle restrictions). East of the tunnel, the geology changes into slickrock, with many carved and etched formations, of which the mountainous **Checkerboard Mesa** is a memorable example. The road travels for about 10 miles from the Zion Canyon turnoff to the eastern exit of the park, with several parking areas along the road. Only one, just east of the mile-long tunnel, has a marked trail – the **Canyon Overlook Trail** (a half-mile long, which climbs more than 100ft and offers fine views into Zion Canyon, 1000ft lower.

Backpacking

You can backpack and wilderness camp along more than 100 miles of trails in Zion. Starting from Lee Pass on the Kolob Canyons Rd in the north, you can backpack along a number of connected trails emerging at the eastern entrance of the park. This entire traverse of the park is about 50 miles. Park rangers can suggest a variety of shorter backpacking options.

The most famous backpacking trip is through **The Narrows**, a 16-mile journey through canyons along the North Fork of the Virgin River. In places, the canyon walls are only 20ft apart and tower hundreds of feet above you. The hike requires wading (sometimes swimming) the river many times. It is usually started at Chamberlain's Ranch (outside the park) and completed via the Riverside Walk Trail at the northern end of Zion Canyon, to allow hikers to move with the river current. The trip takes about 12 hours and camping overnight is recommended. This hike is only open from June to October, but may be closed from late July to early September due to the danger of flash-flooding. The few miles at the northern end of Zion Canyon can get very crowded with hundreds of day hikers.

Backpackers need a permit ($5 per person per night) from either of the visitor centers (see the Information section). These are usually issued the day before or the morning of the trip; problems with selecting a route are rare (although there may be a day or two wait for The Narrows). Camping is allowed in most areas; ask a ranger. Zion's springs and rivers flow year-round, but the water must be boiled or treated for drinking. Day hikes do not require a permit, with the exception of people attempting the entire trip in one day.

Campfires are not allowed, so carry a camping stove or food that doesn't need to be cooked. Sun protection is essential sunblock, hat, dark glasses and long sleeves. Insect repellent is priceless in spring and early summer.

Many backpacking trips require either retracing your footsteps or leaving a vehicle at either end of the trip. If you don't have two vehicles, a 'Ride Board' at the main visitor center in Zion Canyon can connect you with other backpackers. Also, Zion Lodge (see Places to Stay & Eat) has a shuttle desk and will arrange a ride for a fee.

Places to Stay & Eat

Between the southern entrance and the main visitor center are two campgrounds: **Watchman** *(reservations taken; sites $16; open year-round)* with 170 sites; and **South** *(no reservations taken; sites $14; open Mar-Oct)* with 141 sites. Both are run by the Park Service (☎ 800-367-2267) and have water and toilets, but no showers.

Zion Lodge *(☎ 435-772-3213, reservations 303-297-2757, 888-297-2757; rooms $107-130, cabins $116)* has motel rooms and cabins, most with views and porches. Book early – summer dates may fill up months ahead. The lodge's restaurants serve breakfast, lunch and dinner.

Zion Ponderosa Ranch Resort *(☎ 435-648-2700, 800-293-5444; tent sites per person $65, cowboy cabins with shared bath per person $99, double log cabins with private bath per person $139; open Mar-Dec)* is outside the eastern entrance and 5 miles north from Hwy 9 on North Fork County Rd. It has a pool, hot tub and restaurants, and offers a cornucopia of activities, including horseback riding, mountain biking and a climbing wall. Rates include three meals a day and most activities.

Pioneer Lodge *(☎ 435-772-3233, 888-772-3233; 838 Zion Park Blvd, double rooms $59-99, apartments $139-180)*, in nearby Springdale, is a popular spot, with about 40 standard rooms and several apartments. Prices fluctuate with the day of the week, season and holidays.

Canyon Ranch Motel *(☎ 435-772-3357; 668 Zion Park Blvd; doubles $69-88 per room)* has rooms in homey cottages; rooms with kitchenettes cost an additional $10.

BRYCE CANYON NATIONAL PARK

The **Grand Staircase** – a series of steplike uplifted rock layers stretching north from the Grand Canyon – culminates in the **Pink Cliffs** formation at Bryce Canyon. These cliffs were deposited as a 2000ft-deep sediment in a huge prehistoric lake some 50 to 60 million years ago, slowly lifted up to over 7000ft and 9000ft above sea level, and then eroded into wondrous ranks of pinnacles and points, steeples and spires, cliffs and crevices. And then there are the wondrous 'hoodoos,' phalanxes of oddly luminous stone towers that line up as if awaiting some kind of blessing. It's a Stonehenge perspective rendered in roseate stone. The oddly shaped 'hoodoos' are made up of reddish-pink rock that is incredibly variable; a shaft of sunlight can suddenly transform the view from merely magnificent to almost otherworldly.

Climate & When to Go

The park is open year-round, with 75% of the approximately 1.6 million annual visitors arriving between May and September. Summer high temperatures at the 8000ft to 9000ft elevation of the rim may reach into the 80°s F – and even hotter below the rim – so carry water and sun protection. Summer nights have temperatures in the 40°s F. June is relatively dry, but July and August see sudden, though usually brief, torrential storms.

Snow blankets the ground from about November to April, but most of the park's roads remain open. A few are unplowed and designated for cross-country skiing or snowshoeing. The main Rim Rd is occasionally closed after heavy snow, but only until the plows have done their job. January is the slowest month.

Orientation

From Zion National Park, it takes about two hours to drive to Bryce Canyon; follow Hwy 9, then turn north on Hwy 89 before turning east onto Hwy 12. Scenic Hwy 12 is the main paved road to the park and cuts across its northern portion. (There's no entrance fee for driving across the northern corner.) Follow Hwy 12 for 14 miles east of Hwy 89 to Hwy 63, which heads south to the official park entrance, 3 miles away. From here, an 18-mile dead-end drive continues along the rim of the canyon. Rim Rd climbs past turnoffs to the visitor center (at about 8000ft), the lodge, campgrounds, viewpoints and trailheads, ending at Rainbow Point, 9115ft above sea level. Trailers are allowed only as far as Sunset Campground, 3 miles south of the entrance. Vehicles over 25ft in length have access restrictions to Paria View in summer.

The 122-mile-long Hwy 12 is one of the most scenic roads in Utah. It continues northeast past Bryce Canyon and terminates at Torrey on Hwy 24, about 4 miles from Capitol Reef National Park, where more red-rock cliffs await. This road is not conducive to fast driving.

Information
The **Visitor Center** (☎ 435-834-5322; W www.nps.gov/brca; open 8am-4:30pm daily, extended hours late Spring-early Fall, closed Thanksgiving, Christmas & New Year's Day) is the first main building along Hwy 63 after you officially enter the park. Entry to the park is $15 per person if arriving by shuttle, or $20 per car. Tickets are valid for seven days, and Golden Age, Eagle and Access passes are honored. The entrance station and visitor center provide free maps and brochures. Anyone planning on staying in the backcountry will need to pay an additional $5 per day.

Places to Stay & Eat
Inside the Park The Park Service operates the **North Campground** (sites $10; open year-round), near the visitor center, and

Sunset Campground (sites $10; open May-10 Oct) about 1 mile south. Each campground has toilets and drinking water. There are no hookups at the 200-odd sites and generator hours are restricted. A dump station is available during the summer months. Some motorhome sites are available at the North Campground. Sites often fill up by noon in summer.

Between the two campgrounds is a **General Store**, for basic food and camping supplies, coin-operated showers and a laundry in summer. Visit Ruby's Inn (see Outside the Park) for a winter shower.

Bryce Canyon Lodge (☎ 435-834-5361, reservations 800-367-2267; units $99-122; open Apr 1-Oct 31), near the visitor center, opened in 1924 and has 114 units, a restaurant and coin-operated laundry. Reservations are more or less essential.

Outside the Park On Hwy 63 about a mile north of the park entrance is **Bryce View Lodge** (☎ 435-834-5180, 888-279-2304; W www.bryceviewlodge.com; rooms $55-65), which has more than 100 recently renovated air-con rooms with bathrooms and cable TV. Guests are welcome to use the swimming pools and spas located across the street at Ruby's Inn and Ruby's RV Park and Campground.

Ruby's Inn (☎ 435-834-5341, 866-866-6616, fax 435-834-5265; W www.rubysinn .com; doubles $46-95; open year-round) is a huge, popular Best Western hotel opposite Bryce View Lodge. Facilities include a pool, spa, post office and coin-operated laundry. Horse, bike and ski rentals are available. The coin-operated showers and laundry stay open all year. There are pleasant rooms at the motel, where prices are halved from January to March (make reservations early).

EXCURSIONS

LONELY PLANET

ON THE ROAD

Travel Guides explore cities, regions and countries, and supply information on transport, restaurants and accommodation, covering all budgets. They come with reliable, easy-to-use maps, practical advice, cultural and historical facts and a rundown on attractions both on and off the beaten track. There are over 200 titles in this classic series, covering nearly every country in the world.

 Lonely Planet Upgrades extend the shelf life of existing travel guides by detailing any changes that may affect travel in a region since a book has been published. Upgrades can be downloaded for free from **www.lonelyplanet.com/upgrades**

For travellers with more time than money, **Shoestring** guides offer dependable, first-hand information with hundreds of detailed maps, plus insider tips for stretching money as far as possible. Covering entire continents in most cases, the six-volume shoestring guides are known around the world as 'backpackers bibles'.

For the discerning short-term visitor, **Condensed** guides highlight the best a destination has to offer in a full-colour, pocket-sized format designed for quick access. They include everything from top sights and walking tours to opinionated reviews of where to eat, stay, shop and have fun.

CitySync lets travellers use their Palm™ or Visor™ hand-held computers to guide them through a city with handy tips on transport, history, cultural life, major sights, and shopping and entertainment options. It can also quickly search and sort hundreds of reviews of hotels, restaurants and attractions, and pinpoint their location on scrollable street maps. CitySync can be downloaded from **www.citysync.com**

MAPS & ATLASES

Lonely Planet's **City Maps** feature downtown and metropolitan maps, as well as transit routes and walking tours. The maps come complete with an index of streets, a listing of sights and a plastic coat for extra durability.

Road Atlases are an essential navigation tool for serious travellers. Cross-referenced with the guidebooks, they also feature distance and climate charts and a complete site index.

LONELY PLANET

ESSENTIALS

Read This First books help new travellers to hit the road with confidence. These invaluable predeparture guides give step-by-step advice on preparing for a trip, budgeting, arranging a visa, planning an itinerary and staying safe while still getting off the beaten track.

Healthy Travel pocket guides offer a regional rundown on disease hot spots and practical advice on predeparture health measures, staying well on the road and what to do in emergencies. The guides come with a user-friendly design and helpful diagrams and tables.

Lonely Planet's **Phrasebooks** cover the essential words and phrases travellers need when they're strangers in a strange land. They come in a pocket-sized format with colour tabs for quick reference, extensive vocabulary lists, easy-to-follow pronunciation keys and two-way dictionaries.

Miffed by blurry photos of the Taj Mahal? Tired of the classic 'top of the head cut off' shot? **Travel Photography: A Guide to Taking Better Pictures** will help you turn ordinary holiday snaps into striking images and give you the know-how to capture every scene, from frenetic festivals to peaceful beach sunrises.

Lonely Planet's **Travel Journal** is a lightweight but sturdy travel diary for jotting down all those on-the-road observations and significant travel moments. It comes with a handy time-zone wheel, a world map and useful travel information.

Lonely Planet's eKno is an all-in-one communication service developed especially for travellers. It offers low-cost international calls and free email and voicemail so that you can keep in touch while on the road. Check it out on **www.ekno.lonelyplanet.com**

FOOD & RESTAURANT GUIDES

Lonely Planet's **Out to Eat** guides recommend the brightest and best places to eat and drink in top international cities. These gourmet companions are arranged by neighbourhood, packed with dependable maps, garnished with scene-setting photos and served with quirky features.

For people who live to eat, drink and travel, **World Food** guides explore the culinary culture of each country. Entertaining and adventurous, each guide is packed with detail on staples and specialities, regional cuisine and local markets, as well as sumptuous recipes, comprehensive culinary dictionaries and lavish photos good enough to eat.

LONELY PLANET

OUTDOOR GUIDES

For those who believe the best way to see the world is on foot, Lonely Planet's **Walking Guides** detail everything from family strolls to difficult treks, with 'when to go and how to do it' advice supplemented by reliable maps and essential travel information.

Cycling Guides map a destination's best bike tours, long and short, in day-by-day detail. They contain all the information a cyclist needs, including advice on bike maintenance, places to eat and stay, innovative maps with detailed cues to the rides, and elevation charts.

The **Watching Wildlife** series is perfect for travellers who want authoritative information but don't want to tote a heavy field guide. Packed with advice on where, when and how to view a region's wildlife, each title features photos of over 300 species and contains engaging comments on the local flora and fauna.

With underwater colour photos throughout, **Pisces Books** explore the world's best diving and snorkelling areas. Each book contains listings of diving services and dive resorts, detailed information on depth, visibility and difficulty of dives, and a roundup of the marine life you're likely to see through your mask.

OFF THE ROAD

Journeys, the travel literature series written by renowned travel authors, capture the spirit of a place or illuminate a culture with a journalist's attention to detail and a novelist's flair for words. These are tales to soak up while you're actually on the road or dip into as an at-home armchair indulgence.

The range of lavishly illustrated **Pictorial** books is just the ticket for both travellers and dreamers. Off-beat tales and vivid photographs bring the adventure of travel to your doorstep long before the journey begins and long after it is over.

Lonely Planet **Videos** encourage the same independent, tough-minded approach as the guidebooks. Currently airing throughout the world, this award-winning series features innovative footage and an original soundtrack.

Yes, we know, work is tough, so do a little bit of deskside dreaming with the spiral-bound Lonely Planet **Diary** or a Lonely Planet **Wall Calendar**, filled with great photos from around the world.

TRAVELLERS NETWORK

Lonely Planet Online. Lonely Planet's award-winning Web site has insider information on hundreds of destinations, from Amsterdam to Zimbabwe, complete with interactive maps and relevant links. The site also offers the latest travel news, recent reports from travellers on the road, guidebook upgrades, a travel links site, an online book-buying option and a lively travellers bulletin board. It can be viewed at **www.lonelyplanet.com** or AOL keyword: lp.

Planet Talk is a quarterly print newsletter, full of gossip, advice, anecdotes and author articles. It provides an antidote to the being-at-home blues and lets you plan and dream for the next trip. Contact the nearest Lonely Planet office for your free copy.

Comet, the free Lonely Planet newsletter, comes via email once a month. It's loaded with travel news, advice, dispatches from authors, travel competitions and letters from readers. To subscribe, click on the Comet subscription link on the front page of the Web site.

Lonely Planet Guides by Region

Lonely Planet is known worldwide for publishing practical, reliable and no-nonsense travel information in our guides and on our Web site. The Lonely Planet list covers just about every accessible part of the world. Currently there are 16 series: Travel guides, Shoestring guides, Condensed guides, Phrasebooks, Read This First, Healthy Travel, Walking guides, Cycling guides, Watching Wildlife guides, Pisces Diving & Snorkeling guides, City Maps, Road Atlases, Out to Eat, World Food, Journeys travel literature and Pictorials.

AFRICA Africa on a shoestring • Botswana • Cairo • Cairo City Map • Cape Town • Cape Town City Map • East Africa • Egypt • Egyptian Arabic phrasebook • Ethiopia, Eritrea & Djibouti • Ethiopian Amharic phrasebook • The Gambia & Senegal • Healthy Travel Africa • Kenya • Malawi • Morocco • Moroccan Arabic phrasebook • Mozambique • Namibia • Read This First: Africa • South Africa, Lesotho & Swaziland • Southern Africa • Southern Africa Road Atlas • Swahili phrasebook • Tanzania, Zanzibar & Pemba • Trekking in East Africa • Tunisia • Watching Wildlife East Africa • Watching Wildlife Southern Africa • West Africa • World Food Morocco • Zambia • Zimbabwe, Botswana & Namibia
Travel Literature: Mali Blues: Traveling to an African Beat • The Rainbird: A Central African Journey • Songs to an African Sunset: A Zimbabwean Story

AUSTRALIA & THE PACIFIC Aboriginal Australia & the Torres Strait Islands •Auckland • Australia • Australian phrasebook • Australia Road Atlas • Cycling Australia • Cycling New Zealand • Fiji • Fijian phrasebook • Healthy Travel Australia, NZ & the Pacific • Islands of Australia's Great Barrier Reef • Melbourne • Melbourne City Map • Micronesia • New Caledonia • New South Wales • New Zealand • Northern Territory • Outback Australia • Out to Eat – Melbourne • Out to Eat – Sydney • Papua New Guinea • Pidgin phrasebook • Queensland • Rarotonga & the Cook Islands • Samoa • Solomon Islands • South Australia • South Pacific • South Pacific phrasebook • Sydney • Sydney City Map • Sydney Condensed • Tahiti & French Polynesia • Tasmania • Tonga • Tramping in New Zealand • Vanuatu • Victoria • Walking in Australia • Watching Wildlife Australia • Western Australia
Travel Literature: Islands in the Clouds: Travels in the Highlands of New Guinea • Kiwi Tracks: A New Zealand Journey • Sean & David's Long Drive

CENTRAL AMERICA & THE CARIBBEAN Bahamas, Turks & Caicos • Baja California • Belize, Guatemala & Yucatán • Bermuda • Central America on a shoestring • Costa Rica • Costa Rica Spanish phrasebook • Cuba • Cycling Cuba • Dominican Republic & Haiti • Eastern Caribbean • Guatemala • Havana • Healthy Travel Central & South America • Jamaica • Mexico • Mexico City • Panama • Puerto Rico • Read This First: Central & South America • Virgin Islands • World Food Caribbean • World Food Mexico • Yucatán
Travel Literature: Green Dreams: Travels in Central America

EUROPE Amsterdam • Amsterdam City Map • Amsterdam Condensed • Andalucía • Athens • Austria • Baltic States phrasebook • Barcelona • Barcelona City Map • Belgium & Luxembourg • Berlin • Berlin City Map • Britain • British phrasebook • Brussels, Bruges & Antwerp • Brussels City Map • Budapest • Budapest City Map • Canary Islands • Catalunya & the Costa Brava • Central Europe • Central Europe phrasebook • Copenhagen • Corfu & the Ionians • Corsica • Crete • Crete Condensed • Croatia • Cycling Britain • Cycling France • Cyprus • Czech & Slovak Republics • Czech phrasebook • Denmark • Dublin • Dublin City Map • Dublin Condensed • Eastern Europe • Eastern Europe phrasebook • Edinburgh • Edinburgh City Map • England • Estonia, Latvia & Lithuania • Europe on a shoestring • Europe phrasebook • Finland • Florence • Florence City Map • France • Frankfurt City Map • Frankfurt Condensed • French phrasebook • Georgia, Armenia & Azerbaijan • Germany • German phrasebook • Greece • Greek Islands • Greek phrasebook • Hungary • Iceland, Greenland & the Faroe Islands • Ireland • Italian phrasebook • Italy • Kraków • Lisbon • The Loire • London • London City Map • London Condensed • Madrid • Madrid City Map • Malta • Mediterranean Europe • Milan, Turin & Genoa • Moscow • Munich • Netherlands • Normandy • Norway • Out to Eat – London • Out to Eat – Paris • Paris • Paris City Map • Paris Condensed • Poland • Polish phrasebook • Portugal • Portuguese phrasebook • Prague • Prague City Map • Provence & the Côte d'Azur • Read This First: Europe • Rhodes & the Dodecanese • Romania & Moldova • Rome • Rome City Map • Rome Condensed • Russia, Ukraine & Belarus • Russian phrasebook • Scandinavian & Baltic Europe • Scandinavian phrasebook • Scotland • Sicily • Slovenia • South-West France • Spain • Spanish phrasebook • Stockholm • St Petersburg • St Petersburg City Map • Sweden • Switzerland • Tuscany • Ukrainian phrasebook • Venice • Vienna • Wales • Walking in Britain • Walking in France • Walking in Ireland • Walking in Italy • Walking in Scotland • Walking in Spain • Walking in Switzerland • Western Europe • World Food France • World Food Greece • World Food Ireland • World Food Italy • World Food Spain **Travel Literature:** After Yugoslavia • Love and War in the Apennines • The Olive Grove: Travels in Greece • On the Shores of the Mediterranean • Round Ireland in Low Gear • A Small Place in Italy

Lonely Planet Mail Order

Lonely Planet products are distributed worldwide. They are also available by mail order from Lonely Planet, so if you have difficulty finding a title please write to us. North and South American residents should write to 150 Linden St, Oakland, CA 94607, USA; European and African residents should write to 10a Spring Place, London NW5 3BH, UK; and residents of other countries to Locked Bag 1, Footscray, Victoria 3011, Australia.

INDIAN SUBCONTINENT & THE INDIAN OCEAN Bangladesh • Bengali phrasebook • Bhutan • Delhi • Goa • Healthy Travel Asia & India • Hindi & Urdu phrasebook • India • India & Bangladesh City Map • Indian Himalaya • Karakoram Highway • Kathmandu City Map • Kerala • Madagascar • Maldives • Mauritius, Réunion & Seychelles • Mumbai (Bombay) • Nepal • Nepali phrasebook • North India • Pakistan • Rajasthan • Read This First: Asia & India • South India • Sri Lanka • Sri Lanka phrasebook • Tibet • Tibetan phrasebook • Trekking in the Indian Himalaya • Trekking in the Karakoram & Hindukush • Trekking in the Nepal Himalaya • World Food India **Travel Literature:** The Age of Kali: Indian Travels and Encounters • Hello Goodnight: A Life of Goa • In Rajasthan • Maverick in Madagascar • A Season in Heaven: True Tales from the Road to Kathmandu • Shopping for Buddhas • A Short Walk in the Hindu Kush • Slowly Down the Ganges

MIDDLE EAST & CENTRAL ASIA Bahrain, Kuwait & Qatar • Central Asia • Central Asia phrasebook • Dubai • Farsi (Persian) phrasebook • Hebrew phrasebook • Iran • Israel & the Palestinian Territories • Istanbul • Istanbul City Map • Istanbul to Cairo • Istanbul to Kathmandu • Jerusalem • Jerusalem City Map • Jordan • Lebanon • Middle East • Oman & the United Arab Emirates • Syria • Turkey • Turkish phrasebook • World Food Turkey • Yemen **Travel Literature:** Black on Black: Iran Revisited • Breaking Ranks: Turbulent Travels in the Promised Land • The Gates of Damascus • Kingdom of the Film Stars: Journey into Jordan

NORTH AMERICA Alaska • Boston • Boston City Map • Boston Condensed • British Columbia • California & Nevada • California Condensed • Canada • Chicago • Chicago City Map • Chicago Condensed • Florida • Georgia & the Carolinas • Great Lakes • Hawaii • Hiking in Alaska • Hiking in the USA • Honolulu & Oahu City Map • Las Vegas • Los Angeles • Los Angeles City Map • Louisiana & the Deep South • Miami • Miami City Map • Montreal • New England • New Orleans • New Orleans City Map • New York City • New York City City Map • New York City Condensed • New York, New Jersey & Pennsylvania • Oahu • Out to Eat – San Francisco • Pacific Northwest • Rocky Mountains • San Diego & Tijuana • San Francisco • San Francisco City Map • Seattle • Seattle City Map • Southwest • Texas • Toronto • USA • USA phrasebook • Vancouver • Vancouver City Map • Virginia & the Capital Region • Washington, DC • Washington, DC City Map • World Food New Orleans **Travel Literature**: Caught Inside: A Surfer's Year on the California Coast • Drive Thru America

NORTH-EAST ASIA Beijing • Beijing City Map • Cantonese phrasebook • China • Hiking in Japan • Hong Kong & Macau • Hong Kong City Map • Hong Kong Condensed • Japan • Japanese phrasebook • Korea • Korean phrasebook • Kyoto • Mandarin phrasebook • Mongolia • Mongolian phrasebook • Seoul • Shanghai • South-West China • Taiwan • Tokyo • Tokyo Condensed • World Food Hong Kong • World Food Japan **Travel Literature:** In Xanadu: A Quest • Lost Japan

SOUTH AMERICA Argentina, Uruguay & Paraguay • Bolivia • Brazil • Brazilian phrasebook • Buenos Aires • Buenos Aires City Map • Chile & Easter Island • Colombia • Ecuador & the Galapagos Islands • Healthy Travel Central & South America • Latin American Spanish phrasebook • Peru • Quechua phrasebook • Read This First: Central & South America • Rio de Janeiro • Rio de Janeiro City Map • Santiago de Chile • South America on a shoestring • Trekking in the Patagonian Andes • Venezuela **Travel Literature**: Full Circle: A South American Journey

SOUTH-EAST ASIA Bali & Lombok • Bangkok • Bangkok City Map • Burmese phrasebook • Cambodia • Cycling Vietnam, Laos & Cambodia • East Timor phrasebook • Hanoi • Healthy Travel Asia & India • Hill Tribes phrasebook • Ho Chi Minh City (Saigon) • Indonesia • Indonesian phrasebook • Indonesia's Eastern Islands • Java • Lao phrasebook • Laos • Malay phrasebook • Malaysia, Singapore & Brunei • Myanmar (Burma) • Philippines • Pilipino (Tagalog) phrasebook • Read This First: Asia & India • Singapore • Singapore City Map • South-East Asia on a shoestring • South-East Asia phrasebook • Thailand • Thailand's Islands & Beaches • Thailand, Vietnam, Laos & Cambodia Road Atlas • Thai phrasebook • Vietnam • Vietnamese phrasebook • World Food Indonesia • World Food Thailand • World Food Vietnam

ALSO AVAILABLE: Antarctica • The Arctic • The Blue Man: Tales of Travel, Love and Coffee • Brief Encounters: Stories of Love, Sex & Travel • Buddhist Stupas in Asia: The Shape of Perfection • Chasing Rickshaws • The Last Grain Race • Lonely Planet ... On the Edge: Adventurous Escapades from Around the World • Lonely Planet Unpacked • Lonely Planet Unpacked Again • Not the Only Planet: Science Fiction Travel Stories • Ports of Call: A Journey by Sea • Sacred India • Travel Photography: A Guide to Taking Better Pictures • Travel with Children • Tuvalu: Portrait of an Island Nation

LONELY PLANET

You already know that Lonely Planet produces more than this one guidebook, but you might not be aware of the other products we have on this region. Here is a selection of titles that you may want to check out as well:

Las Vegas map
ISBN 1 74059 428 2
US$5.99 • UK£3.99

Las Vegas condensed
ISBN 1 74059 453 3
US$11.99 • UK£6.99

USA phrasebook
ISBN 1 86450 182 0
US$6.99 • UK£4.50

Calafornia
ISBN 1 86450 331 9
US$21.99 • UK£13.99

Los Angeles
ISBN 1 74059 021 X
US$15.99 • UK£9.99

San Francisco
ISBN 1 86450 309 2
US$15.99 • UK£9.99

Texas
ISBN 1 86450 375 0
US$19.99 • UK£12.99

Arizona
ISBN 1 74059 458 4
US$15.99 • UK£9.99

Hiking in the Sierra Nevada
ISBN 1 74059 272 7
US$17.99 • UK£11.99

USA
ISBN 1 86450 308 4
US$24.99 • UK£14.99

Drive Thru America
ISBN 0 86442 506 6
US$12.95 • UK£6.99

Travel Journal
ISBN 186450 343 2
US$12.99 • UK£7.99

Available wherever books are sold

Index

Text

Bold indicates maps.

Places to Stay

Places to Eat

Boxed Text

Las Vegas Map Section

MAP 1 GREATER LAS VEGAS

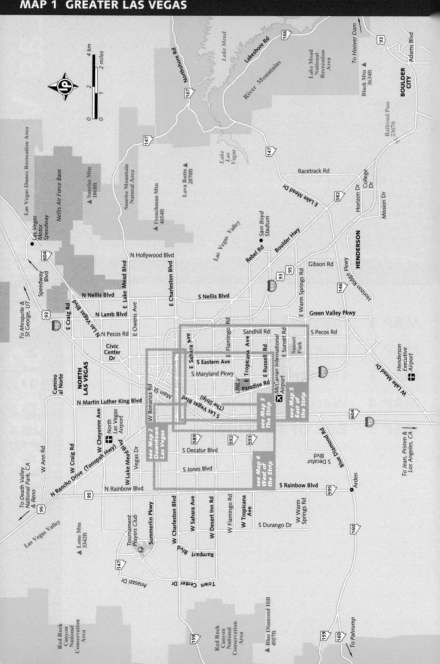

MAP 2 DOWNTOWN LAS VEGAS

PLACES TO STAY
6 Main Street Station; Triple 7 Brew Pub; The Pullman Grille
9 California
10 Jackie Gaughan's Plaza; Center Stage
14 Golden Nugget; Hand of Faith Nugget; Carson Street Café
15 Fremont; Second Street Grille; Tony Roma's: A Place For Ribs
19 Budget Inn
20 Victory Hotel
23 Las Vegas International Hostel
30 USA Hostels - Las Vegas

PLACES TO EAT
12 Golden Gate
13 Binion's Horseshoe Coffee Shop; $1 Million in Cash
16 Hugo's Cellar
18 Limerick's
21 Andre's
26 Dona Maria Tamales
32 Rincon Criollo

SHOPPING
17 Harley-Davidson
24 Gamblers General Store
27 Gambler's Book Club
28 Antique Square Shopping Center
29 Toys of Yesteryear
31 A Slightly Sinful Adventure

OTHER
1 Old Las Vegas Mormon Fort
2 Las Vegas Natural History Museum
3 Cashman Field
4 Lied Discovery Children's Museum
5 Reed Whipple Cultural Center
7 CAT Bus Station
8 Post Office
11 Greyhound Lines
22 Bunkhouse Saloon
25 Arts Factory Complex

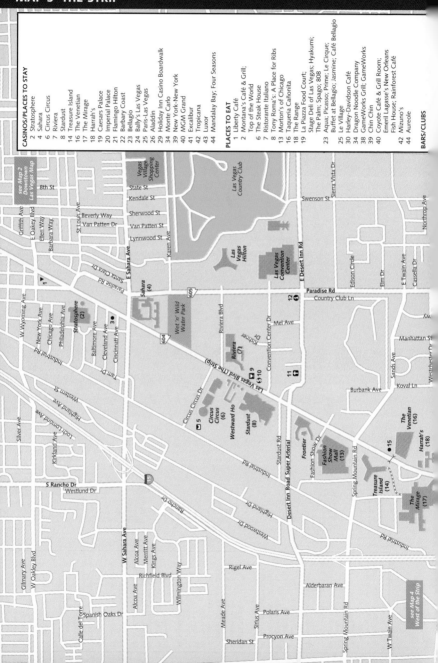

MAP 3 THE STRIP

CASINOS/PLACES TO STAY

2 Stratosphere
4 Sahara
6 Circus Circus
7 Riviera
8 Stardust
14 Treasure Island
16 The Venetian
17 The Mirage
18 Harrah's
19 Caesars Palace
20 Imperial Palace
21 Flamingo Hilton
22 Barbary Coast
23 Bellagio
24 Bally's Las Vegas
25 Paris-Las Vegas
26 Aladdin
29 Holiday Inn Casino Boardwalk
34 Monte Carlo
39 New York-New York
40 MGM Grand
41 Excalibur
42 Tropicana
43 Luxor
44 Mandalay Bay; Four Seasons

PLACES TO EAT

1 Liberty Café
2 Montana's Café & Grill;
   Top of the World
6 The Steak House
8 Ristorante Italiano
8 Tony Roma's: A Place for Ribs
13 Morton's of Chicago
16 Taqueria Cañonita
18 The Range
19 La Piazza Food Court;
   Stage Deli of Las Vegas; Hyakumi;
   The Palm; Spago; 808
23 Aqua; Picasso; Prime; Le Cirque;
   Buffet at Bellagio; Jasmine; Café Bellagio
25 Le Village
30 Harley-Davidson Café
34 Dragon Noodle Company
38 GameWorks Grill; GameWorks
39 Chin Chin
40 Coyote Café & Grill Room;
   Emeril Lagasse's New Orleans
   Fish House; Rainforest Café
42 Mizuno's
44 Aureole

BARS/CLUBS

MAP 3 THE STRIP

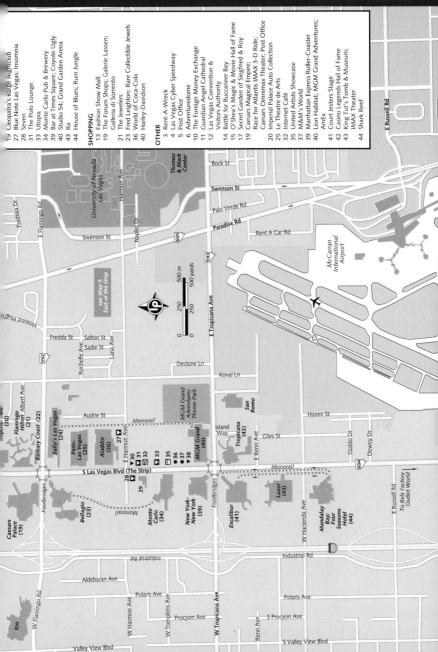

19 Cleopatra's Barge Nightclub
27 Blue Note Las Vegas; Insomnia
28 Seven
31 The Polo Lounge
33 Utopia
34 Monte Carlo Pub & Brewery
39 Bar at Times Square; Coyote Ugly
40 Studio 54; Grand Garden Arena
43 Ra
44 House of Blues; Rum Jungle

SHOPPING
13 Fashion Show Mall;
19 The Forum Shops; Galerie Lassen;
    Galleria di Sorrento
21 The Jewelers
23 Fred Leighton: Rare Collectible Jewels
36 World of Coca-Cola
40 Harley-Davidson

OTHER
4 Rent-A-Wreck
4 Las Vegas Cyber Speedway
5 Post Office
6 Adventuredome
10 The Foreign Money Exchange
11 Guardian Angel Cathedral
12 Las Vegas Convention &
    Visitors Authority
14 Battle for Buccaneer Bay
15 O'Shea's Magic & Movie Hall of Fame
17 Secret Garden of Siegfried & Roy
19 Caesars Magical Empire;
    Race for Atlantis IMAX 3-D Ride;
    Caesars Omnimax Theater; Post Office
20 Imperial Palace Auto Collection
25 Le Theatre de Arts
32 Internet Café
35 United Artists Showcase
37 M&M's World
39 Manhattan Express Roller-Coaster
40 Lion Habitat; MGM Grand Adventures;
    AmEx
41 Court Jesters Stage
42 Casino Legends Hall of Fame
43 King Tut's Tomb & Museum;
    IMAX Theater
44 Shark Reef

MAP 4 WEST OF THE STRIP

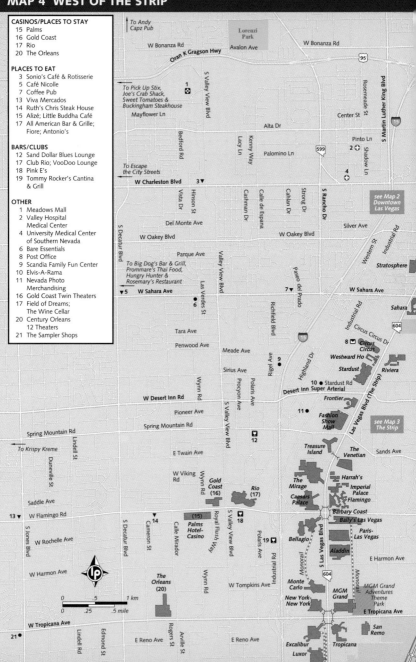

CASINOS/PLACES TO STAY
15 Palms
16 Gold Coast
17 Rio
20 The Orleans

PLACES TO EAT
3 Sonio's Café & Rotisserie
5 Café Nicolle
7 Coffee Pub
13 Viva Mercados
14 Ruth's Chris Steak House
15 Alizé; Little Buddha Café
17 All American Bar & Grille;
   Fiore; Antonio's

BARS/CLUBS
12 Sand Dollar Blues Lounge
17 Club Rio; VooDoo Lounge
18 Pink E's
19 Tommy Rocker's Cantina
   & Grill

OTHER
1 Meadows Mall
2 Valley Hospital
   Medical Center
4 University Medical Center
   of Southern Nevada
6 Bare Essentials
8 Post Office
9 Scandia Family Fun Center
10 Elvis-A-Rama
11 Nevada Photo
   Merchandising
16 Gold Coast Twin Theaters
17 Field of Dreams;
   The Wine Cellar
20 Century Orleans
   12 Theaters
21 The Sampler Shops

MAP 5 EAST OF THE STRIP

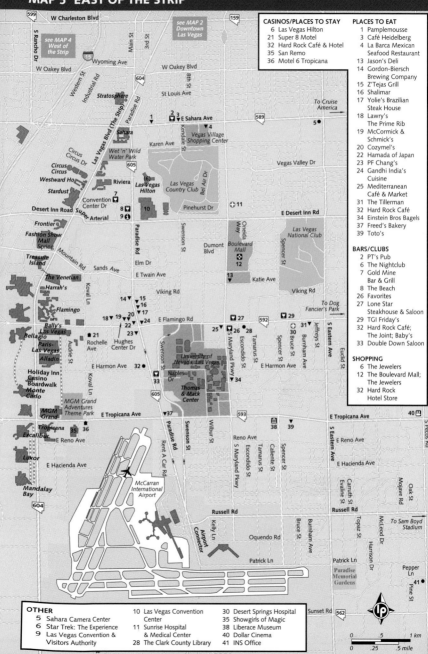

CASINOS/PLACES TO STAY
6 Las Vegas Hilton
21 Super 8 Motel
32 Hard Rock Café & Hotel
35 San Remo
36 Motel 6 Tropicana

PLACES TO EAT
1 Pamplemousse
3 Café Heidelberg
4 La Barca Mexican Seafood Restaurant
13 Jason's Deli
14 Gordon-Biersch Brewing Company
15 Z'Tejas Grill
16 Shalimar
17 Yolie's Brazilian Steak House
18 Lawry's The Prime Rib
19 McCormick & Schmick's
20 Cozymel's
22 Hamada of Japan
23 PF Chang's
24 Gandhi India's Cuisine
25 Mediterranean Café & Market
31 The Tillerman
32 Hard Rock Café
34 Einstein Bros Bagels
37 Freed's Bakery
39 Toto's

BARS/CLUBS
2 PT's Pub
6 The Nightclub
7 Gold Mine Bar & Grill
8 The Beach
26 Favorites
27 Lone Star Steakhouse & Saloon
27 TGI Friday's
32 Hard Rock Café; The Joint; Baby's
33 Double Down Saloon

SHOPPING
6 The Jewelers
12 The Boulevard Mall; The Jewelers
32 Hard Rock Hotel Store

OTHER
5 Sahara Camera Center
6 Star Trek: The Experience
9 Las Vegas Convention & Visitors Authority
10 Las Vegas Convention Center
11 Sunrise Hospital & Medical Center
28 The Clark County Library
30 Desert Springs Hospital
35 Showgirls of Magic
38 Liberace Museum
40 Dollar Cinema
41 INS Office

MAP LEGEND

ROUTES

City Regional

.............Freeway
.............Toll Freeway
.............Primary Road
.............Secondary Road
.............Tertiary Road
.............Dirt Road

.............Pedestrian Mall
.............Steps
.............Tunnel
.............Trail
.............Walking Tour
.............Path

TRANSPORTATION

.............Monorail Line

HYDROGRAPHY

.............River; Creek
.............Canal
.............Lake

.............Spring; Rapids
.............Waterfalls
.............Dry; Salt Lake

ROUTE SHIELDS

Interstate Highway
Nevada Highway
US Highway
California Highway

BOUNDARIES

.............International
.............State

.............County
.............Disputed

AREAS

.............Airport
.............Building
.............Campus

.............Cemetery
.............Garden; Zoo
.............Golf Course

.............Military
.............Park
.............Plaza

.............Shopping Area
.............Sports Field
.............Swamp; Mangrove

POPULATION SYMBOLS

○ NATIONAL CAPITAL ...National Capital
◉ STATE CAPITAL ....State Capital

● Large City ....Large City
● Medium City ....Medium City

● Small City ....Small City
● Town; Village ....Town; Village

MAP SYMBOLS

■.............Place to Stay
▼.............Place to Eat
●.............Point of Interest

.............Airfield
.............Airport
.............Archeological Site; Ruin
.............Bank
.............Baseball Diamond
.............Battlefield
.............Bike Trail
.............Border Crossing
.............Buddhist Temple
.............Bus Station; Terminal
.............Cable Car; Chairlift
.............Campground
.............Castle
.............Cathedral
.............Cave

.............Church
.............Cinema
.............Dive Site
.............Fishing
.............Footbridge
.............Fountain
.............Hospital
.............Information
.............Internet Access
.............Lighthouse
.............Lookout
.............Mine
.............Mission
.............Monument
.............Mountain

.............Museum
.............Pagoda
.............Park
.............Parking Area
.............Pass
.............Picnic Area
.............Police Station
.............Pool
.............Post Office
.............Pub; Bar
.............RV Park
.............Shelter
.............Shipwreck
.............Shopping Mall
.............Skiing - Cross Country

.............Skiing - Downhill
.............Stately Home
.............Surfing
.............Synagogue
.............Temple
.............Taxi
.............Telephone
.............Theater
.............Toilet - Public
.............Tomb
.............Trailhead
.............Tram Stop
.............Transportation
.............Windsurfing
.............Winery

Note: Not all symbols displayed above appear in this book.

LONELY PLANET OFFICES

Australia
Locked Bag 1, Footscray, Victoria 3011
☎ 03 8379 8000 fax 03 8379 8111
email: talk2us@lonelyplanet.com.au

USA
150 Linden St, Oakland, CA 94607
☎ 510 893 8555 TOLL FREE: 800 275 8555
fax 510 893 8572
email: info@lonelyplanet.com

UK
10a Spring Place, London NW5 3BH
☎ 020 7428 4800 fax 020 7428 4828
email: go@lonelyplanet.co.uk

France
1 rue du Dahomey, 75011 Paris
☎ 01 55 25 33 00 fax 01 55 25 33 01
email: bip@lonelyplanet.fr
www.lonelyplanet.fr

World Wide Web: www.lonelyplanet.com *or* AOL keyword: lp
Lonely Planet Images: www.lonelyplanetimages.com